ESSAYS ON REALISM

Essays on Realism

GEORG LUKÁCS

edited and introduced by Rodney Livingstone
translated by David Fernbach

The MIT Press
Cambridge, Massachusetts

This collection first published in German
in Georg Lukács, *Werke*, Vol. 4: *Essays über Realismus*,
Hermann Luchterhand, West Germany, 1971
© Ferenc Jánossy
This English-language edition first published 1980
© 1980 by Lawrence and Wishart Ltd, London
First MIT Press edition, 1981
Library of Congress catalog card number 80-83788
ISBN 0-262-12088-7

Printed in Great Britain

Contents

Introduction *Rodney Livingstone*   1

The Novels of Willi Bredel [1931/2]   23
1. FOR DIALECTICS AS A LITERARY PRINCIPLE   23
2. AGAINST THE THEORY OF SPONTANEITY IN LITERATURE   28

'Tendency' or Partisanship? [1932]   33

Reportage or Portrayal? [1932]   45
1. CRITICAL REMARKS À PROPOS A NOVEL BY OTTWALT   45
2. A VIRTUE OF NECESSITY   63

Expressionism: its Significance and Decline [1934]   76
1. THE IDEOLOGY OF THE GERMAN INTELLIGENTSIA IN THE IMPER-
   IALIST PERIOD   78
2. EXPRESSIONISM AND THE IDEOLOGY OF THE USPD   91
3. EXPRESSIONISM'S CREATIVE METHOD   102

Marx and the Problem of Ideological Decay [1938]   114

A Correspondence with Anna Seghers [1938/9]   167
Anna Seghers, 28 June 1938   167
Georg Lukács, 29 July 1938   175
Anna Seghers, February 1939   185
Georg Lukács, 2 March 1939   189

Tribune or Bureaucrat? [1940]   198
1. THE GENERAL SIGNIFICANCE OF LENIN'S ANTITHESIS   198
2. BUREAUCRACY AS A BASIC FORM OF DEVELOPMENT OF
   CAPITALIST CULTURE   205
3. TRAGEDY AND TRAGICOMEDY OF THE ARTIST UNDER
   CAPITALISM   213
4. THE ACTUALITY OF LENIN'S ANTITHESIS   227

Notes   238

Name index   246

Publishers' note: Notes by Lukács are marked: [G.L.'s note.] All other notes are by the editor. Lukács's reference notes have been retained; some references incorporated in the text are to sources unidentified by Lukács supplied by the translator. In all cases English-language sources have been used where available.

Introduction

Lukács in the thirties

The essays collected in this volume are among the major contributions to literary theory and literary criticism published by Georg Lukács in the nineteen-thirties. They differ in character, therefore, from the writings which had made his name in the previous decade, since these had been almost entirely political.

During the twenties, after his active participation in the abortive revolutionary government in Hungary, Lukács lived in exile in Vienna, where in 1923 he produced his epoch-making contribution to Marxist theory, *History and Class Consciousness*.[1]* This book proved immensely influential as a critique of reformist Marxism but also made Lukács a highly controversial figure, attracting criticism from, among others, Bukharin and Zinoviev at the Fifth Comintern Congress in 1924. Throughout the twenties Lukács was involved in political activity and controversy, and his political career was ended for three decades by the debate following the publication of his 'Blum Theses' in 1928 (see *Political Writings, 1919–1929*, pp. 227–53), in which he proclaimed the need for a 'democratic dictatorship' in Hungary, i.e. an alliance of peasantry and proletariat, at a time when the Comintern had just moved to the left and embarked on its Third Period policy of condemning collaboration with social-democratic and other left-wing bourgeois parties. Forced to retract, Lukács withdrew from all political activity.

From 1929 to 1931 Lukács lived in Moscow where he worked at the Marx–Engels–Lenin–Institute, directed by David Riazanov. Here he was shown the typescript of Marx's *Paris Manuscripts of 1844* before their publication. They confirmed Lukács in the views he had expounded in *History and Class Consciousness*, and also strengthened the classical humanism he was to defend in his writings during the thirties.

In 1931 he moved to Berlin where he stayed until the Nazis came to

* See Notes on p. 238.

power. Here he became a leading member of the League of Proletarian-Revolutionary Writers, a literary and political organization affiliated to the International Association of Revolutionary Writers in the USSR. It was for the *Linkskurve*, the journal of the League, that the essays in this volume attacking Bredel and Ottwalt, as well as '"Tendency" or Partisanship' were written. *Linkskurve* was one of the three German-language periodicals to which Lukács contributed during the thirties. The others were *Internationale Literatur*, which generally reflected official Soviet views, and *Das Wort*, an international journal published from Moscow, which was designed to express the views of exiled writers and, broadly speaking, had a popular-front ideology. It was in *Das Wort* that the Expressionism debate appeared.

Throughout this period Lukács was involved in literary debates. He took up a position critical both of socialist realism, which became official Soviet policy after the Writers' Congress of 1934, and of 'Proletcult' and modernist or experimental writers. The ambiguity of Lukács's position is suggested by the fact that he was a member of the editorial board of *Internationale Literatur* from 1935 on, whilst at the same time he could publish in it works as critical of Stalinist bureaucracy as 'Tribune or Bureaucrat?'.

During the thirties Lukács completed some of his principal literary and philosophical works. In 1938 he was awarded a doctorate in philosophy by the Soviet Academy of Sciences for *The Young Hegel*, which was not published, however, until 1948, and in the same period he also completed *The Historical Novel* (1936/7). Other major works of the period were the essays on Russian and French realist writers, published in English as *Studies in European Realism*, and various contributions to literary theory (published in English under the title *Writer and Critic*). Of the major work as yet untranslated, particular mention should be made of the studies in German realism – including essays on Heinrich Heine, Georg Büchner, Gottfried Keller and Theodor Fontane – which have drawn favourable comment even from hostile critics like Theodor Adorno and which undoubtedly contain some of Lukács's finest work.

With the Nazi takeover in 1933 Lukács moved back to the Soviet Union where he remained until the end of the war. Regarded by some, for instance Brecht, as a powerful and more or less official spokesman of Soviet literary policy, his true position seems to have been rather more fragile. He was arrested and jailed for some months in 1941 on a charge of having been a Trotskyist agent, but was finally released on the intervention of Dimitrov. Although Lukács did not lack an authoritarian side to his personality, he seems to have regarded himself, not without justice, as a 'partisan', in broad agreement with Soviet policies, making concessions which he thought justified by the prime need to combat fascism, but for all this retaining an independent and critical line. Precisely because of this uneasy accommodation, Ferenc Feher's reference to the 'partisan's feeling of icy isolation'[2] is perhaps the most fitting description of the Lukács of these years.

Romantic Anti-Capitalism

The picture of Lukács that emerges in his literary essays of the thirties is of a dualistic thinker. His approach is to set up contrasting concepts – the 'partisan' as opposed to the tendentious writer, the realist writer who 'portrays' as opposed to the modernist who practises 'reportage', the tribune of the people as opposed to the bureaucrat. These pairs could be augmented by reference to other works: Thomas Mann or Kafka, the writer who narrates or the writer who describes, and so on. However, this picture is over-simple, since it generally turns out that Lukács sees himself as mediating between two extremes. Thus the realist who practises dialectical portrayal is contrasted on the one hand with the superficial naturalist writer who records immediate experience, and on the other with the no less superficial expressionist whose works register utopian protest. But the dualism is then usually restored by Lukács's frequent argument that the vulgar materialism of the one is simply the obverse of the subjective idealism of the other. Each has got hold of one side of a dilemma, the key to which is in the possession of the true dialectician.

In the upshot, then, we are confronted by a body of work strangely compounded of subtlety and crudeness. On the one hand, a complex mind, attempting to forge a theory of literature with the conceptual apparatus developed in *History and Class Consciousness*, a theory with a 'democratic' bias and values rooted in the tradition of German classicism. On the other hand, the constant lapse into dualism has the Manichean overtones which point to the apparently Stalinist Lukács, the mind in chains, whose 'every criticism contains a threat' (Brecht). To strike a balance between these two aspects is not easy, but recent commentators have attempted to use Lukács's own term 'romantic anti-capitalism' as a tool to disentangle the muddle. Even though the term itself is, as we shall see, open to objection, it is perhaps reasonable to think of Lukács as a Marxist who developed out of the tradition of romantic anti-capitalism, importing some of its themes into his major work, *History and Class Consciousness*. In the following period, he retained some of its most important insights, in particular the theory of reification. At the same time, in line with his repudiation of *History and Class Consciousness*, he turned against elements of his own past, and also against writers whose opposition to capitalism may be suspected of being 'romantic'.

What was romantic anti-capitalism? Following Löwy's account,[3] we may think of it as a wide spectrum of opposition to capitalism, ultimately tracing its roots back to the romantic movement, but acquiring a new impetus in the latter part of the nineteenth century. It includes such disparate figures as Ferdinand Tönnies, Georg Simmel, Max Weber, Thomas Mann, Stefan George and Ernst Toller. Capitalism is attacked for a variety of reasons, including machine-production, the modern division of labour, the depersonalization of individuals (Nietzsche), the growth of large towns and the break-up of small communities (Tönnies) and the inexorable growth of rational calculation (Weber). It may be summed up in the polar opposites of 'culture' versus 'civilization', the plea for a universe governed by qualitative values as opposed to the logic of rationality and the cash nexus.

The anti-capitalism of the turn of the century may be distinguished from earlier critiques by the realization that capitalism had become an irreversible process. A nostalgia for earlier, traditional societies was now joined by a mood of resignation, a 'tragic consciousness'. Overall there was a 'feeling of "spiritual impotence" when faced with an uncultured barbarian-civilized and vulgar-materialist "mass society"' (Löwy, p. 67).

The early Lukács fully shares in these attitudes though they are sharpened in his case by a greater radicalism and by the genuine revolutionary potential which characterized the Hungarian intelligentsia. In the words of a contemporary, Paul Honigsheim, Lukács was irreconcilably opposed to 'the bourgeoisie, liberalism, the constitutional state, parliamentarianism, revisionistic socialism, the Enlightenment, relativism and individualism' (quoted in Löwy, p. 95).

Lukács's two early books testify to the potency of the themes of romantic anti-capitalism. *Soul and Form* (1911) develops systematically the tragic vision already explored in *A History of the Development of Modern Drama* (written between 1906 and 1909, published 1911) where he had argued that the conflict between the desire for personal fulfilment and the reified reality of capitalism formed the basis of modern drama. Similarly, in *The Theory of the Novel* (1916), the novel expresses the unbridgeable gulf between the individual and the community; it is the 'form of absolute sinfulness'. Both books explore a sense of tragic doom founded on the irreparable inhumanity of capitalist society and the absence of any adequate way out at least for individuals. *Soul and Form* does consider a number of attempts to achieve 'authenticity' – Theodor Storm's attitude of resignation, Stefan George's haughty rejection of society, Kierkegaard's cultivation of 'the art of living'. At the same time the rejection of these private solutions is accompanied by a search for an authentic collective which proceeds via Tolstoy and Dostoyevsky to a commitment to the proletariat as the agency which will overcome the inhumanity of capitalism by overthrowing capitalism itself. Lukács's road to Marxism involves a sharpened critique of capitalism coupled with the ultimate rejection of the ideology which had enabled him to launch that critique. But equally, certain features of that ideology survive into his Marxism.

History and Class Consciousness

The central importance of romantic anti-capitalism in Lukács's thought is immediately evident from a consideration of *History and Class Consciousness* (1923). Lukács's most fertile idea, the concept of reification, comes into being as the result of a marriage between his critique of capitalism and the Marxian analysis of commodity fetishism. Lukács's innovation here is to extend Marx's analysis beyond the market place and to apply it to the institutions and forms of thought of capitalist society. This is the first real attempt to elaborate Marx's own suggestive but fragmentary insights, and to construct from them a major theory of ideology.

Reification is Lukács's term for the process by which capitalism permeates the whole of society.

> Its basis is that a relation between people takes on the character of a thing and thus acquires a 'phantom objectivity', an autonomy that seems so strictly rational and all-embracing as to conceal every trace of its fundamental nature: the relation between people (*H & CC*, p. 83).

Reification, then, makes a given social formation appear natural and permanent, solidifying time into space, and so denying process, upheaval, change. But whereas Marx emphasized exploitation in the production process, the alienation of the worker's labour power and the material degradation of the worker, Lukács stresses instead the 'principle of rationalization based on what is and can be calculated' (ibid., p. 88). The rational nature of the division of labour becomes for Lukács an ever-intensifying revolutionary force which breaks with 'the organic, irrational and qualitatively determined unity of the product' (ibid.). This opposition between rational calculation and the organic and qualitative comes from the vocabulary of romantic anti-capitalism and clearly shows his debt to it.

The same is true of the principal object of his analysis. Just as the process of production increasingly fragments the worker, reducing him to a mere appendage of the machine, so too the rationalized superstructure of society reifies human institutions, as well as stamping its imprint on 'the whole consciousness of man' (ibid., p. 100).

However, the dehumanization of man at the hands of capitalism in effect reinterprets the dilemma that had faced the romantic anti-capitalist. The latter had felt an invincible despair about the state of the world in general. By providing this diagnosis with a socio-economic explanation Lukács made it possible to discover a way out of the impasse, and was now able to argue that the processes of intensified rationalization would produce their own contradiction in the shape of the proletariat. Just as for Marx the proletariat had been the secret of capitalist production, so for Lukács, proletarian class consciousness is the secret of the reified consciousness of capitalism.

This consciousness is in the first instance neither actual nor simply desirable: it is an objective possibility appropriate to 'a particular typical position in the process of production' (ibid., p. 51). It forms itself initially in a vanguard party, whose function however is simply that of a catalyst; its task is to express and propagate the scientific truth about capitalism and to develop methods of organization and political struggle. In contrast with the *putschist* actions of utopian socialists or the reformist activities of social democrats, the working class makes this possible consciousness actual by the interaction of theory and practice in the course of its experience of struggle.

The structure of consciousness which emerges from *History and Class Consciousness* continues, albeit with significant amendments, to determine Lukács's thought in the nineteen-thirties. He delivers a searching critique of bourgeois thought and of the contradictions which result from the bourgeoisie's inability to transcend the ideological limitations which arise from its role as the prime cause of capitalist reification. At the same time, he considers and rejects the vulgar materialism of social democracy as well as the subjective idealism of utopian socialists. The position from which he pronounces judgement is that of a dialectical materialism powerfully influenced by the critique developed by romantic anti-capitalism. In the following years a similar structure asserts itself in the field of literary debate, but with significant shifts of emphasis, since Lukács comes increasingly to commit himself to a 'classical' aesthetics based on closed mimetic forms, and to denigrate romantic anti-capitalism as 'unrealistic', full of good will, but purblind. At the same time, but also in a significantly altered way, the concept of reification is carried over into literary criticism.

As will be evident from the foregoing, the concept of romantic anti-capitalism may be said to have a function in drawing attention to certain persistent preoccupations among writers and thinkers in the earlier part of the century. But its limitations as an analytical concept are also apparent. In Lukács's own application it rapidly acquires derogatory connotations functioning as the opposite of 'Marxist', and a fairly narrow definition of Marxist at that. While it may be useful to point to the petty-bourgeois origins, the nostalgic, backward-looking values of its adherents, the term is too general to be ultimately effective. To consider it just from the point of view of political involvement, it is evident that there is a world of difference between Stefan George's proud abstentionism and Toller's active commitment to pacifism and socialism. Even more seriously, the pejorative associations of 'romantic' devalue the seriousness of the critique of capitalism. As Raymond Williams has recently noted:

If the diffuse anti-capitalism of those days spent so much time analysing the problems of state bureaucracy, of the relations between a modern industrial system and quantitative kinds of thinking and administration, of the differences between actual communities and a centralized monetary social order, we can hardly, from the end of the seventies suppose that they were wasting their time or missing some simple truth.[4]

Reconciliation with Reality

The late twenties brought about significant shifts in Lukács's thought. Lukács himself puts it in this way:

After 1924 the Third International correctly defined the position of the capitalist world as one of 'relative stability'. These facts meant that I had to rethink my theoretical position. In the debates of the Russian Party I agreed with Stalin about the necessity for socialism in one country and this shows very clearly the start of a new epoch in my thought (*H & CC*, pp. xxvii–xxviii).

The far-reaching identification with Stalinism proclaimed here, albeit with many reservations and qualifications, was to last throughout the thirties and forties. The stabilization of the international situation led Lukács to abandon revolutionary perspectives and to stress instead the need for 'realism', i.e. reconciliation with an existing reality. This expressed itself in his tendency to use the term 'utopian' as a pejorative epithet in his account of writers like Fichte, Ernst Toller or Moses Hess (see the essay on Hess in *Political Writings, 1919–1929*, pp. 181–223), who are contrasted unfavourably with Goethe, or with Hegel whose tendency to reconcile himself with reality is a mark of his 'grandiose realism' and his 'rejection of all utopias'. Even though Lukács recognized that Hegel's acceptance of Prussian reality was reactionary, he nevertheless argued that this realism was closer to materialism and hence intrinsically more progressive than the apparently more revolutionary outlook of, say, Fichte or Hess. His most developed statement of this position comes in a comparison between Hegel and Hölderlin in 1935.

> Hegel comes to terms with the post-Thermidorian epoch and the close of the revolutionary period of bourgeois development, and he builds up his philosophy precisely on an understanding of this new Thermidorian reality; he remains faithful to the old revolutionary ideal of renovating the 'polis' democracy and is broken by a reality which had no place for his ideals, not even on the level of poetry and thought. While Hegel's intellectual accommodation to the post-Thermidorian reality . . . led him into the main current of the ideological development of his class . . . Hölderlin's intransigence ended in a tragic impasse . . . The world-historical significance of Hegel's accommodation consists precisely in the fact that he grasped . . . the revolutionary development of the bourgeoisie as a unitary phase, one in which the revolutionary Terror as well as Thermidor and Napoleon were necessary phases. The heroic period of the revolutionary bourgeoisie becomes in Hegel . . . something irretrievably past, but a past which was absolutely necessary for the emergence of this unheroic phase of the present to be considered progressive (see *Goethe and His Age*, pp. 137–9).

Lukács justified his own accommodation to reality, an instance of which was his cynical recantation of the 'Blum Theses', as a self-sacrifice made necessary by the fascist threat:

> I was indeed firmly convinced that I was in the right, but I knew also – e.g. from the fate that had befallen Karl Korsch – that to be expelled from the Party meant that it would no longer be possible to participate actively in the struggle against Fascism. I wrote my self-criticism as an 'entry-ticket' to such activity . . . (*H & CC*, p. xxx).

Heine had used the phrase about the 'entry-ticket', not so much to justify his pro forma conversion to Christianity as to expose the scandal such a conversion implied. He did not abandon one faith for another, but the appearance of Judaism for an outward conformity with Christianity. If his apostasy was hypocritical, the blame was less his than that of the society that imposed it. Lukács's use of the phrase conceals the fact (possibly from himself) that he had made a real accommodation to Stalinism, even though in some ways he preserved his intellectual independence.

Stalinism

As with many of the leading Marxists of the thirties, not excluding obvious dissenters like Bertolt Brecht or Ernst Bloch, Lukács's relationship with Stalinism is full of ambivalence. In his case, of course, the fact that he spent the period in the USSR makes it difficult to define his position with any precision. Acts of homage cannot always be taken at their face value and genuine dissent may have smouldered beneath apparent acquiescence and the obligatory quotations from Stalin. 'Tribune or Bureaucrat?', for example, has often been taken for an outspoken attack on the bureaucracy, all the more remarkable for the fact that it was published in 1940. And no doubt that is how it should be read. But at the same time, the bureaucracy is assailed in Stalin's name, and is conceived not as something integral to the Stalinist system, but as a vestige of capitalism (see below, pp. 228–9). Moreover, in literary terms, it soon becomes apparent (cf. p. 228 below) that by 'bureaucratic phenomena' Lukács refers to the survival in Soviet literature of the very trends towards formalism and naturalism that he castigates throughout his critical essays.

Since he remained in the Soviet Union it is reasonable to assert that his acceptance of Stalinist Russia cannot have been wholly formal. Thus he writes in 1936:

> Even today, *when a socialist society has become a reality*, it would be a mistake to think that we have nothing further to learn from Gorky (*Studies in European Realism*, p. 241; my emphasis, R.L.).

His writings abound in such remarks and, whether insincere or not, they cannot simply be discounted. Löwy points out that Lukács was not opposed to the show trials and even when it became possible to speak out more clearly, after the Twentieth Congress, he went no further than the statement that they were 'superfluous' (Löwy, p. 206).

But equally, to identify Lukács wholly with Stalinism would be an even greater mistake than to stylize him into a hidden dissident. The 'reconciliation with reality' and his own beliefs undoubtedly led him to give his support to the Soviet Union and this was more than a tactical necessity exacted by the threat of fascism. At the same time, it is hard to disagree with his own subsequent assessment of the matter as expressed in the Preface to *Writer and Critic*:

> It is not hard to see today that the main direction of these essays was in opposition to the dominant literary theory of the time. Stalin and his followers demanded that literature provide tactical support to their current political policies. Accordingly, all art was to be subordinated both in the positive and negative sense, to these needs. Only acceptable characters and situations, ideas and emotions were to be introduced, only material adapted to their policies and nothing going beyond these policies. As everyone knows, no open polemics were possible during that period. Yet I did protest consistently against such a conception of literature. A revival of Marx's and Lenin's views regarding the complicated dialectic, rich in contradiction, between the political and social positions of writers and their actual works, ran counter to Zhdanov's prescriptions. In expounding such and similar views through analyses of a Balzac or a Tolstoy, I not only offered a theory in opposition to the official line but also by clear implication a critique of the official literature. As many documents attest, those I criticized were well aware of what I was doing (ibid., p. 7).

How are these two accounts to be reconciled? Both Löwy and Feher argue convincingly (though with varying emphases) that Lukács managed to retain his independence despite concessions and compromises. According to Löwy:

> Lukács was in opposition whenever Stalinism was in sharp conflict with Western (bourgeois) democracy and culture; which is why he was criticized as a right-opportunist by the Comintern and the Hungarian Communist Party in 1928–30 and why he was arrested in Moscow in 1941 (Löwy, p. 203).

And he believes that a coherent strategy may be discerned in Lukács's political and intellectual career from 1928: 'it was a consistent attempt to "reconcile" Stalinism with bourgeois democratic culture' (ibid., p. 204).

We may conclude that if the authoritarian features in Lukács himself were powerful enough to induce him to submit to Stalinism, they were also strong enough to enable him to stand up for his own — bourgeois-democratic — version of Stalinism. This helps to explain why Brecht and others could see him as an official Soviet spokesman at the same time as he was stressing his own internal opposition.

Realism

Lukács's accommodation to Stalin's reality took the form of an attempt 'to build his personal Weimar — a cultural island among power relations unambiguously hostile to any democratic culture' (Feher, op. cit., p. 114). In this effort realism played a pivotal role. Although the earlier Lukács had always resolutely opposed modern art, his early preference was essentially for art, such as the works of Tolstoy or Dostoyevsky, which contained 'solutions' to the impasse of modern culture. In the early twenties, however, his taste begins to change. In the *Theory of the Novel*, for example, Balzac is criticized because his work does not constitute a genuine totality:

> None of the parts, seen from the viewpoint of the whole, possesses an organic necessity of existence; if it were not there at all, the whole would not suffer; conversely, any number of new parts might be added and no evidence of inner completeness would prove them superfluous (*The Theory of the Novel*, p. 111).

By 1922, however, he was praising Balzac, contrasting him in his latest manner with Zola and Flaubert on the basis of the theory, to be expanded in 'Marx and the Problem of Ideological Decay', that they belong to the bourgeois decadence that dates from the collapse of the 1848 revolutions. Thus Balzac has now become 'the literary expression of the ascendant, progressive bourgeoisie', and he is praised because he

> not only knew how to describe human passions simply or to analyse them psychologically, but was able also to grasp their essence, their relationship to the totality of social life and to understand how they interacted.[5]

The scene was set, therefore, for his later advocacy of classical realism — Balzac, Scott, Tolstoy and in modern times, Thomas Mann and Gorky.

In Lukács's programme for realism, art fills the gap left vacant by the collapse of his confidence in the proletariat. It is now art and specifically realist art whose function it is to de-reify reality; it is the realist who is the '"defetishized" man who sees through the veils of reification, penetrates appearances to arrive at their essences' (Feher, p. 126).

Lukács's view of realism as defined in these essays and elsewhere is then a form of essentialism. The underlying assumption is that actual consciousness, that which is immediately 'given', is not enough. For if under capitalism all consciousness is reified, then the immediate reflection of appearances can never transcend that reification.

Realism, then, is to be distinguished from traditional definitions, such as that of George Eliot who declared that her aim was 'to give a faithful account of men and things as they have mirrored themselves in my mind' (*Adam Bede*, Chapter 17), or that of Erich Auerbach for whom it was 'the serious treatment of everyday reality'.[6] For although realism must satisfy these requirements, the crucial fact for Lukács is that what we see is only appearance, whereas the great novelist reveals 'the driving forces' of history which are invisible to actual consciousness.

It is perhaps less important at this stage, now that Lukács's ideas have acquired a certain currency, to spell out the details of his position.[7] It can be seen clearly enough in the essays published here, above all in the defence of Tolstoy in 'Reportage or Portrayal?', in '"Tendency" or Partisanship?', and the clarifications in the correspondence with Anna Seghers. What should be emphasized rather is the central vision. The elision of realism and essentialism in effect invokes the message of German classicism: the hope that art can somehow break through the limitations of actual consciousness and for a moment overcome human alienation. Feher has rightly emphasized the democratic inspiration here. He draws attention to Lukács's constant invective against merely formal democracy. Lukács's praise is reserved for the small community of sophisticated individuals in *Wilhelm Meister* but more especially for the Switzerland of Gottfried Keller which, because it had not been fully penetrated by capitalism, allowed a glimpse of a more genuine democracy:

> Nevertheless, the free atmosphere in which Keller's heroes move radiates an idea of self-governed mankind: a regulative theoretical idea without which socialism is impossible (Feher, p. 118).

This democratic vision may be flawed by the authoritarian overtones of a theory in which art is presented as a closed universe, handed down to the consumer, but it is nevertheless at the core of Lukács's defence of realism.

The Linkskurve *Essays*

The first three essays, 'The Novels of Willi Bredel', ' "Tendency" or Partisanship?' and 'Reportage or Portrayal?' appeared in 1931 and 1932 in the *Linkskurve*, the official organ of the League of Proletarian-Revolutionary Writers. The League had been founded in 1928 as the German branch of the International Bureau for Revolutionary Literature, which had provided it with funds. Although it unreservedly supported the policies of the German Communist Party, it was strictly independent of it and pursued its own cultural policy. The Communist Party, in the literary pages of its own daily, *Die Rote Fahne*, still retained views on art that went back to the Second International; that is to say, it promoted a Kantian view of 'pure' art: 'art is too sacred a matter to permit its name to be used for propaganda purposes. What the workers need today is powerful art . . . such art may be of bourgeois origin as long as it is art'.[8]

In contrast to this the League had borrowed most of its programme from RAPP (the Russian Association of Proletarian Writers), its sister organization in the Soviet Union, which had its roots in the Proletcult movement of 1917. Its main points were: to foster a proletarian-revolutionary literature; to develop a proletarian-revolutionary theory of literature; to criticize bourgeois literature and prove that its claims to be 'pure art' were a fiction; to provide a rallying point for all proletarian-revolutionary writers; and to give support to the Soviet Union. Most of the writers for the *Linkskurve* were worker correspondents, but a number of well-known bourgeois writers, such as the editor, Johannes R. Becher, Anna Seghers and Erwin Piscator contributed to it. The proletarian emphasis is visible in the attitude of the magazine to intellectuals.

Initially, this was summed up in the 'midwife' theory: intellectuals were denied any creative role and had to accept the extinction of their own personality as well as a total submission to party discipline. Their sole function was to assist proletarians in the writing and publication of their works. This position was modified in 1930 in favour of a vanguard role for intellectuals, but the history of the journal reflects all the current debates about the nature and function of workers' literature, the role of sympathizing intellectuals, and the value to be placed on the bourgeois cultural heritage.

From the summer of 1931 Lukács, who had been sent to Berlin as a Comintern emissary,[9] took an increasingly active role in the affairs of the League and the policy of the *Linkskurve*. Apart from Karl Witt-fogel, who had made a first attempt at formulating a Marxist aesthetics, there was no one in the *Linkskurve* who could compete with Lukács's unrivalled grasp of theoretical issues. In October 1931 Becher had signalled a change of direction. Vanguard literature with the emphasis on factory reportage and industrial themes was to be abandoned in favour of a mass literature designed to act as a counterweight to the pulp literature, penny-dreadfuls and other types of kitsch for the masses. This was in line with the recently declared policy of the Communist Party which with the aid of the slogans of 'people's revolution' and 'Red Unity' was attempting to widen its appeal to the broad masses and saw literature as a useful ally. At the same time, Becher also argued that proletarian literature had overcome its teething troubles and was now strong enough to enter into a phase of self-criticism. This self-criticism began in the next issue (November 1931) with Lukács's critique of the novels of Willi Bredel.

Willi Bredel was a worker novelist and a protégé of the leader of the German Communist Party, Ernst Thälmann. The two novels criticized by Lukács, *Maschinenfabrik N & K* (1930), written while he was in gaol for 'literary treason', and *Rosenhofstraße* (1931) are typical examples of the proletarian novels produced under the auspices of the League. Lukács's criticism focuses on Bredel's language, in particular on his use of a mixture of fictional and non-fictional techniques. However, Lukács is eager to stress that he does not just want to reproach Bredel with a failure in craftsmanship. The technique is itself symptomatic of something deeper: his lack of a dialectical approach to his subject. By 'dialectical' Lukács clearly means 'realistic': the language Bredel's characters use is not what might be expected of workers, 'it is almost universally that of the newspaper report'.

Essentially, what Lukács arrives at is the rejection both of existing party literature and the alternative of a genuine mass literature in favour of his own vision of popular literature. The subsequent controversy in the *Linkskurve* makes it clear that Lukács's central objection – the absence of dialectics – reflects his disapproval of the spontaneous, immediate consciousness of the workers which shows that they have failed to penetrate the veils of reification. Bredel himself readily accepted Lukács's criticisms, with a haste which fits in all too well with his own message of submission to authority. However, in April 1932 an answer by Otto Gotsche appeared in the *Linkskurve* which began by reproaching Lukács with 'a destructive method of criticism' and went on to report the reactions of workers to whom he had shown both Bredel's novel and Lukács's review. His respondents evidently resented Lukács's intrusion ('The book is good, the other stuff is shit!') and demanded that Lukács should prove himself as a novelist before venturing to criticize the work of others. They obviously felt that Bredel reflected their own lives back to them, whilst Lukács was making extraneous and irrelevant demands for 'art' and 'form'. Lukács never again attacked proletarian literature, but the criticism of its 'spontaneity' was carried over into his essays on official socialist realism. At the same time, the significance of the episode is that 'grass roots' literature was rejected firmly in favour of a bourgeois realism to be 'handed down' to the masses.

Modernism

Of wider implications than the attack on proletarian literature is the criticism of Ottwalt's novel *Denn sie wissen, was sie tun* ('For they know what they do') in 'Reportage or Portrayal?'. This was Lukács's first major assault on experimental literature. Modernist experimentation had played a role in the activities of the League of Revolutionary-Proletarian Writers. Erwin Piscator had maintained that the theatre should not rest content with the depiction of individual, private fates. It was essential to expose the social and economic determinants which made such individual conflicts into social, class conflicts. This could be done by means of technical innovations such as the use of projections, textual commentary on stage actions, statistics, film strips and so on. As far back as 1924 he had started to experiment with 'open' forms when he had arranged a 'satirical-political evening' in support of the German Communist Party in the elections to the Reichstag. After the visit of a Moscow workers' troupe to Germany in 1927 some 180 agitprop troupes had sprung up all over Germany using similar techniques. It was these techniques that were subsequently assembled and theorized by Brecht. At around the same time, and parallel to the tendencies of *Neue Sachlichkeit* (the New Objectivism), writers like Egon Erwin Kisch had called for a proletarian art based on documentary. Workers, it was held, were suspicious of fiction and in his reply to Lukács, in the *Linkskurve* in October 1932, Ottwalt argued that they prefer real fact to fiction. This idea led in Brecht to a view of art as demystification in a sense quite different to the meaning given to it by Lukács: for Brecht art was a process of demystification in which art too was demystified. In 1931 Sergei Tretyakov came to Berlin and gave a series of public lectures in which he defended the views of *Lef* in Russia,[10] attacking the Tolstoyan novel with its sustained story-line, invented action and individual characters. His ideas became influential among radical circles both inside and outside the League. Lukács's essay on Ottwalt's 'literature of facts, of true events' was a response not just to Ottwalt, but to a whole tendency, and it culminates in his first critique of Brecht himself (see pp. 70–1 below).

Ernst Ottwalt has been even more completely forgotten today than Bredel, but he is a far more substantial figure. His novel *Denn sie wissen, was sie tun* is an effective exposure of class justice in the Weimar Republic. His method is to report actual cases in such a way as to highlight the contradictory nature of Weimar justice. By the use of montage, i.e. the juxtaposition of the facts of a case and the various attitudes of the participants, without providing any overall authorial judgement, he creates a type of reportage which throws the burden of thought back to the reader. Thus his technique is radically different from that of Orwell, for example, but instead anticipates the use of alienation effects in Brecht. And in his reply to Lukács he does indeed talk in Brechtian terms, insisting for example that 'It is not the task of our literature to stabilize the reader's consciousness, but to change it', and renouncing for his novels the ambition of granting the reader the 'gentle satisfaction of having read a beautiful book'.

As with Bredel, Lukács is not content to reproach Ottwalt with the faulty application of particular techniques. He rejects the techniques as such. Beginning with the criticism of reportage, he extends his attack in 'A Virtue of Necessity' to embrace montage, documentary and 'epic' forms in general. In his view the use of such devices spells the destruction of fiction because it involves the unwarranted use of non-literary devices. His criticism is really twofold. First, any literature that applies documentary procedures in fiction ends up by fetishizing facts. Ottwalt stands convicted of reproducing surface reality, rather than the essence, the process. Such a non-totalizing approach ends up by distorting the truth: what Ottwalt shows is the invincibility of the bourgeois judicial apparatus, instead of showing how the proletariat is potentially able to overcome it. In short, the category of 'totality' is used to ascribe to Ottwalt the fetishism characteristic of bourgeois thought, an accusation backed up by Lukács's comments on Ottwalt's failure to cast off his petty-bourgeois origins (for failure to grasp the totality is, according to Lukács, the very mark of a petty-bourgeois outlook). In the second place, Lukács's definition of realism leaves no room for any literature that 'lays bare the device'. All such 'abstract' means, as he suggests in '"Tendency" or Partisanship?', undermine the 'objectivity' of realism. They represent arbitrary subjective interventions and so 'end up in idealistic experiment in form'.

In his reply Ottwalt makes a number of telling points. He suggests that it is a mistake to do no more than examine the relationship between an author's 'literary tendency' and his class position. Instead the critic should consider the interactions between a literary work and reality. Ottwalt also argues, like Brecht, that the changed reality of today requires different methods, none of which need be denied the label 'realistic' in advance:

> If, for example, I make it my task to write a novel about farmers, I would have to present the causes of the agrarian crisis and above all I would have to expose the international ramifications of agrarian economics. It would also be necessary to relate the development of the means of production to changes in the thought and behaviour of the farmers. To put it concretely it is impossible to portray this development in terms of the interactions between people, the figures in the novel. I could still, if need be, establish an 'individual' relationship between an East Frisian farmer and the General Manager of the potash trust, but this would be quite idiotic if the manager of the Canadian wheat pool had to be drawn in as well (*Linkskurve*, October 1932, p. 24).

Lukács is able simply to deny this and to point to Gorky's ability to express the essential nature of capitalist exploitation at a given time by portraying the workings of a single factory. However, the issue continues to reverberate in the debate on modernism throughout the thirties.[11]

The Expressionism Debate

Following his attacks on the proletarian novel and experimental modernism, Lukács turned his attention to expressionism. 'Expressionism: Its Significance and Decline' is commonly regarded as the opening shot in the debate on expressionism that filled the pages of *Das Wort* in 1937–8. However, crucial though Lukács's essay was for the subsequent debate, the difference of context must be noted. Lukács wrote this essay in 1934, before the First Soviet Writers' Congress of 1934 in Moscow, where under Zhdanov's influence socialist realism became official policy. When Lukács wrote there was as yet no official 'line', and even though the campaign against modern art had been under way for some time, his essay was of necessity much more individual and controversial than it appeared some years later. In the subsequent debate, the issue had changed: the Popular Front was now official policy, so his subsequent attack on expressionism served the purpose of uniting a Marxist and bourgeois literature, a proletarian *and* a bourgeois literary public, around a common programme which called for a traditional realist mode of writing combined with a progressive, anti-fascist outlook. Such a programme entailed the exclusion of a modernism whose anti-bourgeois experimentalism seemed too private and elitist to make it a suitable vehicle for mass literature.

The intention of the 1934 essay is clear: it is to focus attention on the ideological roots of Nazism and the futility of any opposition to it which is not based on a Marxist analysis. Here he argued that in pre-war Imperial Germany, increasingly a society of parasitical rentiers living off unearned income, the prevailing philosophies (neo-Kantianism, Machism, *Lebensphilosophie*) obliterated the connections between ideology and economics or politics. In consequence no overall critique of capitalism was possible. Would-be oppositional movements were unable to penetrate the veil of mystification; their critiques, while subjectively progressive, remained objectively reactionary, because they could not get beyond the critique of an aspect. The expressionists voiced a general hostility to the bourgeois, but were unable to locate bourgeois vices in any particular class. Thus they discerned capitalist symptoms in the workers and this led them to abolish class struggle in favour of an 'eternal' conflict between bourgeois and non-bourgeois. The latter are seen as an elite that should rule the nation, a misconception that eventually leads to fascism. It follows that, although expressionism purported to be an opposition movement, its adherents shared the ideological preconceptions of their enemies. If this corresponded to any practical political posture, it was that of the German Independent Socialist Party (USPD). They shared the virtues of the USPD, such as opposition to the war, but also its vices: they failed to see its class character and helped to divert the masses from revolution.

Lukács's ideological objections to expressionism are complemented by his critique of its 'creative method'. The expressionists' search for essences was achieved by stylization and abstraction. While professing to lay bare the kernel of reality, they merely give vent to their own passions. Expressionism, according to Lukács, is therefore a subjectivism that verges on the solipsistic, since words are used not referentially but only 'expressively'. The result is an over-emotional and inflated rhetoric. As society stabilized after the war the expressionists found their way to what Lukács regarded as the cynical acquiescence of the New Objectivism, or else – like Johannes R. Becher – abandoned expressionism in favour of a more authentically creative method.

We may note a number of criticisms which have been made of the essay. In the first place it is characteristic of Lukács's critique of National Socialism. As we can see from his later work *The Destruction of Reason* (1954), the decisive battle against fascism had in his view to be fought out at the level of consciousness: it was a struggle for rationalism and humanism against irrationalism and barbarism. To make this issue plain would be to strike a blow for the allegiance of the intelligentsia, to rescue confused men of good will, among whom conceivably the expressionists might be numbered. But only if they saw the error of their ways. Lukács's opposition to fascism is not dissimilar to liberal bourgeois criticisms which focus on its ideological antecedents, rather than on social and political analysis.

A further point is that the animus towards the petty bourgeoisie displayed here and elsewhere in these essays is not simply part of the general and substantially correct view on the left of the crucial role of that class in the formation of the mass base of National Socialism. What is notable here is that Lukács's vantage-point is that of the grande bourgeoisie, and is linked to his defence of the anti-Fascist position adopted by Thomas Mann. As Isaac Deutscher puts it: 'It was rather the antagonism of the cultivated patrician bourgeois to the savage plebeians, the *Kleinbürger* and the *Lumpenproletariat* who were running amok in the shadow of the swastika.'[12]

Conclusion

Lukács has been a controversial figure in the history of literary criticism. In Marxist circles he has been canonized and ostracized in turn, depending on whether his commitment to a humanist version of Marxism has been in fashion or not. Outside Marxism he was the first to gain recognition as the one critic whose cultural credentials were admitted to be at least on a par with those of his non- or anti-Marxist counterparts. How should we regard his achievement today?

Lukács was a highly sensitive, complex and moralistic man, whose own high standards exacted sacrifices which have had a lasting effect on his writings and his reputation. In his early phase despair about the inhuman fate of man under capitalism was mingled with a personal grief at the premature death of his best friend, Leo Popper, and the suicide of his beloved, Irma Seidler, in 1910. His high moral and intellectual standards prevented him from accepting 'solutions' which connived in any way at the state of what Fichte had referred to as the 'absolute sinfulness' of the world. But equally his sensitivity and pride strengthened his distaste for those who flaunt their personal problems. He might have chosen to regard his own torments as exemplary and to display them as wounds inflicted by an inhuman world. In that case his writings, like those of so many modern writers, would have been inscribed in his own flesh, like the crimes of the victims in Kafka's 'Penal Colony'. Instead he chose to suppress them and to deny himself the luxury of an inner life. It is only in this way that we can account for such extreme statements as the following, admittedly from his last years:

> I can say that I have never felt frustration or any kind of complex in my life. I know what these mean, of course, from the literature of the twentieth century, and from having read Freud. But I have not experienced them myself. When I have seen mistakes or false directions in my life, I have always been willing to admit them – it has cost me nothing to do so, and then turn to something else ('An Unofficial Interview' in *New Left Review*, 68, July/August 1971, p. 58).

Such abstinence is little short of heroic and of course scarcely credible from the man who was himself near suicide in 1911. But we may find it suggestive even though we remain convinced that he was self-deceived. We may link it with his persistent search for 'objectivity' and with his increasingly severe criticism of the subjective. He chose as motto to one of his essays a quotation from Heraclitus:

> Those who are awake have a world in common, but every sleeper has a world of his own.

It is evident that his dislike of modernist literature of all kinds is rooted in his belief that any preoccupation with the 'subjective' is an aesthetic or existential self-indulgence on the part of men who are really asleep. Such writers are accused of solipsism, for their fixation on their own private worlds is a denial of the world we all share. This must be borne in mind when reading his critique of the decadent bourgeois tradition, e.g. of Rilke in 'Marx and the Problem of Ideological Decay', or of Hofmannsthal in 'Tribune or Bureaucrat?'.

His hatred of bourgeois decadence is at the same time eloquent testimony of his efforts to emancipate himself from a contemplative passivity. His repudiation of subjectivity obviously goes too far. It expresses itself, for instance, in his style, or rather, his denial of style, a mode of writing which presents the reader with an almost impenetrable coat of armour, a mask of objectivity which scorns to importune the reader with the movements of his hidden thoughts and feelings. Everything must be made public and so the gestures of his writing deny the existence of an inner world. But this inner world persists and the reader who is alert to its presence can discern the internal struggle which continues throughout Lukács's life as a kind of sub-text appended to the overt message.

His commitment to realism is a commitment to the 'world in common' of those who are awake. It is a sustained appeal to all progressive thinkers to abandon their residual private worlds. Realism is then not a substitute for political action: it is the structure of consciousness that accompanies it. It is this that constitutes the strength of Lukács's position.

Lukács undoubtedly overstates the case for realism and his interpretation of it is open to question. It is not, as he thinks, a privileged form of narration. But neither is it merely, as the structuralists maintain, a particular, bourgeois version of reality. Both he and his critics have been too anxious to pin it down ideologically. Lukács was wrong to grant it a near-monopoly of ideological rectitude, but right to defend its ability to disclose reality. As long as it can do that it will be a viable option. Of course, Brecht and the other modernists who attacked Lukács in the thirties could point to the way realist art had lost its cutting edge, and it has long since been integrated into the bourgeois culture industry or domesticated as socialist realism. To that extent they were justified in repudiating the realist tradition. But from our vantage point we can see that while Lukács was wrong to deny any historical development for realism, his insistence on the value of the nineteenth-century novel was not misplaced. Realism may serve, as Brecht thought, as a cultural prop of the ruling classes, but this is no ineluctable fate. Lukács has done more than anyone, perhaps, to demonstrate its 'progressive' potential.

Lukács's humanist Marxist values are of lasting importance. It is true, as we have seen, that the pressures of the day have left their mark on his style and in the harshness with which he has sometimes defended his opinions. But this does not invalidate his contribution. The issues to which he addressed himself are not capable of definitive solution, since they re-emerge in different forms whenever the political and ideological significance of literature becomes an urgent issue. But even though the terms of the debate may have altered somewhat since the thirties, the central article of faith, held in varying forms by all the protagonists, has not. This is the idea that literature is not a mystification, though sometimes it mystifies, but that it can also have a de-reifying, i.e. a humanizing, effect. This idea, rooted in German classical aesthetics, was taken up and developed by Lukács in terms of the Marxist theory of alienation. Through *History and Class Consciousness* it exercised a wide influence over his contemporaries, and thanks both to that influence and to his own extensive writings on literature, it still remains a cornerstone of Marxist literary debate.

Southampton   Rodney Livingstone
May 1980

The Novels of Willi Bredel [1931/2]

1. FOR DIALECTICS AS A LITERARY PRINCIPLE*

Bredel's two novels hold an important place in the development of proletarian revolutionary literature in Germany.[1]† With the happy combination of both genuine talent and militant class standpoint, Bredel has chosen themes that are not only central to the interest of every worker, but open up a new landscape for all readers. Neither of his subjects, the effects of the beginnings of rationalization on the working class, and the everyday life and struggle of a proletarian tenement block, have ever before been depicted in Germany from the proletarian class position.

This is no small thing. And yet it is by no means the whole of Bredel's achievement. In the organization of his subject-matter and the construction of his works, he shows a skilled hand, a sure political instinct and a militant combativeness. His first novel was already well constructed in this way, with its description of the preparation, outbreak and defeat of a strike in a factory. Here Bredel not only creates the outlines of a lively plot, through which the details of everyday working-class life are translated into elements and stages of the class struggle; over and above this, he shows that the entire action is only a single moment in the class war as a whole, which began before the novel opens, and will continue with undiminished vigour after the present battle is lost. This is undoubtedly a correct pattern for a proletarian novel. For it offers the possibility of fitting the whole significant class development within the factory (the struggle of the workers against the capitalists, the intervention of state power, the stratification of the workers, political divisions, the role of the social democrats and the trade union, the life of the Communist cells, etc.) into an artistic composition, which even though it forms a coherent narrative entity, still has no absolute beginning or end, but is portrayed as one part of the overall process.

* First published in *Die Linkskurve*, III/11, 1931, pp. 23–7.
† See Notes at end of book.

The composition of the second novel marks a further step forward in this direction. Here Bredel extends still further the framework of his composition, setting himself the correct and important goal of depicting the life of the workers in concrete interaction with that of the other classes, in particular the petty bourgeoisie. Both politically and artistically this goal is absolutely correct, and an important development. For most works of our proletarian revolutionary literature suffer from the defect of taking as their theme either the contradiction between bosses and workers within the factory, or else that between the workers' state and the bourgeois state in a situation of acute class warfare – a narrowing of the field that sometimes even amounts to 'economism'. In this way, the political horizon is narrowed from one which, while 'national in form', poses the question at an overall level, to the isolated emphasis on a single aspect, no matter how important this might be. And this inevitably leads also to narrowness, insufficiency and impoverishment from the artistic standpoint as well. It is against this tendency that Bredel stands out with such boldness and vigour. The content of this novel is the life of a working-class tenement. Here both workers and petty bourgeois of the most varied levels and political tendencies, Communists, social democrats, Nazis, apolitical, etc., live closely together and come into contact with one another in the most varied of ways in the course of their everyday life. A rent strike, and at the close of the book the Hamburg elections, provide the nucleus of the story around which the most diverse episodes of proletarian and petty-bourgeois life are colourfully hung, both political (Nazi attacks, demonstrations, etc.), and private (an abortion tragedy, childbirth, the pawnshop, etc.). Here again, we have a picture that is correctly conceived from the standpoint of its content, and thus once again has genuine epic potential: once more the framework and pattern for a fine proletarian revolutionary novel.

Unfortunately, however, in both cases it is no more than a framework or pattern, an outline and no more. For Bredel's novels fail to develop far beyond the conception stage. To summarize the basic weakness in Bredel's artistic creation, we can say that there is an artistically unresolved contradiction between the broad narrative framework of his story, which includes everything that it essentially requires, and his manner of telling it, which is partly a kind of journalistic reportage, and partly a kind of public speech. The bare bones of the novel are correct, but there is nothing more than these bare bones. What is needed to make them come alive, i.e. living human beings, with living, changing and developing relationships between them, is as good as completely lacking. True, Bredel does provide sketches of his various characters, describing quite well, even, their external features, and emphasizing certain of their character traits, etc. But the whole thing still remains rigid. His characters fail to grow and develop. At most, they change suddenly overnight. Not that this is inherently impossible, but it works only if it is artistically prepared, if there is a transformation from quantity (i.e. small changes that might well remain unnoticed even for the people who undergo them) to quality, and not just a sudden pistol-shot. This unprepared and sudden transformation fails to ring true in its artistic effect even if it is abstractly possible. Bredel's characters, therefore, turn out to be little more than what in theatrical language used to be called '*Chargen*' [stereotypes]: they possess a fixed and characteristic feature (possibly more than one), which is repeated and underlined at every possible (and even impossible) opportunity. But in this way the characters fail to come alive, even if these features are observed correctly. A novel simply demands a different kind of characterization than a journalistic report: what may be good enough for the one is completely inadequate for the other.

This inadequate characterization is most evident in Bredel's language. With rare exceptions, this is little more than the language of press reports. In some passages this is justifiable. In describing a public meeting or a party cell in session, for instance, it is quite possible to depict this simply and dryly, as a straightforward report, so as to bring out the political content in the speeches, interjections, etc. Even here, however, it should be stressed that real political life is richer and more finely textured and alive than in Bredel's depiction. If Comrades Thälmann or Neumann,[2] for example, speak on the same theme or political line that Bredel portrays, their speeches are completely different in their construction, language, tone, etc. Bredel always gives his political speeches the same tone (simply with the already mentioned stereotyped trimmings, which do not make things any better). In language, too, therefore, he lags behind the reality that he seeks to depict in his art, stuck in a pale reproduction of this.

What is still worse is that he uses the same kind of language outside meetings, sessions and reports. I shall quote just a few random examples. Two workers are discussing literature. One of them says about Emil Ludwig[3]: 'He is certainly an unusually absorbing and instructive historian.' The other answers: 'He is undoubtedly a very interesting literary figure, but an unreliable historian.' In another case, a woman worker goes to the pawn-shop, and Bredel describes her horror at it as follows: 'In the pawnshop she came to know the whole wretchedness of human poverty.' Then again, some workers are listening to the radio, and a woman Communist says: 'The radio is a mouthpiece of the ruling class, and every hour millions of people are manipulated and stupefied by it.' This abstract treatment of language necessarily leads many of Bredel's attempts to come to grips with concrete reality to collapse into absurdity and kitsch. To give yet another example, a Communist wants to get to know a non-party colleague whom he is working with on a committee, and has a little talk with him. All Bredel gives of the conversation are a few fragments, which neither succeed in characterizing the non-party man, nor the developing relationship between the two characters. As he sums it up: 'He now got to know a deeply honest and interesting person, who hid his understanding and heart behind a rough exterior.'

It would be very tempting to conclude from all this that what Bredel lacks is simply the 'technique' of writing. But this is not in fact the problem. Of course, Bredel is short on technique, too. Yet it would be highly misleading for a critic to say to him: Yes, your novels are quite correct in their content and world-view, they are Marxist and politically exemplary, all you need is to improve your 'technique' of writing and master its form, and you will write a great proletarian novel.

In reality, form and content are far more closely linked, and their dialectical interaction – despite the predominance of the class content – is far more intimate, mediated and complex than would permit us to answer the question in so mechanically simple a way.

First of all, the portrayal of human character is not a 'technical' question, it is above all a question of applying dialectics in the field of literature. In every introductory course in dialectical materialism we stress the difference between metaphysical and dialectical thought; we emphasize time and again that dialectical thought dissolves the rigid appearance of things, which obtains also in thinking, into the processes that they really are. Doesn't this basic principle of dialectics hold good for literature as well? In the everyday class struggle, any party cadre would very rapidly come to grief if he treated the milieu in which he had to act, and which is made up of human beings (individuals, groups, masses), metaphysically rather than dialectically. Is it not a correct demand that literature, in its methods of portrayal, should attain at least the same level that is beginning to be generally reached in the everyday practice of class struggle, often by mere instinct, and despite all errors? I would say we are justified in putting higher demands than this. The demand, for instance, that the highest achievements of our literature should be measured, as far as their deployment of dialectics goes, against the highest achievements of KPD [German Communist Party] and Comintern theory and practice.

This lack of dialectics in characterization gives rise to a distortion in content, too. As a result of the mode of presentation we have described, Bredel – quite unintentionally – inevitably makes light of the difficulties that the development of the revolution comes up against. For these difficulties can only be portrayed in literature if our writers succeed in depicting, in a genuinely living and palpable way, the obstacles that keep good workers away from the revolutionary movement, and the currents that drive even the lower and proletarianized stratum of the petty bourgeoisie into the camp of counter-revolution – only if they show us how hard a road these sections of the masses face in attaining ideological clarification. Bredel however takes a short cut – not that this is his alone. He offers results, but not the process with its obstacles, difficulties and setbacks. This is bound to falsify his picture as well. For Bredel does indeed portray the upward course of the revolutionary movement. But by failing to depict the obstacles, he necessarily gives a distorted view. The honest non-party man becomes a Communist over-night; the badly functioning cell suddenly takes on the leadership of the strike; in public meetings, the revolutionary line always prevails against the trade-union bosses, and so on.

All this is in no way a matter of inadequate 'technique', but of lack of dialectics.

Many comrades will certainly think this criticism too hard. But its author is only applying the words that Comrade Stalin expressed in regard to another literary question: 'Since when have Bolsheviks feared the truth?' Our proletarian revolutionary literature has had to fight for its existence, and has proved its right to exist in hard struggle. Our proletarian revolutionary writers are proven and devoted soldiers of their class. And now, when the tasks facing us on all fronts of the class struggle are greater than ever, they must not lag behind the general movement. On the contrary, they must confront their failings by un-sparing self-criticism, unembellished exposure of this backwardness and its causes, and by setting themselves tasks that correspond to the general level of development of the revolutionary class struggle. By tenacious and deliberate work, by learning to deploy materialist dialec-tics in literary creation, they must eliminate these weaknesses as quickly as possible.

This criticism of Bredel's works is also in the fullest sense of the word

a self-criticism. The problem is in no way that Bredel as an individual
has failed to attain the level of our proletarian revolutionary literature,
but rather that we have all failed to match the level of the objective situation in Germany in our literary activity (both creative and critical).
Bredel is one of our best writers, in terms of his talent and his potential
for further development. His failings are less individual failings than the
general failings of the whole literary movement. If we are to uncover
these failings by self-criticism, therefore, we must not fall into the
opposite error of underestimating Bredel and forgetting that his novels,
for all their weaknesses, have also great merits. For a start, the
revolutionary literature of the proletariat has struggled through and
justified its existence. And how could it have done this, without possess-
ing at least some literary qualities? At the start of this essay I expressly
stressed these qualities, and I emphasize here again that Bredel's novels
open up a new landscape, and remain therefore useful, instructive and
stimulating reading, even indispensable reading for anyone who wants
to understand the everyday life of the workers in Germany today.
Secondly, the sharpness of my criticism also implies a recognition of
our achievements so far, and not least Bredel's own achievements. For
if Bredel were simply a modest beginner, without artistic talent worthy
of recognition, it would be necessary to cherish and protect the young
plant from the harshness of the elements. We are beyond that stage,
however, and not least due to the achievements of Bredel himself.
Because Bredel is talented (as are also other proletarian revolutionary
writers), and because his writing has reached a certain level already –
because he deserves to be read! – we must make higher demands of him.
And this is possible only by way of sharp criticism and self-criticism. It
is precisely what is good and worthy of recognition in Bredel's writing
that makes it possible and necessary to take one step further and require
higher achievements of him (and of others of our writers, too), i.e. a real
mastery of materialist dialectics and the matching of the performance of
our movement in other fields. We can and must demand this, as we are
convinced that Bredel is in a position to fulfil such demands.

2. AGAINST THE THEORY OF SPONTANEITY IN LITERATURE*

I can only make a brief reply to Comrade Gotsche's article,[4] for he has
not refuted my criticism of Bredel, but rather confirmed it on all points.
Before I summarize these points, however, I should like to ask Comrade

* First published in *Die Linkskurve*, IV/4, 1932, pp. 30 ff.

Gotsche – in the interest of our discussions, which are designed to be of practical benefit to the literature of the revolutionary proletariat – to discuss with me in a comradely and less naive fashion. If working-class readers demand that the critic should 'produce something better himself', then Comrade Gotsche should explain to them that this is not the critic's task. Views such as this are always widespread in the early stages of any new literature. Bourgeois literature also experienced this infantile disorder (in Germany, before Lessing). But are we really to draw our model from a period of bourgeois literature that has today become actually comic, from the period of its very first stammerings? It can of course happen that a good Marxist critic is also a proletarian revolutionary creative writer, but this is accidental, no matter how desirable it might be that our proletarian revolutionary writers should work with a Marxist consciousness so developed that they are themselves in a position to give a critical presentation of their creative methods. The great writers of the bourgeoisie's revolutionary era, from Diderot through to Stendhal, and from Lessing to Heine, were capable of this almost without exception. Criticism in itself, however, has just as valid a place in the division of labour of our proletarian revolutionary literary movement as does creative writing, with its special allotted tasks: it has the task of applying materialist dialectics in the field of literature, of discovering and helping to elucidate those creative methods that best correspond to the problems of the class struggle at the time (both at the level of the everyday struggle, and in the great struggles of whole epochs), and of establishing their literary validity. In no way can it rest content with simply following critically in the wake of our writers; it must rather seek – with the aid of our whole inheritance – to comprehend the necessary developmental tendencies of the epoch, independently, if need be, and struggle for their realization, when necessary even against the present practice of the writers themselves. A Russian worker would look very surprised if it were suggested to him that he should perhaps demand better novels, short stories, poems, etc., from Comrade Averbach,[5] before the latter might venture to criticize such works.

Comrade Gotsche's notes, in fact, show that he is not clear himself as to what the proper tasks of criticism are. He seems to equate criticism with criticism by the masses. This is the standpoint of spontaneity, one of the several residues of Luxemburgism in the German workers' movement. It is very far from my intent here to underestimate the value of criticism by the masses. This is indispensable for the sake of establishing, broadening and deepening contact between our literature on the one hand, and the masses on the other. It is also of the greatest importance for the literary education of the masses, and for checking whether our literature really does give expression to the things that move the masses, and does so in a correct and penetrating way, rather than lagging all too far behind the development of the masses themselves. It is thus equally instructive and beneficial for both masses and writers. But criticism by the masses is not the same thing as criticism *per se*. And to put forward the idea that Marxist criticism, which leads and guides, pruning off erroneous developments in creative methods and struggling for correct developments, can be replaced by mass criticism, is the same in the field of literary politics as if a party comrade were to propose that the work of central ideological and strategic leadership should be 'replaced' by spontaneous factory discussions. Certainly Comrade Gotsche doesn't want that. He just has not thought the matter through.

Gotsche's viewpoint is still full of elements of bowing to spontaneity. He says: 'We have made a breakthrough in our literature. It will improve and perfect itself only in the constant to and fro of the developmental process as a whole.' Does he mean automatically? Or as the spontaneous result of 'development'? Comrade Gotsche even takes over, without noticing it, the very terminology of the Russian spontaneity worshippers, who used to speak of the 'slow zig-zag course' of development, virtually equivalent to Gotsche's 'constant to and fro'. Any criticism that with relentless candour points out mistakes is obviously 'destructive' for this view of things.

But what concrete arguments does Comrade Gotsche raise against my criticism? In actual fact, he only confirms its central point. He says of Bredel that 'above all . . . he fails to make a dialectical analysis', etc., and his very terminology here (his definition of characters) shows that Comrade Gotsche is still very insecure in questions of materialist dialectics and their application to literature. Can he really maintain that Bredel's books are satisfactory works of art if they are wanting in the application of materialist dialectics? The gist of my criticism was precisely to expose this deficiency, and on this very point Comrade Bredel himself agrees with me. Comrade Gotsche also admits the point, but he resists its concrete applications in criticism. Is this consistent? Is it dialectical? In no way. And it follows from this false point of departure that he is unable to explain to the party cell functionary H. R.,[6] who holds that 'for us it is not only a question of "artistic" form, but of the value of the book in the class struggle', that the contradiction con-structed here between artistic form and impact in the class struggle is a purely bourgeois one. On the basis of spontaneity, it is precisely bourgeois ideologies that make their way into the workers' movement, as Lenin demonstrated in so masterly a way as far back as 1902. Comrade Gotsche makes deep obeisance to this spontaneity, both here and also elsewhere. In this way he drags our literature back, instead of helping it forward. Or does he believe that even if Bredel did have the powerful creative method of Gorky, his works would not have more impact and hence be of greater value in the class struggle? Comrade H. R. seems to equate this improvement with an improvement in sales. But does Comrade Gotsche also believe that the difference in impact between Bredel and Gorky lies only at this level?

Comrade Gotsche bows to spontaneity a further time when he excuses our particular backwardness on the literary front by saying that there is backwardness in other fields as well. But this is hardly a Marxist argument. It would be a pretty pass if one bad factory cell could appeal to the existence of another bad cell, instead of saying: we have fallen behind the possibilities that the objective situation offers, and we must now make up for lost time, catch up and overtake! And this is only possible if we are clearly aware of both the goal to be attained and the difficulties to be faced on the way towards it, of both the favourable ob-jective situation and its possibilities, and of our own strengths and weaknesses – if we consciously resolve to eliminate this backwardness by our own activity, and not by relying on the spontaneity of the movement as a whole.

It is bowing before spontaneity yet a final time, when Comrade Gotsche appeals to the fact that worker readers say: 'This is how people really are'; 'Bredel has depicted all his characters properly', etc. This is to lead the discussion up a wrong path. In my criticism I reproached Bredel for writing a mixture of reportage and public speeches, instead of genuine literary portrayal. This is a question of creative method. The fact that the comrades in Hamburg recognize themselves in Bredel's depictions is neither here nor there. For they would obviously recognize themselves just as well in newspaper reports or public speeches that described their factories and streets, indeed even if these speeches were deficient even in their own terms. Can a bad public spech be made into a good one in this way, or any public speech into a literary por-trayal? Of course not. No more than a photograph becomes a painting just because the person it depicts recognizes himself in it. What should be discussed is rather this, whether speeches or reports can replace literary portrayal? Is reportage perhaps, as certain proletarian writers maintain, both here and in the Soviet Union, the correct 'contemporary' method for our literature? Or is it an inferior creative method, which has been superseded in the Soviet Union, and should be overcome in our case also? This would provide the subject for a very useful discussion. But using the spontaneous method of Comrade Gotsche, we fail even to pose the right questions.

I do not intend to get lost in details. Even though almost every sentence of Comrade Gotsche's needs correction, and especially his basic approach, which can only reinforce working-class readers in sticking to their spontaneous and backward ideas, I would rather call for a discussion on the really burning questions of our literature. For unfortunately both spontaneity and bowing before spontaneity still hold a very great place in it. Until these have been eliminated, we shall not eliminate our backwardness either. For this bowing to spontaneity is a way of papering over the cracks, a way of bowing to our own backwardness, of bowing to those petty-bourgeois ideological residues that exist also among worker readers and writers. Comrade Stalin's criticism of Slutsky,[7] and the articles and speeches by Comrade Thälmann, have given the entire German workers' movement an important push forward. Our task now is to take up the struggle against the ideological inheritance of the Second International concretely and energetically in the field of literature as well, and not to strengthen the workers in their false conceptions, in their clinging to the basis of the spontaneity theory.

'Tendency' or Partisanship? [1932]*

The question as to whether our literature displays 'tendency' is in no way simply a matter of terminology. If we propose to use the word '*Parteilichkeit*' (instead of '*Tendenz*') to denote one of the fundamental characteristics of our literature, it is evident that this implies a new theoretical understanding as to the nature of this literature. We intend in this way to eliminate a complex of theoretical errors and superficialities from our view of literature, and to formulate what is specific about our literature in a clearer and less mistakable way than previously.

What is the meaning of the term '*Tendenz*'? And how did it enter our literary terminology? To start with, '*Tendenz*' is highly ambiguous. It means, first of all, 'a law whose absolute action is checked, retarded and weakened by counteracting circumstances' [*Capital*, Vol. 3, Chapter 14, 1], a meaning of no immediate interest to us here but one which should be mentioned because it above all should not be allowed to disappear from our view.

What is more important and significant for our present question is the sense in which '*Tendenz*' means aspiration or endeavour. In this sense, it already came into widespread use in government and police language in the first half of the nineteenth century. 'Seditious tendency', etc., is a term found in general use in the censorship instructions, proscriptions of books, etc., of the time. What is of fundamental importance for us here is that '*Tendenz*' receives a subjective meaning. In his critique of the new Prussian censorship instructions, the young Marx precisely branded this aspect as characteristic of the arbitrary '*jurisdiction of suspicion*', for such are laws which 'make their main criterion not *actions as such*, but the *frame of mind* of the doer' [*Collected Works*, Vol. 1, p. 119; Marx's emphases]. Unfortunately, I cannot pursue here the precise history of how this legal and police terminology developed into an aesthetic one. (As far as I know, this is a peculiarly German development; the French 'tendency' plays of the mid-nineteenth century were rather known as '*drames à thèse*'.) This shift of meaning, however, already began in the 1840s. In 1841, for example, at a time when he was still under the

* First published in *Die Linkskurve*, IV/6, 1932, pp. 13–21.

influence of the 'Young Germany' movement, Engels referred to Arndt's '*Tendenz*' ('Ernst Moritz Arndt', in *Collected Works*, Vol. 2, p. 137). And among Heine's *Zeitgedichten*, too, we find one with the title '*Die Tendenz*', its last verse reading as follows:

> Peal, resound, thunder daily,
> Till the last oppressor flees –
> Only sing in this direction,
> But do keep your poetry
> As general as possible.

This mocking conclusion of Heine's, who precisely in this very period was further removed from 'pure art' and '*Tendenzlosigkeit*' than before or later, shows how Heine, with a true poetic instinct, had strong reservations about the true nature of the 'tendency' art of his time, and for this very reason objected to the expression in question. Indeed, he struggled both here and in other writings of the same time against the subjectivist, emotion-trapped and hence abstractly general character of 'tendency' literature. We shall go on very shortly to discuss the social reasons for this abstractness. First, we simply want to corroborate the justice of this mocking objection with a further example from another poet, though one who also viewed poetry as a means of struggle.

In the conflict between Herwegh and Freiligrath[1] over the party or non-party stance of the poet (1843), a conflict that had great importance for literary history, Herwegh wrote:

> . . . Let a poem be a sword in your hand.
> Choose a banner, and I am content,
> Even if it is different from my own . . .

Herwegh thus fought for partisanship in general, against the view that Freiligrath held at that time: 'The poet stands on a loftier watchtower than the battlements of party.' Two points are noteworthy here. First, according to Herwegh the question of partisanship or not (i.e. in later terminology 'tendency' art or 'pure' art) was one of subjective decision, not an inescapable law of any literature, as a product and weapon in the class struggle. Second, Herwegh welcomed any partisanship – even one opposed to his own – as a developmental advance, thus conceiving the question of partisanship ('tendency') in a formal manner.

It is not necessary here to depict in detail how this entire view of Herwegh's was based on illusions. Yet it has had to be introduced and analysed in brief, for illusions of this same kind underlie to a greater or lesser extent any bourgeois theory for or against 'tendency art', and the question for us here is not so much to expose these illusions as illusions, but rather to disclose their roots in the existence of the bourgeois class. This is particularly important for us because Franz Mehring's[2] formulation of this complex of questions, which had a decisive influence on the proletarian revolutionary movement in literature, arose under the very strong influence of bourgeois 'tendency art', and despite all Mehring's efforts, did not manage to overcome the contradictions contained in the question itself.

It is understandable, indeed obvious, that the first proletarian literature should have linked up with the 'tendency' literature of what little was left of the literature of the progressive bourgeoisie, and thus took over both the theory and practice of 'tendency'. It did so all the more, in that right from the start it was forced to adopt, in intensified form, the positions held by this progressive bourgeois literature at the time. 'Tendency', in other words, is something very relative. In bourgeois literary theory, as recognized today even officially, a text is seen as displaying 'tendency' if its class basis and aim are hostile (in class terms) to the prevailing orientation; one's own 'tendency', therefore, is not a tendency at all, but only that of one's opponent. The positions of struggle that the various literary factions of the bourgeoisie took up against one another, in which connection, of course, it was generally the more politically and socially progressive trend that was particularly reproached for its 'tendency', rather than the reactionary trend, were assumed with doubled vigour against the first beginnings of proletarian literature. Any depiction of society, whether the society of the proletariat or that of the bourgeoisie, and no matter whether this was presented from the class standpoint of the proletariat itself, or simply from one close to it, was viewed as 'tendentious', and every possible argument as to its 'inartistic' and 'hostile-to-art' character was marshalled against it. At the same time, bourgeois 'pure art' became ever poorer in content and further removed from reality, while simultaneously growing ever more tendentious, so that the prejudice about proletarian 'tendency' art became increasingly hypocritical. Under such conditions, it is only too readily understandable that the young proletarian literature should have taken up the term of abuse applied to it by the class enemy and worn it as a badge of honour, just like the Dutch 'Geusen' (beggars) in the sixteenth and seventeenth centuries, or the 'sans-culottes' of the French revolution. For a long time, therefore, we referred to our literature with pride as a 'tendency literature'.

Yet however understandable it was to take up this theoretical position, this in no way means it is theoretically correct. On the contrary. It takes over unseen, together with the bourgeois formulation of the problem and the bourgeois terminology, the entire bourgeois eclecticism involved in the very terms of the problem itself, its bourgeois-eclectic contradictions, which are not superseded, but rather in part glossed over, and in part rigidly polarized. What we particularly have in mind here is the antithesis between 'pure art' and 'tendency'. On this basis, only two answers are possible. Either, on the one hand, we express contempt for 'pure art' and its perfection of form; literature has a social function in the class struggle, which determines its content; we fulfil this function consciously, and do not worry about the decaying bourgeoisie's questions of form. (This is to restrict literature to everyday agitation, the standpoint of mechanical materialism in literary theory.) Or else, on the other hand, we acknowledge an 'aesthetic' and attempt to reconcile with it a 'tendency' that is taken from the realm of the 'social' or 'political', i.e. a realm that is 'foreign to art'. In this way, the insoluble task of introducing into the work of art a component that is 'foreign to art' is raised in a haphazard manner. On the one hand, therefore, aesthetic immanence is (tacitly) recognized, i.e. the 'pure' autonomy of the work of art, or the domination of form over content; while on the other hand it is demanded that a content which in this view lies outside the artistic ('tendency') should prevail. The result is an eclectic idealism.

These untranscended (and on this basis untranscendable) contradictions are what account for Franz Mehring's lack of sureness on this question. It is well known that Mehring also viewed the Kantian aesthetic that was decisive for the artistic theory of the declining bourgeoisie as a necessary theoretical foundation. The basic conception expressed in this, of 'purposefulness without purpose', and the exclusion of all 'interestedness' from the consideration of art, is evidently a theory of 'pure art'. The further development of this theory by Schiller, which Mehring takes over, that of the 'destruction of the material by the form', only strengthens this tendency of subjective idealism. It is quite consistent, therefore, that the artistic theory of the declining bourgeoisie should make use of these views as a weapon for their struggle against 'tendency'. They could do so all the more successfully, in that the opponents of this practice, the supporters of 'tendency' (in as much as they did not simply represent a vulgarized mechanical materialism), themselves stood on the ground of this theory and were therefore only able to defend themselves against the necessary and unpreventable consequences that were drawn from it in a very inconsistent and eclectic fashion.

This is most blatant with Mehring himself, the most significant German literary theorist of the nineteenth century, who stood far above his bourgeois contemporaries. Mehring's eclecticism finds very clear expression in the way that he could find only an 'on the one hand, on the other hand' solution to the central question of content and form. Mehring is aware that the unconditional recognition of the (subjective idealist) solution of Kant and Schiller leads to acknowledging the 'timelessness' or 'time-transcending' character of art, hence to the primacy of form and a rejection of 'tendency' of any kind. And because he seeks to reject this conclusion, without criticizing its underlying assumptions, he writes that 'taste therefore also depends on the content and not just on the form'. This eclecticism, leading to an absolutely vacuous response on precisely the decisive question, clearly shows how little Mehring was able to go beyond the fundamental problematic of Kant and Schiller, and hence the bourgeois aesthetic in general. The limitation of this conception is shown by the way that the question of 'tendency' is made into a question of the relationship between art and morality, so that the subjective idealist character of 'tendency' clearly emerges: 'tendency' is a demand, an 'ought', an ideal, which the writer counterposes to reality; it is not a tendency of social development itself, which is simply made conscious by the poet (in Marx's sense), but rather a (subjectively devised) commandment, which reality is requested to fulfil. Behind this line of thought lies first of all the rigid and formalized separation of the various spheres of human activity from one another. That is to say, we are confronted by the ideological reflection of the capitalist division of labour. However, instead of thinking of this reflection as the consequence of the division of labour, and subjecting it to Marxist analysis and criticism, it is conceived in purely ideological terms as an 'eternal' law that separates 'essences' and is then made into the starting-point of all further analyses in a quite unhistorical manner. Second, human activity, practice, is conceived not in its real, objective or material production, and as applied to changing society, but rather in its distorted and upside-down ideological reflection (as 'morality'), so that in a similarly ahistorical way, the distorted ideological result has to be made the theoretical starting-point. Third, this counterposing of art and morality contains an uncritical and ideological illusion of the human individual as an 'atom' of society (cf. on this illusion *The Holy Family*), as well as the fetishized conception of society as something 'thing-like', surrounding human beings as an 'alien' reality (the environment theory), rather than being simply the sum and the system, the result of human activity (even if under capitalism this result is not conscious or intended). Fourth, corresponding to this rigid and mechanical counterposing of (individual) man and society, which underlies the entire bourgeois conception of 'morality', we find that the work of art is isolated from social practice, from material production and the class struggle, and the task of art is thought to be that of realizing an 'aesthetic ideal'. And fifth, on this view art and morality are not results of the same social practice, but rather realizations of different, divergent and rigidly counterposed ideals (in Kant's case, 'interest' and 'disinterest'). We can therefore apply to their relationship, and to the solution of the problem of literature and 'tendency' ('morality'), what Hegel wrote about the undialectical conception of body and soul: 'If we take them to be absolutely antithetical and absolutely independent, they are as impenetrable to each other as one piece of matter to another.'[3]

We can take any number of literary works and theories of the nineteenth century, and see that none of them was able to escape the necessary consequences of this approach, which arose from the social being of the bourgeois class, and particularly of its writers (fetishism, etc.). There were only two choices. Either consciously to renounce 'tendency' and create 'pure art' (a renunciation however, that was for this very reason merely apparent), in which case the result was a tendentiously adjusted depiction of reality, i.e. a 'tendency literature' in the worst sense of the term.[4] Or alternatively 'tendency' could be subjectively counterposed to the portrayed reality in a moralizing and preaching fashion, which meant bringing an alien element into the literary portrayal.

Even Mehring was unable to find any escape from this tangle of contradictions, and we can now understand the reason for this. If he accuses Schiller's *Wilhelm Tell*, for example, of an 'inartistic tendency', or Heinrich von Kleist of 'inartistic methods', these are only eclectic solutions, for Mehring was simply in no position, given his premises, to explain in concrete terms what an 'artistic tendency' would be, in theory and in practice. He could not give this explanation, for it follows from the bourgeois conception of art, the basis of which Mehring could not consistently leave behind, that the 'ideal' of art is precisely 'lack of tendency', so that only circumstances that are unfavourable for artistic development (such as the intensification of class conflicts) force on art a 'tendency' character. Mehring's political and class standpoint, however, stands in an insoluble contradiction to his artistic insights. Mehring actually expresses this connection himself, naturally without realizing its full scope: 'In all revolutionary periods, and in all classes struggling for their liberation, taste is always significantly muddied by logic and morality, which is simply a philosophical way of saying that where knowledge and the powers of desire are intense, the power of aesthetic judgement is always jeopardized.'

Here we already have in embryo the literary theory of Trotskyism. For it is clear that when Trotsky writes that 'the dictatorship of the proletariat is not the culturally productive organization of a new society, but rather a revolutionary means of struggle to achieve this', later going on to counterpose rigidly to one another socialism and class struggle, culture accordingly assumes for him, corresponding to the intensification of class struggle and the concretization of all problems in it, the same position that (Kantian) 'pure art' did for Mehring. 'Revolutionary literature must be permeated with the spirit of social hatred . . . (thus it is simply a 'tendency art': G.L.). Under socialism the foundation of society is solidarity (so that a 'pure art', a 'genuine culture' is possible: G.L.) [*Literature and Revolution*, Ann Arbor, 1960, pp. 184 ff.]. It is no accident, then, that the uncritical acceptance of Mehring's writings in our literary and cultural theory has given a boost to Trotskyism. In the same way, any mechanistic reduction of our literary goals, whether conscious and intentional or not, must necessarily end up taking a Trotskyist turn.

It cannot be our task here to analyse in detail all the errors of this conception; this has already been done to a large extent, moreover, in the struggle against Trotskyism. Here we need only indicate the mistake that is decisive for our present question: the false and undialectical view of the subjective factor. Marx and Engels repeatedly gave the dialectic of subjective and objective factors in social development a correct dialectical formulation, in a quite unmistakable fashion. Here I need only quote one such example, which is of particular importance in settling our present question:

The working class . . . have no ready-made utopias to introduce *par décret du peuple*. They know that in order to work out their own emancipation, and along with it that higher form to which present society is irresistibly tending by its own economical agencies, they will have to pass through long struggles, through a series of historic processes, transforming circumstances and men. They have no ideals to realize, but to set free the elements of the new society with which old collapsing bourgeois society itself is pregnant [*The Civil War in France*, *On the Paris Commune*, Moscow, 1971, p. 76].

Thus it is precisely a knowledge of social necessity that determines the correct (and important) place of the subjective factor in the development, contrary to both the mechanistic and the idealist conceptions. Yet it does so for the proletariat in a different fashion than for other classes. The thesis that the working class 'have no ideals to realize' applies only to the proletariat. For other classes, including the revolutionary period of the bourgeoisie, what Engels wrote still holds: 'Ideology is a process accomplished by the so-called thinker consciously, it is true, but with a false consciousness' (letter to Mehring, 14 July 1893). This 'false consciousness' has the subsequent result that conscious human activity in the historical process either has no active significance at all, or else is allotted an inflated independence or leading role, as is also shown in the way that the subjective factor appears in the form of 'morality', its goals taking the form of the 'ideal'. Even those bourgeois writers and thinkers who have penetrated relatively deeply into the dialectic of history, still either get lost in foggy mysticism or remain trapped in contradictions they are unable to resolve. (Hegel, for example, whom Marx saw as affected both by an 'uncritical idealism' and by an 'uncritical positivism'.) Even if they do manage to reach a knowledge of the objective and real driving forces of social development, they still do so only with 'false consciousness', without clear intention, and often actually against their will, consciousness and intent. Thus Engels emphasized in his discussion of Balzac (cf. *Linkskurve*, March 1932) how his conscious intention was to glorify the declining class of the French *ancien régime*, but in actual fact he was 'compelled to go against his own class sympathies and political prejudices', and present a correct and exhaustive picture of the society of his time [letter to M. Harkness, April 1888]. His 'tendency' thus stood in contradiction with his portrayal, and his portrayal was significant despite its 'tendency' rather than because of this. (The situation is similar with Tolstoy and a series of other major bourgeois writers.)

The proletariat, however, does not face this ideological barrier. Its social being allows it (and thus also proletarian revolutionary writers) to transcend this barrier and clearly see the class relationships, the development of the class struggle, that lies behind the fetishized forms of capitalist society. Clarity about these connections and their laws of development also means clarity as to the role of the subjective factor in this development: both the determination of this subjective factor by the objective economic and historical development, and the active function of this subjective factor in the transformation of objective conditions. This knowledge is in no way a mechanical and immediate product of social being. It has rather to be produced. The process of its production, however, is both a product of the internal (material and ideological) disposition of the proletariat, as well as a factor promoting the development of the proletariat from a 'class in itself' to a 'class for itself', i.e. promoting its internal organization for the fulfilment of its world-historical task (the rise of trade unions and the party, their further development, etc.).

If the subjective factor in history is viewed in this way – and this is how it must be viewed by a proletarian revolutionary writer with a command of dialectical materialism – then all the problems we have discussed above in connection with 'tendency' simply cease to be problems at all. Such a writer can reject the dilemma between 'pure' art and 'tendency' art. For in his depiction, a depiction of objective reality with its real driving forces and real developmental tendencies, there is no space for an 'ideal', whether moral or aesthetic. He does not introduce any demands on the portrayal of reality 'from without', for since they are the integral moments of objective reality, from which they emerge and which they help to mould in their turn, any demands that grow concretely out of the class struggle are necessarily an inherent part of the writer's portrayal of reality. This is the necessary result, if the writer seeks to depict reality correctly, i.e. dialectically. He can also reject, therefore, the other dilemma of the 'tendentious' introduction of 'tendency' into the portrayal, the nakedly immediate counterposing of 'tendency' and depiction of reality. He does not need to distort the reality, to adjust it or 'tendentiously' touch it up, for his depiction, if it is correct and dialectical, is precisely built up on a knowledge of those tendencies (in the proper, Marxian sense of the term) that prevail in the objective development. And no 'tendency' can or need be counterposed to this objective reality as a 'demand', for the demands that the writer represents are integral parts of the self-movement of this reality itself, at the same time the results and premises of this self-movement.

It clearly emerges from all this that the rejection of 'tendency' in no way means any 'higher watchtower' of the writer's, in Freiligrath's sense, that would be above 'the battlements of party' (a view which Mehring, for all his eclectic defence of 'tendency', inclines towards despite his dislike of it). On the contrary, a correct dialectical depiction and literary portrayal of reality presupposes the partisanship of the writer. Naturally, again not some kind of 'partisanship in general' as defended by Herwegh, something abstract, subjectivist and arbitrary, but rather partisanship for the class that is the bearer of historical progress in our period: for the proletariat, and specifically for that 'section of the working-class party', the Communists, who are distinguished from other proletarians because 'in the national struggles of the proletarians of the different countries, they point out and bring to the front the common interests of the entire proletariat, independently of nationality', while 'in the various stages of development which the struggle of the working class against the bourgeoisie has to pass through, they always and everywhere represent the interests of the movement as a whole' [*Communist Manifesto, Collected Works*, Vol. 6, p. 497].

A partisanship of this kind, unlike 'tendency' or 'tendentious' presentation, does not stand in contradiction to objectivity in the reproduction and portrayal of reality. It is on the contrary the pre-condition for a true – dialectical – objectivity. In contrast to 'tendency', where a position taken for some cause amounts to an idealistic glorification, and a position against something means simply tearing it to pieces, in contrast also to an 'above party' attitude, whose motto (never kept to in practice) is 'to understand all is to forgive all' – an attitude that contains an unconscious and hence almost always mendacious standpoint – this partisanship champions precisely the position that makes possible knowledge and portrayal of the overall process as a synthetically grasped totality of its true driving forces, as the constant and heightened reproduction of the dialectical contradictions that underlie it. This objectivity, however, depends on a correct – dialectical – definition of the relationship between subjectivity and objectivity, the subjective factor and objective development, and the dialectical unity of theory and practice. The analyses of Marx, Engels and Lenin give us the models of how this dialectical unity should be conceived. To quote again just one example:

> The bourgeoisie makes it its business to promote trusts, drive women and children into the factories, subject them to corruption and suffering, condemn them to extreme poverty. We do not 'demand' such development, we do not 'support' it. We fight it. But *how* do we fight? We explain that

trusts and the employment of women in industry are progressive. We do not want a return to the handicraft system, premonopoly capitalism, domestic drudgery for women. Forward through the trusts, etc., and beyond them to socialism! [Lenin, 'The "Disarmament" Slogan', in *Collected Works*, Vol. 23, p. 97.]

Partisanship in this sense, therefore, is not a new label for an old thing. It is not a question of replacing the term 'tendency' by the term 'partisanship', and leaving everything else as it was. Terminology, in fact, is never accidental. The fact that we took the term 'tendency' from the literary theory and practice of the oppositional bourgeoisie (and not even from the brilliant period of its revolutionary development) was, as we have shown, an indication that we took over along with this term a not inconsiderable ideological baggage. Today, when the ideological legacy of the Second International is being subjected to basic revision at all points of our theory and practice, we must also pay sharp attention in our literary theory and practice that we no longer carry with us the bourgeois baggage handed down by the Second International, which can only hinder our onward march.

We have briefly indicated what the theory of 'tendency' means. By way of conclusion, we want now to ask whether this theory has actually had an influence on our practice. Of course it has. We need not only consider the literary practice of Trotskyism in all its variants, both conscious and unconscious, but also what has up to now been our best literature. Has this really managed the breakthrough to partisanship that makes possible a dialectically objective portrayal of the overall process of our epoch? As soon as this question is clearly raised, it is immediately answered in the negative. Our literature, even in its best products, is still full of 'tendency'. For it does not always succeed, by a long chalk, in portraying what the class-conscious section of the proletariat wants and does, from an understanding of the driving forces of the overall process, and as representative of the great world-historical interests of the working class, portraying this as a will and a deed that themselves arise dialectically from the same overall process and are indispensable moments of this objective process of reality. In place of the portrayal of the subjective factor of revolutionary development, we find all too frequently a merely subjective (because unportrayed) 'desire' on the part of the author: i.e. a 'tendency'. And if the author presents this desire as objective and fulfilled, instead of dialectically portraying the subjective factor as it really is, with its willing and doing, then his depiction becomes 'tendentious'. There is no reason to deny these errors and weaknesses. Still less, to shunt them aside into the field of 'technical mistakes' or 'technical clumsiness'. The method for exposing our errors and disclosing their roots – in the unliquidated legacy of the Second International – is also the method that will help us to overcome these errors: the materialist dialectic, Marxism-Leninism. Partisanship in place of 'tendency' is an important point at which we can and must achieve this breakthrough to the full use of Marxism-Leninism for our creative method.

Reportage or Portrayal? [1932]

1. CRITICAL REMARKS À PROPOS A NOVEL BY OTTWALT[*1]

Ottwalt's new novel[2] is representative of a whole trend in literature, and a quite specific kind of creative method. He works with the methods of journalistic reportage, instead of the 'traditional', 'obsolete' and 'bourgeois' methods of 'invented' plot and 'portrayed' men and women. This trend is very widespread today, on an international scale. The most varied writers are using it, from Upton Sinclair and Tretyakov through to Ilya Ehrenburg. But it is not a trend that has just arisen overnight. In certain respects Zola can already be counted among its forbears and indeed its origins can be traced right back to the social-critical novels of the late Romantic period (Victor Hugo, Georges Sand, Eugène Sue). Historical research into the origins of this literary method would be of great value for the questions we are dealing with here, but unfortunately nothing at all has yet been done in this field. For any definitive conclusions as to its true nature, and its relationship to other literary methods, could only be drawn from a demonstration of how the method arose out of the ideological position of the bourgeoisie at a particular stage in its development. For the time being, however, for want of even preliminary work of this kind, we must rest content with a narrower and hence more abstract framework of discussion.

It is clear, at all events, that even this more limited perspective cannot stop short at Ottwalt's book alone. It would be a simple matter to count the positive aspects of this novel, and if we do not dwell on these here, it is not because we see the book as a bad one. Quite the contrary. It is a good, instructive and useful book. It handles its subject-matter – class justice in Germany in the post-war era – diligently, knowledgeably and systematically. It depicts this subject, moreover, in a lively and stimulating manner. All these good qualities are the individual good qualities of Ottwalt as a writer. What we intend to criticize in Ottwalt's book, on the other hand, is his literary tendency, his creative method, i.e. precisely what he has in common with many other contemporary

*First published in *Die Linkskurve*, IV/7, 8, 1932, pp. 23–30.

writers. Such a criticism must start out, therefore, from these common features. Ottwalt's book, which is thus the occasion for this critique as well as its direct object, is suited precisely by virtue of its merits as the starting-point for that fundamental debate on these questions that has become indispensable in our literary development.

Psychologism

Why do many people, even among proletarian writers and readers, view this form as more contemporary than that of the traditional novel? This is not a hard question to answer, and the response sheds an immediate and clear light on the social provenance of this form and its artistic character. The view arose, and became increasingly influential and widespread, that the bourgeois novel, ever more lost in the psychological depiction of private fates and feelings, was absolutely unsuited to tackling in any way the great and general questions of our time, let alone to adopting an appropriate attitude towards them. Contained in this view was the correct instinct that form and content belong causally together; that the complete failure of the psychological novel cannot be just an accident; that there is a causal relationship between the form, its content (and the world outlook of its author); and that the question is therefore not to try and improve or reconstruct it, but to put something quite different in its place. Dissatisfaction with the content of the psychological novel, which had become vacuous, provoked a justified opposition to its form. And yet this opposition did not go deeply enough into either the question of content, or that of world outlook. There were class reasons – as we shall show – why it could not go deep enough, so that it became simply a renewal of form. It would not be an adequate explanation of the failure of the psychological novel if the cause were sought solely in the insufficient courage of its authors to speak the truth about present-day society (as Upton Sinclair does, for example), or even in these writers' inadequate knowledge of social conditions. This is all evidently a factor, and is even of decisive importance. The apologetic character of bourgeois literature in the era of its decay, and even long before this decay became pronounced, is fundamental for any assessment of it. And yet it does not explain why the apologetic tendency takes the precise form of psychologism. For there is also a more overt apologetic tendency in bourgeois literature that does not resort to psychologism; Kipling, for example, as herald of British imperialism, or more crudely, detective stories, etc. On the other hand, there is a variant of the psychological novel that does not derive from an apologetic base, its earliest and greatest representatives, such as Flaubert and Jacobsen,[3] in fact making a sharp criticism of capitalist society, even if inconsistently and with an unsuitable world outlook. Psychologism, as one form of the apologetic tendency, a special and 'superior' form, must therefore be grasped in terms of the social being of the bourgeois class, in terms of the capitalist division of labour and the commodity fetishism that arises on this basis, the 'reification' of consciousness. We should particularly consider, in studying this literary development, the way that under capitalism the division of labour also operates in certain fields of ideological production, so that 'another new and independent sphere is opened up which, for all its general dependence on production and trade, has also a special capacity for acting upon these spheres'.[4] Psychologism, in literature, is one case of this 'special capacity'. The principal expression of 'reification' in the case of writers, and in general of those intellectuals who are not directly connected with material production, is that existing reality appears to them as 'mechanical', 'soulless', and dominated by 'alien' laws. This conception exhibits the most diverse variations ranging from a 'meaningless' system of laws to that of chaos, according to the phase of development of capitalist production, which itself constantly eludes comprehension. To this 'vacuous' reality, the bourgeois writer counterposes the 'life of the soul', which is 'alone decisive'. This life of the soul then becomes the centre of gravity, and sometimes the sole content, of his portrayal. The creative method that arises on this basis is psychologism. It arose in the case of its first and most important representatives as a romantic opposition to the dehumanizing effects of capitalism, although even here the reflection of the real state of affairs was not merely upside down, but quite distorted. For even these writers regard the ideological effects as the reality immediately given to them, and proceed from this starting-point to combat the unfathomed and hence mythologized causes of what they view as harmful and dehumanizing. As the development proceeds, this romantic anti-capitalism increasingly loses its cutting edge. It becomes pure apologetics, in part preaching and glorifying capitulation to old ideologies (Dostoyevsky, Bourget, Huysmans, etc), in part, by depicting only the 'inner life', carrying on a more or less conscious education in the direction of political and social indifferentism, of ignoring and pushing aside the 'inessential', 'external' struggles of the world, in favour of the 'life of the soul', which is all that matters (Hamsun, and Anatole France in his early writings).

The Reportage Novel as an Opposition to Psychologism

Reportage, as a literary method, came into being from a justified op-position to such conceptions and their literary expression. These op-positional writers, who stood in greater or lesser proximity to the workers' movement, some more clearly so than others, sought to depict in objective fashion, faithful to the actual state of affairs, the evils of capitalist society they were concerned to combat. The initial starting-point for this tendency was thus an attitude towards capitalist society different from that of the psychological novelists: a standpoint of petty-bourgeois radicalism, sometimes bordering on socialism. Depictions of the objective facts, which formed the highest goal of this tendency, were thus never an end in themselves, but were designed to serve the exposure of the most crying abuses and grievances. The result of this intention was naturally that in depicting the objective facts in an exposé of this kind, the individual men and women involved in it, with their particular individual experiences, destinies, etc., could only play a subordinate role. In sharp contrast to the psychological novel, its art of 'dissection' and the incessant reflection of its author on the feelings, experiences, etc., of his characters, not to mention the reflections of the characters on their own experiences – in sharp contrast to the entire sceptical, if poetic, caprice of psychologism (Dostoyevsky himself called psy-chology a 'double-edged weapon') – what was now to be depicted was simply and resolutely the objective, the purely typical, that which was independent of the individual. In contrast to psychologism, therefore, a purely social content.

This contradiction, however, was and is still not a dialectical but a mechanical one. As we have already stressed, most representatives of the reportage novel, and especially its inventors, were petty-bourgeois opponents of capitalism, and not proletarian revolutionaries. Thus they had no materialist or dialectical understanding of capitalism's laws of motion, and the contradictions that move it. They could only recognize certain isolated facts, or in the best case groups of facts – never the con-tradictory unity-in-process of the totality – and pass moral judgements on these facts. The fetishistic dismemberment of reality, and the in-ability to see relations between people (class relations) in the 'things' of social life, is therefore as much present in their works as in those of their artistic antipodes, the psychologists, even though for a different reason. While the psychologists, as subjective idealists, fall into the illusion in which 'the egoistic individual of bourgeois society . . . inflates himself in his nonsensical view and lifeless abstraction into an isolated atom', the new school commit the typical mistake of the old materialism and do not recognize the dialectic through which the 'driving forces' of society and history operate 'in the brains of the actors' (Engels, *Ludwig Feuerbach*). They want the objective to be purely objective, the content pure content, without any dialectical interaction with the subjective and formal factors, and in this way they fail to grasp and give adequate expression to both the objective and the content too. The subjective factor they push aside appears in their work as the unportrayed subjectivity of the author, as a moralizing commentary that is superfluous and accidental, an attribute of the characters that has no organic connection with the plot. And this mechanical and one-sided exaggeration of the content leads to an experiment in form: to the attempt to renew the novel with the means of journalism and reportage.

What is Reportage?

Reportage is an absolutely legitimate and indispensable form of journalism. At its best, it makes the right connection between the general and the particular, the necessary and the contingent, that is appropriate to its particular purpose. Genuine reportage is in no way content simply to depict the facts; its descriptions always present a connection, disclose causes and propose consequences. (The materialist dialectic, therefore, as a basic world outlook, can provide opportunities for reportage, too, that are impossible on a bourgeois basis.) Yet the way that facts and their interconnections are combined, i.e. the particular and the general, the individual and the typical, the accidental and the necessary, is fundamentally different here from what happens in creative literature. In good reportage, the fact, i.e. the individual case, is depicted concretely and individually in a way that makes it really come to life; sometimes it really is portrayed, in the sense of creative literature. But here the individual case serves simply as example and illustration of the general, and whether it is depicted more or less scientifically, it is always depicted conceptually and verified (supported by statistics), in a way that directly puts it in a more general context. The intention of reportage, in other words, is to convince by reason alone that the implications it draws from the facts are correct.

Reportage does indeed appeal to our feelings, both in its depiction of the facts and in the call to action that it implies. But it does so by convincing us intellectually. In this respect, therefore, reportage, like all other kinds of journalism, operates principally with the methods of science. The dirtinction between these methods and the methods of art has nothing to do with the modern (bourgeois-decadent) mechanical separation between understanding and feeling (and experience, etc.). Both appeal equally to the understanding and to feeling, and so both call us to action. But in accordance with their differing aims and objectives, they use different methods, and our task is to investigate this difference.

A good reportage is based on thorough and comprehensive study, embraces a large and well-organized body of facts and presents its examples clearly. The better it does all this, the more evident it becomes that the examples produced are no more than examples, simply illustrations of the overall connection that is recognized and presented. They are then all the more readily exchangeable for other examples from the great arsenal of facts, examples and illustrative cases that the author of the reportage has observed, collected and arranged. They must of course be typical cases, if they are correctly to support and elucidate the conditions in question and the implications drawn from them. But they are typical in a way that is fundamentally different from what is typical in literary portrayal. Here the individual and his destiny has to appear typical as such, i.e. to contain its class-type features within it as individual features. The concrete totality of literary portrayal deals only with individuals and individual destinies, whose living interactions illuminate, complement and make each other comprehensible, the connection between such individuals being what makes the whole typical. In reportage, on the other hand, the individual case only keeps its really typical character, in an all-round way, in the conceptual summary and explanation of the conditions that it serves to illustrate, even if this summary is either necessarily or deliberately kept to a minimum. The concreteness of reportage, as of every conceptual (scientific) reproduction of reality, is only achieved with the conceptual disclosure and presentation of causes and inter-connections. What Engels says of the scientific method in general, holds good also for reportage and journalism in general: 'The general law of change in the form of motion is far more concrete than any specific "concrete" example of it.'

Reportage as Creative Method

In no way does this distinction imply any criticism of reportage. It is simply the distinction between two specific methods for two specific fields. The question is quite different, however, if reportage comes to be used as a creative method in literature. It is then necessary to investigate meticulously whether the method that is perfectly correct in reportage proper, as its particular way of reproducing reality, does not become an obstacle for literary portrayal. This seems to me to be precisely what actually happens. The methods of depiction that underlie science and art respectively exclude one another, however much their ultimate basis, the reproduction of reality in thought, might be the same, and however profitably each of them can and sometimes must use elements of the other − subordinated to its own underlying method and organically inserted into it. Yet an 'artistic' depiction with scientific goals will always result in both a pseudo-science and a pseudo-art, while a 'scientific' solution of specifically artistic tasks similarly produces a pseudo-science, from the point of view of content, and a pseudo-art, from the point of view of form. But this is precisely what reportage as a creative method in literature strives to do, whether consciously or otherwise. It seeks to overcome caprice and subjectivism. But since it arises on a class basis from which a method of objective comprehension and reproduction of reality as an overall process is either no longer, or else not yet attainable,[5] it finds itself clinging to a method of objectivity that can serve in literature only as a surrogate.

This surrogate, this replacement of the authentic by the inauthentic, is simply the empirical reality itself − however paradoxical this may sound. In reportage, what matters above all is that the facts adduced agree in every detail with the actual situation. If a writer says that the worker Franz Müller in Wedding [a working-class suburb of Berlin] has had his unemployment assistance unjustifiably withdrawn, then this must actually have happened to a real Franz Müller, born on such and such a date, living at a certain address, etc. Here the successful, palpable and concrete depiction of the case makes no new contribution to the actual state of affairs, it simply serves to enhance the impression it makes on people. Even the best depiction cannot add to the actual circumstances of the Müller case, and the worst depiction cannot take anything away from it. If on the other hand this case is something to be portrayed in fiction, then it is quite immaterial how many details may not coincide with the underlying empirical reality. They may all agree exactly, and yet the literary result may be quite worthless; on the other hand they may not agree at all, and yet the literary result may still be perfect. And this alone is what matters here. For the creative writer does not create in perfect freedom, simply out of his own mind, as bourgeois-idealist aesthetics claims. He is on the contrary closely tied to the reproduction of reality in a manner faithful to its true content. This tie, however, means that he has to reproduce the overall process (or else a part of it, linked either explicitly or implicitly to the overall process) by disclosing its actual and essential driving forces. The reality of a particular character, a particular destiny, etc., now depends on the expression of this overall process and its driving forces – the degree to which this is successfully achieved, its truth and penetration, concreteness, palpability and typicalness. 'Realism, to my mind, implies, beside truth of detail, the truth in reproduction of typical characters under typical circumstances' [Engels, letter to M. Harkness, April 1888]. Whether the particular features appear in the same combination as in empirical reality is completely immaterial, and indeed, apart from certain particularly fortunate exceptions, it is highly improbable that combinations of individual features should appear in empirical reality in such a way as to indicate pervasive features that show clearly, and in a palpable and concrete fashion, the connection to the essential and the driving forces.

The reportage novel takes its methods of depicting reality from eye-witness journalism. From a class point of view, this is completely understandable. While the proletarian revolutionary writer, since he takes dialectical materialism as the basis of his creative method, always has in mind the driving forces of the overall process,[6] the writer who finds himself in petty-bourgeois opposition to capitalist society cannot proceed from this overall process and its driving forces, of which he understands nothing. He wants to expose certain details. What is of overriding importance to him, therefore, is that these details are correct. For given that he is unable to portray the process as a whole, he is forced to demonstrate his particular case (or complex of particular cases). And all he can present as evidence is its agreement with empirical reality. Ottwalt explicitly says as much in the Preface to his book, with commendable frankness:

> There are reasons in the history of the German republic why these facts may sometimes strike the reader as quite unbelievable. The writer asks the reader therefore to apply to him, via the publishers, should he have any doubt as to the documentary character of this or that detail depicted in this book. All inquiries of this kind will be answered by production of the factual material on which the points in question are based.

Fetishism

Let us now consider somewhat more closely what implications follow from this difference in methods of depiction. We should note first of all that the merits of reportage in its own field now disappear, and its limitations – which in its own field are the organic limitations of a method of depicting reality that, while restricted, is justified and effective – now transform themselves into barriers to the possibilities of portrayal.

Genuine reportage, in other words, permits a lively, effective and penetrating depiction of a section of reality, even without any insight into the overall process and its interconnections. If the particular cases are correctly observed and depicted, and the generalization goes at least as far as to show that these are typical of the section of reality that is described, then they have a power of conviction even when the overall connection is not recognized at all, or is even misconstrued (e.g. Knickerbocker's peculiar account of conditions in Germany.).[7] The very precondition for the correct construction of a novel, however, is the portrayal of this overall connection. This may be portrayed with 'false consciousness', i.e. in such a way that the author condemns the present in which he lives and which he describes, consciously affirming either a past and perishing society or a utopia present only in his imagination, but nevertheless in his portrayal still recognizing, indicating and portraying the driving forces in their interconnection, which Engels considered 'one of the greatest triumphs of Realism' (letter on Balzac [ibid.]; cf. also Lenin on Tolstoy, where the limitations of a portrayal from the standpoint of this 'false consciousness' are exposed in masterly fashion).

Portrayal of the overall process is the precondition for a correct construction. Why is this? Because only portrayal of the overall process can dissolve the fetishism of the economic and social forms of capitalist society, so that these appear as what they actually are, i.e. (class) relations between people. 'To them, their own social action takes the form of the action of objects, which rule the producers instead of being ruled by them' [*Capital* Vol. 1, Moscow, 1961, p. 75]. If for instance – to turn also in content now to Ottwalt's theme – the capitalist judicial system is described in a journalistic account as a 'machine', on the basis of bourgeois ideology, demolishing people with inhuman 'impartiality' and 'objectivity', this may well be very useful and effective in certain circumstances, the fetishism of this world outlook only restricting the mode of presentation, and not destroying it. But when this fetishistic conception becomes the basis on which a novel is constructed, then its one-sided and mechanical nature emerges with full clarity. The judicial system is now seen as a finished product, not as a moment in a process, as itself in process and development, in constant vital interaction with its preconditions and consequences, as the living result of the (class) human relations between those people whose activity provides both its subject and object. Rigid and mechanical, moved (in a circle) by its 'own' laws, it is seen rather as confronting invincibly and indomitably all those individuals who in part serve this machine – and moreover in such a way that they become themselves simply cogs in its works – and in part fall unresisting victims to it, just as corn to the mill. This is the first characteristic aspect of the reportage novel that we want to stress here: it conceives a social product as ready-made and final, and precisely describes it as such ('objectively' and 'scientifically'). Here the acquisition of a very relative autonomy by the products of the overall development, which Marx and Engels indicated as characteristic of capitalist society, is made into something absolute. Since the dialectical interconnection of such a social product is invisible both to the social stratum that 'serves' this product, i.e. whose activity is what makes up its existence, and to the social totality in whose class struggles it intervenes to perform specific functions (which is the reason why it can acquire this autonomy), the dialectical surface appearance hardens into an illusory reality. This fetishistic appearance of autonomy, which as a moment of the totality ought to be dialectically superseded,[8] remains in fact unsuperseded. It becomes, in fact, a 'thing-like' product, i.e. no longer just the dialectical appearance of a product, becoming genuinely autonomous, and no longer playing in the dialectical process the necessary, but also necessarily superseded, role of a moment that simply becomes 'autonomized'.

A whole series of important ideological and artistic defects follow from these necessary implications of reportage as a creative method. Firstly, the exposure of the bourgeoisie's repressive apparatus, which is made with good revolutionary intent, is given a false emphasis politically. It appears all-powerful and invincible. What is missing is the struggle and resistance of the working class. The proletariat is depicted as the impotent object of the judicial system. Indeed, in most cases what we see are not genuine representatives of the class, but rather characters who have already been worn down and had the life beaten out of them, people incapable of resistance who have fallen into the lumpenproletariat. Even where workers in struggle do become the object of the judicial machinery (e.g. the Cheka trial in Leipzig),[9] they are still mere objects of the system, and their class-conscious and combative attitude cannot find effective expression. Yet this is neither an accidental failure of Ottwalt's, still less his weakness as a writer in general, but rather a necessary consequence of his creative method. Only if the overall process is portrayed, and the class struggle of the proletariat is the depicted pre-condition for the existence and specificity of this class justice, can the struggle of the workers before the court, which in actual fact is only one moment in the class struggle, appear as such a moment. Divorced from the general struggle, what triumphs in the portrayal is simply the fetishistic and rigidified form of appearance. It is certainly not untrue that no matter what the revolutionary worker might say or do in court, the verdict is a foregone conclusion and he is simply an object for the class-justice machine. It is not untrue, but it is only a part of the truth, and 'the truth is the whole' (Hegel). Any partial truth that is separated from the whole and fixed rigidly on itself, while giving itself out as the whole truth, is necessarily transformed into a distortion of the truth. The same political mistake can be found in all novels constructed with this method. I do not intend to discuss Ehrenburg, with whom the connection between a sceptically corroded, intellectualist and anti-revolutionary world outlook, and the ever more deliberate avoidance of all methods of portrayal, is evident at first sight. But even with Upton Sinclair we can clearly see how his lack of clarity in questions of class struggle, and his fluctuation between petty-bourgeois moralizing social criticism and genuine adherence to the proletarian class struggle, also finds expression as a fluctuation between realistic portrayal and reportage. Whenever he gets closer to the concrete class struggle, his literary portrayal is also stronger (*Jimmy Higgins*), and the further removed he is from it, the more pronounced reportage becomes as his method of construction (*Petroleum*). In the latter case, there is a high degree of similarity with Ottwalt in the description of the proletariat. With Ottwalt, too, it seems to us that what finds expression in these political consequences of his creative method are precisely the social roots that led him to choose this method: a rapprochement to the revolutionary proletariat that arises from the critique of bourgeois society, but which up till now has developed only into a criticism of the bourgeoisie, not into a real coalescence with the revolutionary class, so that it remains stuck halfway even as a simple critique of bourgeois society, a mechanical and not a dialectical critique.

Accident and Necessity

The lack of dialectics we have demonstrated in Ottwalt's critique of bourgeois society must necessarily show itself in the depiction of the actual characters in his story and in the connections between them, i.e. in construction, plot and characterization. It is Ottwalt's intention, and this much is completely justified, to present a comprehensive picture of all branches of the German judicial apparatus. He accordingly has us follow the career of his hero from a student just after the war up to a high judicial position, so as to illuminate German justice from all sides in the course of this development. This pattern of construction and plot is designed on the one hand to offer as complete a presentation as possible of all branches and levels of the German judiciary, which indeed it does (from the faculty of law through to corporal punishment), while on the other hand demonstrating the complete adaptation of the central character to the existing system in the course of this 'development', despite his occasional remonstrations. Construction and plot hang closely together, and are carried through with the same – pseudo-scientific – system. The hero's 'development' is taken right from the start as a text-book case. The novel opens with the hero already content in his complete adaptation, before showing us the precise map on which his way towards this is marked point by point. Just as in a mathematical theorem, we have first the thesis, then the proof. Or as in a chess problem, where white is to move and mate in three. The systematic and almost pedantic arrangement of the various elements in the judicial system fits completely into this plan: it is like a collection of butterflies, where neat examples of the public prosecutor, the high-court judge, the capitalist lawyer, etc., are given, each with a tidy label. The plot is geared completely to the construction. With the same pedantic system, the author not only leads his 'hero' through all these stages, but also gives him corresponding 'lessons': at university, a liaison with a working-class girl, a little participation in the killing of workers during the Kapp putsch, and the various types of student (a member of an aristocratic students' association, a poor scholar, a rich sceptic); then during his term as junior barrister, a liaison with an 'enlightened', 'left-wing' Jewish woman, etc.; as provincial judge a liaison with a nymphomaniac aristocratic lady, and acquaintance with various Junker types, etc., etc. Everything that the prescribed content demands is certainly there, and everything systematically arranged in its necessary place. Anything accidental is ruled out. Nothing comes about that is not prescribed by the plan. White moves and mates in three.

This mechanical exaggeration of necessity, however, collapses into its opposite. 'Hence chance is not here explained by necessity, but rather necessity is degraded to the production of what is merely accidental . . . chance is not elevated into necessity, but rather necessity degraded into chance' [Engels, *Dialectics of Nature*, Moscow 1972, pp.

219–20]. What does the antithesis between accident and necessity, and its dialectical supersession, imply for the creative method in literature? Let us seek to make things somewhat clearer with the aid of a concrete example. Tolstoy, in his final novel *Resurrection*, chose a theme that is closely related in content to Ottwalt's book, but he portrayed this theme with a diametrically opposed creative method. Tolstoy also gives us a comprehensive picture of the Russian judicial system. But he does so in particular by illuminating this constantly from two sides, from above and below, within and without. His male hero, on the one hand, is a member of the ruling class, and involved in a jury trial that is of decisive importance for the plot, subsequently seeking to make good the injustice that has been done, etc. His experiences, as we follow them, illuminate the system from 'above' and 'within'. The heroine, on the other hand, is the victim of the judicial system. From her side we acquire a picture from 'below', and experience the hideous arbitrariness and bestial cruelty of tsarist 'justice'. Both these characters are people of flesh and blood. Tolstoy does everything to arouse in his reader a passionate interest in their development, their personality and their fate. And by genuine portrayal in both cases, he does indeed succeed in doing so. In the course of the plot, which is so gripping because we share in it from within, we get to know the most diverse types of victims of the judicial process, as well as its executors. These characters are typical ones, and in their totality they give a far more complete picture of the Russian judicial system than Ottwalt does of the German, without the form of the novel being in any way denatured and reduced to pedantic systems. They give, moreover, a picture with which we can empathize. Just to give one example, both Tolstoy and Ottwalt describe the infliction of corporal punishment. In Ottwalt's case, however, all we get are some informed discussions between lawyers and a fleeting visit to the penitentiary by a judge. With Tolstoy, the suffering of the prisoner, from the stinking, bug-ridden cell through to the actual chastisement, is portrayed in terms of the real suffering of real people. Ottwalt, in other words, has a great deal to say about miscarriages of justice, its arbitrary character, class nature, etc. But he always only speaks about these things, he never gives us the things themselves. When Tolstoy's hero, on the other hand, a Russian aristocrat, appeals to a lady of his own class on behalf of a political prisoner who has already spent seven months in prison on remand, and this lady, in the interest of a little flirtation with him, accedes to his request and writes to him: 'I have spoken with my husband. It seems that this person can immediately be released. My husband has already instructed the commandant . . .' [Book Two, Chapter 18; French in the orginal], these lines illustrate the whole class character of the system far better, more strikingly and devastatingly than a hundred pages of data and reflections, no matter how authentic the documentary material. The question as to why this is so cannot be answered simply by saying that Tolstoy is a 'greater writer'. This would be an evasion of the issue. Tolstoy is indeed the greater writer, but he is so because he presents the question more comprehensively, and in a more all-round, materialist, and dialectical fashion, than does Ottwalt.[10] Tolstoy treats the judicial system as one part of the overall process. To the extent that he writes 'from the standpoint of protest against advancing capitalism, against the ruining of the masses, who are being dispossessed of their land . . . [and] happens to express the specific features of our revolution as a *peasant* bourgeois revolution',[11] to this extent, though only to this extent, does he portray the social process in its dynamic totality and unity; to this extent is the judicial system for him simply a part of this – original – dialectical unity and totality, and does everything in his writing resolve into interaction between individuals, class, class struggle and society as a whole, and does he supersede everything accidental in his characters and their fates, raising it to the level of necessity.

Tolstoy, indeed, treated the accidental in a far more sovereign fashion than does Ottwalt. It is the crassest accident conceivable that his prince sits as a juror over the very girl whom he himself seduced, and as a result of this seduction drove into prostitution. But why does this train of coincidence not strike the reader as a disturbing accident, while with Ottwalt even the most carefully motivated things remain accidental? This difference lies in the overall construction, which, as we have shown, is directly dependent on the world outlook of the writer, and thus ultimately on his class situation and the position he takes up in the class struggle. Tolstoy seeks to use the purely personal (however typical) fate of his character in order to broach a whole series of decisive questions of his time. Since he portrays the living interaction between living human beings, and hence their interaction with the society in which they live and with which they have to battle, he simultaneously portrays the living and dialectical combination and inextricable coalescence of accident and necessity. Accident does not cease to be accident because necessity finds expression through it, nor does necessity cease to be necessary because it is occasioned by an accident. (Recall the above example of the political prisoner.) Engels placed particular emphasis on Hegel's thesis that 'the accidental has a cause because it is accidental, and just as much also has no cause because it is accidental; that the accidental is necessary, that necessity determines itself as chance, and on the other hand, this chance is rather absolute necessity' [ibid., p. 220]. In Ottwalt's case, however, necessity and accident confront one another inflexibly and exclusively. The intelligible content of his book is one of rigid and mechanical necessity; mechanical because, as we showed, the interaction with the overall process, the insertion of the partial field into the totality, is lacking. Every particular, every character, every fate and every event is thus purely accidental, an example that can be exchanged at will, and replaced by another example. At the very most, the choice is determined by the accident that certain particular cases can be documented, or seem best suited, out of a wealth of examples that is evidently far greater than those which Ottwalt actually selects, to serve as illustration of the judicial system. There is simply no connection between the particular elements and steps in the series of examples, disguised as characters, who comprise the novel. While with Tolstoy each particular feature both 'has a cause' and 'has no cause', and is therefore alive, with Ottwalt the abstract idea of the whole is mechanically overdriven; every particular is necessarily drawn into this lifeless, supra-sensible, abstract centre; every particular is unconnected and unnecessary as a particular; it is left one-sidedly and mechanically to accident, just as the abstract whole is one-sidedly and mechanically given the attributes of necessity.

Content and Form

We have now returned to our starting-point, the question of content and form. We said that the mechanical and one-sided exaggeration of the content led to an experiment in form. The grounds for this we have already shown in the analysis of particular problems. To resume once again, in this case the form is independent of the content, confronting it rigidly from outside as something foreign; form and content are kept quite separate from one another. And in this way mechanical materialism collapses into idealism, just as it always does when it seeks to master the process as a whole. In the field of literature, we get an experiment in form. For in the materialist dialectic content is the overriding moment that ultimately determines form, in the living dialectical interaction between the two. For all its dialectically necessary activity, autonomy and inherent dynamic, form is only the essence of the content become visible, palpable and concrete. And form and content are constantly changing places, 'so that content is nothing but the revulsion of form into content, and form nothing but the revulsion of content into form. This mutual revulsion [*Umschlag*] is one of the most important laws of thought'.[12] It only arises if the dialectically dynamic whole is concretely portrayed with all its determinations. If partial moments are allowed to acquire a rigid autonomy, then content and form similarly come to stand in a rigid relation to each other, and the mode of depiction becomes indifferent to the matter depicted. This indifference destroys the unity of content and form, and in this way it leads to the form's autonomy, to an experiment in form. Thus the exaggeration of the content, which was originally intended as materialist, even if mechanically so, ceases to be in any way a possible support for the materialist principle. On the contrary, this exaggeration is what comprises the very essence of the formal experiment; the form, which in this case cannot become the portrayed expression of the content, cannot coalesce with the content and change places with it, must therefore acquire an autonomy of its own. The application of the reportage method to the novel, which was originally intended to give pure expression to the content, ends up in an idealistic experiment in form.

This is most clearly to be seen in the relation between plot and characters. The transformation of form into content and vice versa finds its clearest expression here, in the case of genuine portrayal. If we consider, for example, the example of Tolstoy, as discussed above, we can see that the destinies of his characters are inseparable from their 'psychology'. The characters develop on the basis of actions and events, as the result of these; while conversely these actions and events only exist as actions and events in which these particular people are involved. And the social environment, as it appears in the actions of living human beings, as it is resolved into the actions of these concrete human beings, confronts them as an independent power only in as much as this is the necessary form of appearance of the social environment in capitalist society. This is typical, therefore, but in a way that supersedes the individual and the concrete in the dual dialectical sense, i.e. abolishing and preserving, raising to a higher level. It is quite different with Ottwalt, as we have shown, his construction being simply a systematic presentation of the German judicial system. This can be demonstrated from any element in Ottwalt's plot. He chooses the career of the son of a judge, from a student to a high judge himself. But this 'free' choice of the author's, this 'experimenting' with the material, turns out to be illusory at every step. Since at each stage in the development, one or other category of the same documentary material is presented, discussed and legally processed, the way in which the stages in the plot follow on from one another, i.e. the arrangement of the material, is in fact quite independent of action and construction, following certain abstract political ideas of the author that are not actually rooted in the story itself. The climax in the presentation of the material follows from a different perspective than that of the plot. Equally independent of one another are the plot and its protagonists. Any other character could follow the same career, which is no more than a simple guided tour through the various branches of the judicial system, and all the more so in that the main protagonist is not in fact the 'travelling' main character, but rather the author himself, writing his report on this guided tour. The main character, and still more so the subsidiary characters, are nothing more than objects of demonstration for the presentation of a certain factual content.

(In this point, too, the mistake is not just a personal one of Ottwalt's. All representatives of this method show the same indifference between mode of presentation and contents. With Tretyakov,[13] for example, this is still more crass than in Ottwalt's case. In his most recent novel, for example, Tretyakov relates the life of a Chinese revolutionary in the form of an autobiography.[14] The narrator is only five or six years old when his father, a supporter of Sun Yat-sen, returns home and takes part in organizing the Chinese revolution. The young boy is present at a meeting, at which his father gives an analysis of the various tendencies in the revolutionary party and investigates their social basis. Tretyakov presents all this – from the boy's own memory, and in his own milieu – in proper party language, as a completely well-formed speech. Then again, a few years later the boy describes a journey by boat. He says: 'The coolies bend over the oars or wearily pull on the ropes. We do not see them, they do not interest us.' There follows a precise analysis, i.e. that the sons of the coolies do not go to school, etc. There is simply no relationship between the mode of presentation and the contents.)

But with Ottwalt's main character it is precisely this lack of connection that has such fatal repercussions on the content (as also with Upton Sinclair), in a way that shows the social roots of this creative method, as we have already explained them. The personality of this character is completely contingent, as far as construction and plot are concerned, but he is still a necessary product of this creative method and of the social factors that led to its development. Just as Upton Sinclair with the capitalist petrol industry, so Ottwalt, too, cannot bring this judicial system to life, even in dialogue, because he fails to give any life to his main character. If he really was a class-conscious representative of present-day German justice, i.e. a really typical character, then his social milieu would necessarily be untypical. The author would have to introduce new interlocutors at every step, with doubts, vacillations, qualms of conscience, etc., in relation to whom the main character would then present his consistent class standpoint. For Ottwalt, however, the preferred form is the very reverse of this. The hero's milieu is made up of typical class jurists, his father being the most consistent of these. (Upton Sinclair's construction is again similar, and certainly not by accident.) The main character, on the other hand, is hollow and vacillating; morally repelled by the theory and practice of his environment, and yet incapable of breaking with his class, he swings incessantly back and forth between 'scruples' and resignation, until at last his adaptation is complete. From time to time these fluctuations provide both occasion and theme for conversations in which the reportage material is unfolded and discussed. No long explanations are needed to see quite clearly why 'heroes' of this kind, though of course they can by no means just be identified with their creators, still reflect their authors' class position very faithfully. In both cases, Ottwalt and Upton Sinclair, we have honest intellectuals stemming from the bourgeoisie, who are not only intensely aware of that class's decay, but seek by their practice and literary production to spur on the bourgeoisie's deserved demise. They are aware, too, that the path leading in this direction is precisely the path to the proletariat. But they are not aware – at least not yet – that the break with their own class must be complete in all areas, including that of ideology, and that only such a complete break will provide the preconditions for a fusion with the working class, for the appropriation and ability to use the world outlook of the revolutionary proletariat, i.e. dialectical materialism. As long as this point is not reached, the class basis of these writers remains restricted; they are already estranged from their own class of origin, but are not yet at home in the class that they want to adhere to. This is what leads to the abstractness, rigidity, lifelessness and poverty of their depictions. They have distanced themselves from the everyday life of the bourgeois class, and they view this with justified criticism. But since they have no access to the non-political, non-public life of the proletariat, since they see its class struggle only in its public results and not also in its interaction with the everyday life of the workers, which is what forms the basis of these struggles, they develop the conception that only this final result of the life and struggles of the working class, which is most visible on the surface of public life, provides an interesting theme for their writing. This disdain for the 'private life' of the workers, which even if it is unconscious, is a pervasive feature of reportage novels, is just as fetishistic as the exclusive description of private feelings and destinies practised by psychologism.[15]

In Ottwalt's vacillating 'hero' – and those of many other writers – we have clear and direct expression, expression in the content, of precisely that class position whose consequences we have sought to demonstrate from the standpoint of form and the manifold mediations this involves. This demonstration, this struggle against Ottwalt's creative method, is in no way a struggle against Ottwalt himself. On the contrary, it is a struggle for Ottwalt, the attempt to ease the path towards the working class for an intellectual who is sincerely striving in this direction.

2. A VIRTUE OF NECESSITY*

I can only be grateful to Comrade Ottwalt for his rejoinder.[16] He only confirms everything I wrote in my article, both in what he does say, and in what he does not. He fails to object to the decisive point in my criticism of his book, i.e. that 'the struggle and resistance of the working class is lacking; the proletariat is depicted as the impotent victim of the judicial process . . ., etc.'. I can only assume, therefore, that Ottwalt has no answer to this. What Ottwalt actually does say, however, is more important. For here we have a cohesive system of the false ideas that make up the ideological underpinning of his creative method. It will be most instructive to examine this system under the microscope.

Methodological Questions

Comrade Ottwalt repeatedly reproaches me for concerning myself only with 'aesthetic judgements' and questions of 'creative method', putting forward the opinion that: 'The object to be analysed is not the creative method, but rather the functional significance that a book has in a specific situation, determined by specific economic and political circumstances.' I do not intend to dwell here on Ottwalt's terminology, reminiscent of Machism, though this terminology is in no way accidental, and shall confine myself to pinning down three important aspects of this formulation. First, creative method and economic reality are counterposed here in a rigid and exclusive manner ('not . . . but rather').

* First published in *Die Linkskurve*, IV/11–12, 1932, pp. 15–24.

Second, the task of criticism is defined exclusively as that of investigating the conditions of effectiveness, and not as that of asking: where, from which class position, does the work arise? (Comrade Ottwalt even repeatedly objects to my actually trying to raise this question and, given his rigid and one-sided emphasis on the effect, it is hard not to recall Mach's 'complexes of perceptions' which, according to him, are what make up 'our reality'.) Third, and this follows from the above, the effect is confined to the most immediate actuality, with literature conceived exclusively as agitation, and not even as propaganda.

This view is very widespread today, though in no way does this mean it is either Marxist or correct. On the contrary. Any critique that Marx, Engels or Lenin made of an ideological product, no matter in what field, will show that they saw the effect as a necessary result (even if complexly mediated, and 'uneven' in its expression) of the determinate class factors in its development, i.e. that for them the central object of investigation is always the method with which a specific kind of ideological product is produced. This in no way means, as Ottwalt objects to me, that they remained stuck in 'aesthetic', 'philosophical', 'economic', etc., investigations of a specialist character, being in this way divorced from 'reality'. On the contrary: first, because the objective class base clearly reveals itself in the method and indeed can in no way be understood without it, and second, because the method of treating the material is also a uniquely important link in transmitting a work's effect, the nature and degree of which is most closely connected to the method. Do these general considerations apply also to literature? Or is literature rather a special field of its own, in which the lessons we have drawn from the way that Marx, Engels and Lenin worked in the fields of economics, philosophy, etc., no longer apply? I believe that such a conclusion would be so misguided as to need no discussion here, the less so in that the masters of materialist dialectics themselves used this very same method in questions of literature, it needing only proper application to the specific field in question. Ottwalt's objection that in my view 'reality . . . only presents itself in connection with aesthetic judgements' is thus shown in its true light. It is the self-evident and specific task of a Marxist literary critic to analyse the question of method – i.e. creative method! – in detail. If he fails to do this, then all appeals to reality, to the facts – not to speak of appeals to 'functional significance' – remain mere phrases, which do not bring us a step closer to our specific problem.

A 'Radically' New Art

'Practicism' of this kind, the result of which is a one-sided and exclusive emphasis on agitation, neglect of propaganda and scorn for methodological investigations, runs through Comrade Ottwalt's treatise like a red thread. He takes literature to be a kind of reserve force, to be deployed 'at the point of the class struggle where pamphlets fail, door-to-door agitation is inappropriate, and particular psychological requirements have to be taken into account'. It is in close connection with this that Ottwalt restricts the 'functional' significance of literature in the class struggle to the most immediate level, and is either unwilling or unable to recognize that precisely the present stage of development of the class struggle sets higher tasks for proletarian revolutionary literature, i.e. to create works that encompass the basic developmental tendencies of the period as a whole, works which, without neglecting the immediate here and now, also take into consideration the persistent, longer-term and genuinely typical features of the period – the great proletarian work of art. And when this demand is raised correctly and in Marxist fashion, it in no way contradicts the needs of agitation. On the contrary, the higher the level – i.e. the theoretical level in understanding and the literary level in the portraying these developmental tendencies – the more agitation will also improve; while the one-sided and 'practicist' confinement to agitation actually reduces the level of agitation itself, and thus weakens its force of penetration.

Marx, whom even Ottwalt would hardly see as a one-sided aesthetician, nor as a theorist divorced from the class struggle, went so far as to investigate the effect of works of art that were created in periods quite removed from our own. He even concerned himself – imagine this! – with Homer. And he sought to disclose the reasons that 'they still afford us artistic pleasure and that in a certain respect they count as a norm and as an unattainable model' [*Grundrisse*, Harmondsworth, 1973, p. 111]. This is surely a most heretical view on Marx's part. He was surely a 'barbarian' – as Lenin also confessed himself, in his conversations with Clara Zetkin – unable to keep pace with the 'new art'. And I mean this not as a joke. For Marx, Engels and Lenin repeatedly spoke of artistic pleasure, whereas the 'new school' see this as a completely outdated and bourgeois concept. To quote a characteristic passage from Ottwalt:

> The goal of these works is portrayal, the striving after a closed-in work of art that is content and complete in itself, and before which the reader is automatically transformed into a hedonist consumer, drawing no conclusions and being satisfied with what is given him, with the emotional stimulation and the pious satisfaction of having read a good book.

This exactly expresses the opposition that Bert Brecht makes between the old and the new theatre. The old theatre 'gives the spectator feelings and an experience, the spectator is led to identify himself with the characters', whereas the new theatre 'forces him to make decisions' and presents a 'world view', so that the spectator is 'confronted'. In other words, the 'new' art signifies a radical break with all old art. For in the old art 'perceptions are conserved' (Brecht), 'only aesthetic conclusions are drawn in a literary reality, and not practical ones' (Ottwalt); 'Can we call the work of this man (Balzac) propaganda?' (Upton Sinclair), etc.

It would not be sufficient, of course, simply to content ourselves with having shown that Comrade Ottwalt's ideas stand in diametrical opposition to the ideas of Marx, Engels and Lenin. We must still show, at least briefly, precisely why they are untenable. Above all, they depend on constructions that are false and arbitrary, not in accordance with the objective reality. For in the first place, it is incorrect to make an exclusive antithesis between any kind of 'artistic pleasure' and active propaganda effect. This can only be done by simply identifying the bourgeoisie of today, which has become completely parasitic, with all earlier classes, from the citizens of the Athenian polis through to the Puritan burghers of the English revolution or the Jacobins of the French revolution. Only in this way is it possible to maintain that the creative writers of these classes, who worked always by genuine portrayal, afforded them 'artistic pleasure' at the price of diverting them from action and leading them into sensuous indolence.

But apart from this ahistoric and uncritically generalized basic point, the anti-portrayal theory makes a further theoretical mistake that reveals quite clearly its undialectical character. Ottwalt says: 'Our literature does not have the task of stabilizing the consciousness of its readers: it seeks to alter it.' And Brecht counterposes the 'unchangeable human being' of the old theatre to the 'changeable and changing human being' of the new. Is this correct? Not in my view. If we look at class struggles in concrete terms, and do not simply rest content with social-democratic or liberal stereotypes of 'reaction' – the 'peace of the grave', etc. – we can clearly see that the economic and political condition of every class is continuously changing, and that for this reason every class is constantly forced, on pain of disappearance, incessantly to change the consciousness of both its own members and of the members of other classes that it influences. Anyone who is not blind must see that the ideology of the present-day Centre Party, for example, or the German

National party, is in no way identical with that of the Centre or the Conservatives before the war. The fundamental class interests have certainly remained the same; there are indeed interests that hold good for entire periods. But on the one hand these interests have themselves undergone substantial modifications, while, on the other, the same interests have to be pursued in a different manner, given that circumstances have changed. If the consciousness of the present-day bourgeois is to be 'conserved', then it has to be continuously changed; naturally, in such a way that the kind, content, direction and pace of change correspond to the change of a class development that is genuinely 'conserving', i.e. which seeks to preserve capitalist exploitation with different means to suit the changed conditions. If Comrade Ottwalt finds something paradoxical here, then I would ask him first of all to study the question of the dialectic of rest and motion in the writings of Hegel, Marx, Engels and Lenin, and then to check out historically how little the 'maintenance' of a given state of affairs really is a rigid conservation, or a 'restoration' the unchanged reestablishment of what is restored. Consider the restoration of the English Stuart monarchy after Cromwell, for example, or that of the Bourbons in France after Napoleon.

This theory evidently thinks it can gain support from the last of Marx's *Theses on Feuerbach*, where the well-known counterposing of 'interpreting' and 'changing' reality is presented as the line of separation between previous philosophy and dialectical materialism. But the opposition that we are dealing with now is a mechanical one, and vitiates the real meaning of the Marxian thesis. The idea that before Marx reality was only 'interpreted', and that since Marx we merely want to change it, is a superficial vulgarization of Marx's views in which not only does the dialectic disappear, but materialism as well. How indeed did people manage to live at all before Marx if, amid an ever-changing reality, they 'acted' in the way our more recent literary theorists mistakenly say? It goes without saying, therefore, that there was both a 'changing' of reality and necessarily also of consciousness, i.e. a praxis, before Marx as well. The vital point here, however, is that this was a praxis with 'false consciousness' (Engels). Marx, who also indicated in the first of the *Theses on Feuerbach* that, as a result of the one-sidedness of the old philosophical materialism, 'the *active* side, in contradistinction to materialism, was set forth by idealism . . . but only abstractly', i.e. with false consciousness, also gives us the correct presentation of this connection and its underlying basis. In the section on Feuerbach in the *German Ideology*, he writes: 'Division of labour only becomes truly such from the moment when a division of material and mental labour appears. From this moment onwards consciousness *can* really flatter itself that it is something other than consciousness of existing practice . . .' [*Collected Works*, Vol. 5, pp. 44–5]. The basic turning-point that Marx achieves here is thus not that of putting 'praxis' in place of 'non-praxis' – which would be to far outbid Hegel in idealism – but rather that of recognizing the possibility objectively contained in the class position of the proletariat of transforming the formerly 'unconscious' or 'falsely conscious' praxis into a conscious praxis, a praxis with correct consciousness. The rigid counterposing of the two phases, which though unrecognized and unconscious, is what lies at the basis of Ottwalt's views and those of his fellow-thinkers, must lead to both mechanistic and idealist consequences if followed to its logical conclusion.[17]

Heritage

I have had to go into the philosophical roots of these conceptions in some detail, as otherwise Comrade Ottwalt's key theoretical theses would remain quite incomprehensible. The first of these is the question of heritage. Ottwalt says in his reply to me:

> The question of 'heritage', for example, is far from playing the same role in our case as it does in the Soviet Union. The reason for this is simply that what we have to 'inherit' is for the time being still alive; that we come up against the bourgeois ideologues of classicism and humanity in the daily struggle, not as a dead 'heritage', but as living elements of reaction.

This, too, is a real farrago of theoretical errors. What strikes us first of all is the mechanical adherence to the legal form of the analogy. But behind this question of form there is something very fundamental. For in Ottwalt's eyes, the heritage is simply dead matter, which for the moment the bourgeoisie possesses, and which we shall 'inherit' from it only after its death. Ottwalt overlooks the fact that if Marx and Engels had followed his recipe, then dialectical materialism would never have come into being at all; he also overlooks the fact that the history of proletarian ideology, from its very beginnings, has been one of struggle for all those elements and tendencies, all those achievements of bourgeois development, that were suited to further development once they were dialectically reworked, 'inverted' and 'superseded' by the proletariat – achievements that only the proletariat is in a position to carry forward, and that in the hands of the bourgeoisie only fall back into a reactionary use, if indeed they are used at all. He has to overlook, therefore, that this struggle has to be waged all the more energetically, the further the revolutionary workers' movement develops, and the higher the tasks it is faced with. It is in this sense that Engels speaks of the German workers' movement at the close of his book on Feuerbach as 'the heir of classical German philosophy'. And it is in the same sense that Lenin repeatedly stresses most emphatically the connection of Marx's thinking to classical philosophy and economics, and sees the strength of Marxism as lying precisely in the way that 'it in no way rejected the most valuable acquisitions of the bourgeois epoch', but on the contrary appropriated and reworked them. Ottwalt's view thus contains a triple error. First, by abandoning the heritage, he abandons the real development of all elements of proletarian culture, and even the very struggle for these elements of proletarian culture before the seizure of power by the proletariat. (Points of contact with Trotsky's theory of culture.) Second, he hands over this heritage without a struggle to the bourgeoisie, in as much as he accepts it without examination for what it is in the hands of the bourgeoisie, and as falsified by them: as 'living elements of reaction'. Third, he accordingly requires proletarian literature and – since this is only one part of proletarian culture – he requires proletarian culture as a whole, to arise out of nothing without any connection to the past. He represents therefore a similar tendency to the Proletcult of a few years ago ('conjuring up a special, unique culture of its own'). It goes without saying that this 'special, unique culture' in the imagination of its inventors only arises from the void. In reality, however, cut off from the great stream of revolutionary development and tradition, it feeds on the ideological products of the bourgeoisie's decay (neo-Machism, etc.).

This inheritance – taken over unconsciously – is far greater than is generally believed. To disclose it fully we would naturally need a fundamental Marxist investigation of the literature, literary theory and philosophy of the last fifty or sixty years, of which we do not as yet have even the beginnings. I must therefore confine myself here to a few points bearing directly on the anti-portrayal theory. From the standpoint of its social content, Zola begins to raise these questions in his theoretical writings, though of course only in a relatively indecisive way that corresponds to the far less developed situation of his time. For although on the one hand the theory of the experimental novel already contains certain elements of the reportage form in opposition to portrayal, on the other hand Zola still attempted most forcibly to preserve continuity with the realist inheritance of portrayal (Diderot, Balzac), and to conceive his own practice as a further development of this heritage. The division of the realism of the period of the bourgeoisie's rise was still at this time in its beginnings.[18] Flaubert, Goncourt, also Maupassant, with whom the tendency of this subjectivist transformation of realism begins in France, were themselves still more or less strongly connected with the old realism, more or less phenomena of transition. Only later, with Bourget and Huysmans, did the genuinely subjective and psychologistic tendency clearly emerge. Upton Sinclair, on the other hand, condemns portrayal, even though he sees himself linking up with Zola; his connection with Zola's great qualities of realistic portrayal is already very loose.

This development, which is of course far more complex than in this rough sketch, and should be studied in connection with the period of bourgeois demise as a whole, is not sufficient, however, to explain the anti-portrayal theory in Germany. For besides this aspect of social criticism in its content, we must also take note of a bourgeois-decadent tendency in its form. This appears most strikingly in Germany in the field of art history. Wilhelm Worringer, who later became very important in the development of the expressionist theory of art, presented 'abstraction and empathy' as the two fundamental 'types of approach' towards art, and his depiction of 'empathy' is very closely related to Ottwalt's depiction of the 'traditional form of the novel', or Brecht's 'Aristotelian drama'. Only on the surface, moreover, are these two tendencies distinct, for Worringer already did battle against 'empathic' art and thus achieved his importance in the struggle of tendencies in art and literature. (Here, too, a detailed history is badly needed. Worringer's theory, and the revival of Gothic and – above all – Oriental art, derives on the one hand directly from the Vienna art historian Alois Riegl, while on the other hand it is also determined by the practical – anti-portrayalist – adhesion to Oriental art, from imitation of the Japanese styles through to Negro sculpture. A single line runs through from here, via 'expressionism' and the 'New Objectivism'[19] through to the later theory of non-portrayal, and even if this line is not a straight one, it can still be traced through all its twists and turns.)

This development does undoubtedly express the growing strength, ideological level and force of attraction of the revolutionary workers' movement, especially in Germany. And while expressionism, caught up in the revolutionary wave of the immediate post-war period (partly influenced already by the revolutionary resistance of the working class during the imperialist war), only managed to reach a sham-revolutionary 'literature of humanity', which got stuck once again in bourgeoisdom with the ebb of this revolutionary wave, we now have a far more serious attempt to come to grips with the problems of the proletarian revolution. The more energetic and fundamental revolutionary upswing that is now following on from the period of relative stabilization (which brought with it a new rapprochement of the left intelligentsia to the bourgeoisie – New Objectivism), compels these writers to engage in serious debate with the contents of the proletarian revolution. But since for them these contents still remain abstract, despite a recognizable concretizing tendency, i.e. immediate surface phenomena and not the objective driving forces of the revolution, their revolutionary disposition also remains an abstract preaching, a 'tendency'. We could refer for instance to Brecht's play *The Measures Taken*, where the strategic and tactical problems of the party are narrowed down to 'ethical problems'. From the starting-point of this world outlook, it is impossible to really recognize and portray the driving forces. It is only understandable, therefore, that these writers formally adhere to the creative method sketched out above, and proclaim this, remoulded according to the changed circumstances, as something 'radically' new.

Ottwalt's rejection of the literary heritage thus has a weak theoretical footing, as well as a weak practical one. The self-deception that follows from his unclear theoretical premises can be quite clearly seen in the way he has failed to note that the 'uncle' whose death we are supposedly awaiting for our inheritance is actually dead already as far as our real heritage is concerned: i.e. the revolutionary bourgeoisie. On the other hand, however, Ottwalt takes possession of the inheritance of a still living 'uncle', the decadent bourgeoisie of the imperialist epoch.

Fact, Totality and Portrayal

Comrade Ottwalt thinks he has posed the question very precisely when he says that the workers seek to grasp reality in a highly concrete fashion, even when this is clad in literary garb; that given the alternative between 'fact' and 'literary portrayal', they always decide unconditionally for fact, and must do so out of practical necessity. Unfortunately, however, the matter is far from being as clear as Ottwalt believes. Firstly, his alternative is a false one, as he does not really mean fact or portrayal at all, but rather fact or psychology. That I am not doing Comrade Ottwalt an injustice here can be seen from the way that a few lines further on he equates Tolstoy with Jacob Wassermann,[20] i.e. a genuine portrayer, who develops the consciousness of his characters out of their being, with a subjective idealist, for whom consciousness actually determines being. And even this confusion is not accidental, but rather a dogma (not professed, but more likely unconscious) of the tendency to which Ottwalt belongs. Tretyakov, for instance, who is certainly competent to speak here, says ironically in the course of a polemic: 'What is valued in a writer is his ability "to see into people's hearts"' (i.e. psychology! G.L.), 'but not his knowledge in the field of collective theory and practice' (i.e. Ottwalt's fact). Since dialectical materialist portrayal completely escapes Ottwalt's alternative, he can well celebrate an easy, if somewhat premature, triumph. The answer to his alternative can only be: neither – nor; *tertium datur*: there is still a third possibility!

Comrade Ottwalt is wrong again in identifying the Marxist conception of reality with his own 'facts'. Lenin, in his *Philosophical Notebooks*, quotes the thesis of Hegel's that: 'It is, however, at once apparent that this [the empiricist method] turns things upside down, and that cognition which wishes to take things as they *are* thereby falls into contradiction with itself'. Lenin calls this remark 'very correct', and refers to Marx's *Capital*. There Marx says that 'in appearance, things often present themselves upside down', and demonstrates this using a series of categories ('facts! facts!') taken from everyday economics, such as the 'price of labour'. This is why Lenin says: 'Thought proceeding from the concrete to the abstract – provided it is *correct* . . . does not get away *from* the truth but comes closer to it. The abstraction of *matter*, of a *law* of nature, the abstraction of *value*, etc., in short *all* scientific (correct, serious, not absurd) abstractions reflect nature more deeply, truly and *completely*. From living perception to abstract thought, and from *this to practice*, – such is the dialectical path of the cognition of *truth*, of the cognition of objective reality' [*Collected Works*, Vol. 38, pp. 235 and 171]. Ottwalt omits the link between fact and practice, i.e. the recognition of objectively operating dialectical laws. He ties 'fact', i.e. surface appearance not yet understood as conforming to law, to an immediate reality without the necessary mediation with praxis, which is therefore deformed into mere 'practicism'. The same heedlessness towards the decisive dialectical mediations leads Ottwalt to confuse the totality with the sum of 'facts' (in his sense). He says: 'It goes without saying that the judicial system cannot be portrayed as a total process.

There is no other solution, then, but to give a compendium of a materialist history of law in the form of a novel.' It goes without saying that no one asked him for this nonsense. It would follow from Ottwalt's ideas that one could hardly ever speak of totality at all, for in the best of cases this can only be provided by encyclopedias, dictionaries, etc. Here, too, the Marxist standpoint is diametrically opposed. Consider the definition of 'social-democratic' (in today's terms 'communist') class-consciousness that Lenin gave in *What is to be Done?*, or his interventions on the trade-union question in 1921. 'If we are to have a true knowledge of an object we must look at and examine all its facets, its connections and "mediacies". That is something we cannot ever hope to achieve completely, but the rule of comprehensiveness is a safeguard against mistakes and rigidity' [*Collected Works*, Vol. 32, p. 94]. It may well be terrible, but it is a fact, that on so eminently practical a question as this Comrade Lenin considered it necessary to return to the basic problems of dialectics. We can take courage from this and add that Marx and Lenin have precisely shown us the way in which it is possible, despite the incompleteness of our knowledge, to meet this demand that we should understand the totality. Marx often speaks of the 'predominant moment' that is objectively present in a dialectical relationship of interaction, and can be extracted by knowledge and practice. Lenin repeatedly used the fine image of the 'link in a chain' that must be grasped in order to take hold of the chain as a whole and prepare a firm transition to the next link. It is understandable now why I can well find the totality in Tolstoy (even though, as Ottwalt reproaches him, he never dealt at all with 'civil jurisdiction'), and do not miss it in Ottwalt just because he has taken no account of the 'interim injunction'. For Tolstoy, as I stressed before, in so far as he gives expression to the specific character of the Russian bourgeois revolution as a peasant revolution, portrays the judicial system in living interrelation with the life of those classes for whom it functions as an apparatus of repression, both actively and passively, i.e. 'the totality of the moments of reality, which proves in its development to be necessary'. In Ottwalt's case, precisely this living, moving, cohesive and unifying principle is missing. And necessarily so. For as long as Ottwalt sticks simply to 'fact', as a matter of deliberate policy, i.e. the immediately given surface appearance, he cannot grasp this 'totality of the moments of reality', which does not lie on the surface, and is not immediately given.

It is now clear why Ottwalt believes that 'the absolutely convincing treatment of this material' (he refers to the agricultural crisis) 'must necessarily burst the bounds of the traditional novel form'. Ottwalt's example is a good one, for it can serve to illuminate almost any material for a novel. He argues that since it is above all 'the international inter-connection of the agricultural economy' that would have to be depicted, this is impossible in terms of the relation of people and characters in a novel. It might be possible to 'connect individually' an old-fashioned Friesian peasant and the general manager of the potash trust, but this would become quite idiotic if the manager of the Canadian wheat pool had to be drawn in as well. Given the way that Ottwalt raises the question, he is obviously right (cf. Ehrenburg's works). But the way the question is posed is itself false. At the root of it we find the same confusion of the totality with a mere 'sum of facts' that we have already demonstrated. And any 'traditional' novelist such as Gorky or Panferov[21] would reply by asking Ottwalt why he needs the director of the potash trust, let alone the manager of the Canadian wheat pool? Gorky portrayed the exploitation and oppression of the Russian workers, as well as the beginnings of their revolt against this, in his novel *The Mother*, in the 'traditional' way, and in no way found it necessary to bring in the factory-owners, the board of directors, the landowner, the home secretary or the tsar. His intention was to portray exploitation as it was in the factory itself, and by so doing also to portray the stage of development Russian capitalism had reached at that time; and through the reprisals of the police against the workers, Gorky portrays the whole vileness of absolutism. Or to take Panferov, he portrayed the foundation of collective farming in a single village, i.e. the process itself and not just the results, and it would have been quite superfluous for him directly to introduce a session of the politburo, a deliberation in the people's commisariat for agriculture, etc. His intention was, by portraying the social forces struggling for and against collectivization, both in the village and in the town, in a really comprehensive way, thus grasping the 'totality of the moments of reality', to thereby portray in a particular section of reality the genuine driving forces of the overall development, and hence the overall development itself. For Lenin too repeatedly stresses that Hegel was right in describing the dialectic as 'a circle of circles' [*Philosophical Notebooks*, *Collected Works*, Vol. 38, p. 233].[22]

I cannot tell, of course, what Comrades Panferov or Gorky might really say to Comrade Ottwalt in an actual conversation. But it is clear that their actual practice as writers gives him the answer he needs. And if I have now disentangled at least the most important false premises and questions of Comrade Ottwalt, if necessarily in a rather round-about way. I should like to repeat once again the closing words of my original article: 'This struggle against Ottwalt's creative method is in no way a struggle against Ottwalt himself. On the contrary, it is a struggle for Ottwalt, the attempt to ease the path towards the working class for an intellectual who is sincerely striving in this direction.' This path must necessarily lead via the appropriation of dialectical materialism, Marxism-Leninism. On the basis of Marxism-Leninism, comradely discussions on various different creative methods are necessary and useful. It must, however, be said – in complete friendship, but very decisively – that the proletarian revolutionary movement in literature cannot be brought to abandon its hard-won theoretical level simply because some comrades, however talented, make a virtue (a creative method and a literary theory) out of their necessity (the narrowness of their class basis), and seek to force it upon this movement.

Expressionism: its Significance and Decline [1934]*

... the unessential, seeming, superficial, vanishes more often, does not hold so 'tightly', does not 'sit so firmly' as 'Essence' . . . [e.g.] the movement of a river – the foam above and the deep currents below. But even the foam is an expression of essence!

[Lenin, *Philosophical Notebooks, Collected Works*, Vol. 38, p. 130].

In October 1920, a deeply shattered Wilhelm Worringer, one of its theoretical forerunners and founders, pronounced a funeral oration over expressionism. He tackled the question in broad terms, even if marked by that rather comic professorial generalization that immediately sees general problems of humanity in all the affairs of its own intellectual stratum: 'What is ultimately at stake is not expressionism – that would be only a matter of the studio. It is rather the organ of our present-day existence in general that is put in question, and today there are many people who are bankrupt expressionists who know nothing at all about art' (*Künstlerische Zeitfragen*, Munich, 1921, pp. 7–8). In Worringer's eyes, therefore, the collapse of expressionism is far more than just the business of art. It is the collapse of the attempt to master the 'new reality' (the reality of imperialism, the epoch of World War and world revolution) from the standpoint of the bourgeois intellectuals, in thought and in art. Worringer, of course, has no inkling of the concrete class content of his efforts. All he is aware of is that what he was striving for, what was a central element of world outlook for himself and his stratum, has collapsed. 'But precisely because the legitimation of expressionism lies not in the realm of the rational, but rather in the vital, we stand today before its crisis. . . . It is from the standpoint of the vital that it has exhausted itself, not from that of the rational' (ibid., p. 9). And in confessing this despair, Worringer betrays to us both what he had hoped for from expressionism, and the dawning afterthought, as a mystically concealed insight, that these expectations were in fact condemned to non-fulfilment from the start.

* First published in *Internationale Literatur*, no. 1, 1934, pp. 153–73.

With a phial filled with ultimate essences, we sought to let the ocean of the world, the entire world feeling, flow in. We believed *we could get hold of the absolute if we were to carry the relative* ad absurdum. To give a name to the profound tragedy concealed behind this, *those hopelessly alone sought to make common cause*. But this remained mere simulation. Even here, with a desperate philosophy of 'as if' (ibid., p. 16; my emphases: G.L.).

For all the mysticism of his terminology, and in what lies behind the terminology, this is a fairly clear statement. And the idea expressed in it, that the destiny of expressionism, from the bourgeois intelligentsia through to those intellectual circles in touch with the workers' movement, is viewed not just as a literary or artistic event, is also found among many writers who otherwise might well not agree completely with Worringer's views. Thus Ludwig Rubiner[1] wrote at the time of highest hopes: 'The proletarian frees the world from the economic past of capitalism; the poet (i.e. the expressionist: G.L.) frees the world from the past of capitalism in the sphere of feeling' (Afterword to the anthology *Kameraden der Menschheit*, Potsdam, 1919, p. 176). Between the world-transforming prospect that Rubiner opens up for expressionism, and Worringer's funeral epitaph, there lay only a very short interval of time. But this phenomenon of a sudden collapse is itself characteristic of the destiny of expressionism. The expressionist movement, a relatively narrow one of 'radical' intellectual circles in the years immediately before the war, grew rapidly in the course of the war, particularly during its final years, to become a component part of the German anti-war movement that was by no means ideologically unimportant. To anticipate an argument that I shall later present in detail, it was the literary expression of the ideology of the USPD among the intelligentsia. The harsh questions that were posed during the first years of revolution, the defeats of the proletariat's revolutionary attempts, the development of the left, proletarian wing of the USPD towards communism (its turning-point being the Halle split of 1920),[2] and the parallel development of its right wing into an element of capitalist stabilization, forced such clear decisions between proletariat and bourgeoisie, revolution and counter-revolution, that this ideology could not but be smashed to pieces. A few of its representatives, particularly Johannes R. Becher,[3] made a decision for the proletariat, and took pains to get rid not only of the baggage of expressionist ideology, but of its creative method as well. Most of them, however, landed up in the haven of capitalist stabilization, after the expressionist 'salvation' collapsed. The various paths, transitions, and epigonic preservation or transformation according to fashion of the original creative method are not of fundamental interest to us here. What is important, rather, is to indicate the most general outlines of this development, the historical destiny of expressionism, for this will enable us to disclose the social basis of the movement and the premisses of the world outlook that derive from this, as a step towards evaluating its creative method.

1. THE IDEOLOGY OF THE GERMAN INTELLIGENTSIA IN THE IMPERIALIST PERIOD[4]

The transition to imperialism led to important ideological shifts of alignment among the German intelligentsia, naturally without the agents of ideological transformation being aware of the connection. For the same reason, the internal connections between the reshufflings in the various different fields of ideology remained unrecognized also by bourgeois ideologists and historians of this epoch, which is all the more remarkable in that in this very period the demand for a *Geistesgeschichte*, a history that would embrace philosophy, art, religion and law as forms of appearance and expression of the 'spirit' or 'life style', grew ever louder. This programme was as characteristic of the stage of development of bourgeois ideology in Germany at the time as was the impossibility of fulfilling it. For the reversal that took place in German ideology with the entry into the imperialist period was firstly a striving for content (in contrast to the formalism of the preceding period), for a 'world outlook' (in contrast to the blatant agnosticism of the 'neo-Kantian phase), for comprehensiveness and 'synthesis' (in contrast to the rigid division of labour between the different ideological fields in the 'particular sciences', each strictly confined to its own speciality). On the other hand, however, the epistemological foundations of the earlier, pre-imperialist ideologies could not be abandoned. This turn had necessarily to be effected with the subjective idealist and agnostic ideological foundations preserved (at most perhaps an inessential reformation of certain minor parts). The transition to an objective idealism, which was the object of the exercise, was condemned therefore to failure from the start. For when Hegel made his transition from subjective to objective idealism a century before, the epistemological basis of this transition was a radical break with agnosticism of any kind (the critique of the Kantian conception of the thing-in-itself). There is no need here to criticize the inconsistencies and half measures which Hegel fell into as a result of the idealist way in which he sought to overcome agnosticism –

for every objective idealism falls back into a subjective idealism on certain points of epistemology, because of its basic idealist character. What is involved is rather the peculiarity of this period: why the transition from subjective to objective idealism was necessary, and why this transition had to be effected without the attempt to overcome the agnostic foundations epistemologically.

This contradiction in the epistemological basis is no more than the reflection in thought of the contradiction in the social being of the German bourgeois intelligentsia at the entrance to the imperialist period. The philosophy of the pre-imperialist stage, and the stage of the preparation of imperialism in Germany, was essentially divided into two camps. On the one hand there was the 'unphilosophical' glorification of the 'existent', i.e. the German Reich, as founded in 1871 and subsequently developed. (The school of Ranke in history, and Treitschke and the historical school in economics.) On the other hand, the 'left' wing of the bourgeoisie accepted the Bismarckian and later Wilhelmine regime from the standpoint of Kantian (or Berkeley-Machian) agnosticism: formalist ethics, formalist theory of value, the state as 'mathematical' foundation of ethics, these offered the bourgeoisie and its intelligentsia the possibility of accepting a state that correctly served its economic interest, defended it against the working class, but did not allow it to come directly to power itself – naturally it accepted it in a formalist manner, i.e. in a way that allowed whatever reservations were necessary as far as content was concerned, either keeping these in reserve or putting them forward according to its requirements. This twofold division is of course only a general schema. There was certainly no Chinese wall between the two main bourgeois tendencies and the less so as capitalist development in Germany steadily advanced and the imperialist development progressed further. The transformation of the big aristocratic landowners into rural capitalists, into a section of the imperialist bourgeoisie as a whole, united by finance capital, was necessarily ever more pronounced, and placed the state and its entire policy ever more strongly in the service of the general class interest, even though the form of the state, and the social composition of the state apparatus, changed hardly at all, certainly not fundamentally. This development in no way ruled out struggles within the bourgeois camp, and these were sometimes quite violent; but it did mean right from the start that their character was simply factional. In particular, this development determined the character of the liberal opposition movement. Its 'struggle' to transform Germany into a constitutional and parliamentary monarchy gradually became more and more blunted, and the attempts of the left-bourgeois ideologies to form a great 'left-wing bloc', 'from Bassermann[5] to Bebel', found a greater echo among the revisionists than they did on the right wing of the liberal opposition. The Bülow bloc between the conservatives and the liberal parties, despite its short life and subsequent fragmentation, showed how far this rapprochement had gone. And the same tendency is evident from the character of parties such as the free conservatives and the Centre Party.

It is quite self-evident, then that, long before the imperialist epoch, ideologies of mediation appeared, both in the direction of a better and more elastic adaptation between apologetics for the existing political system and the ideological requirements of the bourgeoisie, and in that of moving from an acceptance with formal reservations towards acceptance in content too. It is characteristic, however, that these ideologies of mediation only attained general significance in the imperialist period. This was when the Dilthey school of *Geisteswissenschaft* arose, as a mediation between neo-Kantianism and mere 'unphilosophical' history, a psychology that 'understood' its content instead of simply dismembering it. This was when Husserl, who up till then had stood somewhat apart, came to have a general effect – and one that very soon stretched beyond the sphere of pure logic which was what he had himself devoted his entire life to – in the application of new methods that were not merely formal, but agnostic on the question of objective reality. Neo-Kantianism, and especially its right wing (Windelband, Rickert), was very quick to take over both stimuli and results from the Dilthey and Husserl schools; both wings abandoned the 'orthodox' ground of neo-Kantianism and began to develop, via Fichte, in a Hegelian direction, even while stressing that the Kantian foundation should not be abandoned (Windelband, *Die Erneuerung des Hegelianismus*, 1910; J. Ebbinghaus, *Relativer und absoluter Idealismus*, 1910). The liberal tradition of rejecting romanticism (Hettner and Haym) was itself rejected. Romantic philosophy experienced a revival, and Goethe was brought in alongside Kant at the very centre of the tradition, as a philosopher, the creator of a world outlook, a 'philosophy of life'. This philosophy of extreme relativism developed ever more strongly into a mystical irrationalism, while, however, still preserving its agnostic and relativistic foundation (Simmel, and the influence of Bergson). Vaihinger linked Kant with Nietzsche as the basis of an extreme, 'mythforming' relativism (his *Philosophie des 'Als ob'* appeared in 1911).

All these tendencies, which we have certainly not enumerated in full, let alone properly characterized, have in common, through all their variations, the turn towards content, to objective idealism, to a 'world outlook'. And this requirement was precisely the result of the entry into the imperialist epoch. The continuous intensification of both internal and external contradictions, the rapid growth of both state and economy, the increase of rentier parasitism, the growing concentration of capital and economic power in a few great corporations, the expansion of Germany into colonies and spheres of interest, the consequent threat of war and preparation for war – all these things produced a series of questions that needed clear answers. Not in the sense that any of these ideologists, apart from a tiny minority, clearly recognized the problems of imperialism, understood them as problems of this stage of development and accepted or rejected them from this standpoint. And yet the specific kind of ideological distortion changes with the entry into imperialism. Formerly, the question had been to evaporate the social pattern into an abstract generality, for which a formalist ethical position, i.e. acceptance of duty as such, was sufficient (or alternatively, instead of such acceptance, its inconsistent, lame, and hence for the bourgeoisie reliable, rejection), but now everything to do with society had to be abstracted and distorted in a way that was comprehensive in content. This pattern, the mythologized depiction of imperialist society, demanded acceptance of its content. To give an example of this development, the cultural values of the neo-Kantian Rickert, which he saw as linking the historical framework, were still not explicitly acknowledged as identical with the present bourgeois society, being so only from the formal side. The 'value ethics' of Husserl's pupil Scheler, on the other hand, had at its centre 'goods' whose identity with the philosopher's own present was already clear in content and unmistakable.

This development into mystical irrationalism, to a 'philosophy of life', a 'world outlook' full in content, accordingly bears a double face. On the one hand, there arises an ever-more decided apology for imperialist capitalism, while on the other hand this apology is clad in the form of a critique of the present. The more strongly capitalism develops, and the stronger its internal contradictions consequently become, the less possible it is to make direct and open defence of the capitalist economy the centrepiece of an ideological justification of the capitalist system. The social process that led to the transformation of classical economics into a vulgarizing apologetics is at work of course in other fields besides that of economics, and affects both content and form of bourgeois ideology as a whole. There is therefore a general estrangement from the concrete problems of the economy, a concealment of the connections between economy, society and ideology, with the result that these questions are increasingly mystified. The growing mystification and mythologization also makes it possible for the results of the capitalist system, which appear ever more clearly, and cannot be dismissed even by the apologists themselves, to be in part recognized and criticized. For the mythologizing of problems opens a way to presenting what is criticized either outside any connection with capitalism, or else giving capitalism itself so evaporated, distorted and mystified a form that the criticism does not lead to any kind of struggle, but rather to a parasitic aquiescence with the system (Simmel's *Kulturkritik*), and even via this detour to an acceptance deriving from the 'soul' (Rathenau). The ideological transfiguration of Germany's political backwardness that followed from the situation of the German bourgeoisie as here depicted naturally intensified this tendency all the more. A 'critique' of capitalism, brewed up from scraps of romantic anti-capitalism, can very easily be turned round into a critique of the 'Western democracies', with a view to stylizing the German situation – in as much as its stands aloof from this 'poison' – as a higher form of social development.

It goes without saying that these critical movements were in no way all apologetic in intention. Even in the period of imperialism, there were in Germany intellectuals who honestly attempted, at least subjectively, either a critique of German political and social conditions, or even a critique of the capitalist system. But since they thought they could make such a critique without examining the general economic, social and ideological foundations of the epoch – which is simply the ideological reflection of the fact that they had not broken with the imperialist bourgeoisie – this critique, too, stood on the same basis as German imperialism, as far as its world outlook was concerned. Even in the best case, it remained unclear, confused, and unable to offer a dialectical solution to the divorce between objective basis and subjective intention, simply patching this up eclectically. At most, even this criticism, with its subjectively good intentions, developed into an unconscious and unwilled component, a particular nuance, of the basic ideological tendency of the epoch: an indirect apology, an apology by way of a mystifying critique of the present.

This development, therefore, was nothing more than an ideological preparation for the mobilization of the intellectuals for the war effort.

But like any ideological development, it proceeded unevenly. The subordination of the bourgeois intelligentsia to an imperialism that was spreading and developing was not affected immediately or without contradiction; opposition movements also arose, and above all sham-oppositional movements, which shared the same ideological foundations as the tendencies they were struggling against, and hence were only able to wage a 'fractional' struggle – no matter how radical their airs, or how convinced they were of this 'radicalism'. We have already pointed out how the general and manifold movement towards content, towards a 'world outlook', overlooked the underlying question in a subjective idealist manner: i.e. knowledge of the objective, material actuality as this exists independent of us, of man. By clinging, therefore, to the basic doctrine of the subjective idealist theory of knowledge, the dependence of the objectivity of the known object on the knowing subject, its 'superseding' of formalism, agnosticism and relativism necessarily remained either pure illusion (as in the Husserl school), or else it collapsed into a mystically exaggerated philosophy of intuition (the followers of Bergson, Simmel, and the Dilthey school).

The character of the opposition movements was determined by this commonality of existential foundation, and hence of forms and contents of consciousness. If they set out to criticize the 'abstract', culture-destroying effects of capitalism, this led in the best of cases to a romantic opposition, with all the internal contradictions of the earlier romantic critique of capitalism, yet far inferior to this in that they were much less able to criticize the capitalist economic system, even from a romantic standpoint (as Sismondi had done), remaining trapped in its ideological surface appearances. If an opposition movement attacked Germany's political backwardness from a 'democratic' standpoint, or developed a polemic against its cultural reaction, this led in the best of cases to a rhetorical, ideologically self-important vulgar democratism, a defence of 'big-city poetry', etc. Even this attitude was restricted by German conditions. With a very few exceptions, for example, big-city poetry in Germany was devoid of that, albeit bourgeois, breadth and range which marked its Western prototypes; even with the expressionists, it is not much more than a somewhat exaggerated and ironically pointed depiction of the Bohemian café society of the intelligentsia (cf. in particular the anthology *Der Kondor*, Heidelberg, 1912). And this is by no means accidental, for the way that Germany was trapped by the narrow compromise forms of the missing bourgeois revolution and the foundation of the Reich in 1871, left its mark even on the thinking of the extreme 'radical democrats'. Kurt Hiller, for example, the editor of *Der Kondor*, and presenter of the first expressionist cabaret, wrote on the occasion of Wilhelm II's jubilee, when Ganghofer and Lauff were decorated by the Kaiser:[6] 'It is still sad that the ruler of Germany, as this new act once again and frighteningly shows, has not the least trace of connection to what (before God) is Germany's value, i.e. the German spirit. . . . The idea that a German emperor of genuine culture might raise Stefan George and Heinrich Mann to the hereditary nobility is not such a bad one. . . . Is this utopian? *Perhaps less so in a monarchy than in a republic*' (*Die Weisheit der Langeweile*, Leipzig, 1913, II, pp. 54–5. My emphasis: G.L.).

We see clearly here – and I repeat that Hiller was one of the most 'political' and 'left-wing' champions of early expressionism – a similar reactionary prostration before the backward form of the German state, a similar glorification of the monarchy, i.e. the apologetic transformation of German political backwardness into something exemplary, as that made by the official apologists. Hiller's attack on Wilhelm II as an individual means very little in this connection; that can also be found in many opposition writers, including even conservatives.

What we have here, then, is the same common foundation, with the most far-reaching implications for both the content and form of expressionism. The stronger this common basis, then, the narrower the possibility of a new content, and the more the 'opposition' is restricted to formalism, and to the exaggeration of distinctions that are in reality only slight. This is far more the case with expressionism than it was with the naturalism of the 1880s and 1890s, the previous bourgeois opposition movement in the field of ideology, and particularly of literature. The very intensification of external conditions was responsible for this constriction. 'Advanced Europe,' Lenin wrote in 1913, 'is commanded by a bourgeoisie which supports everything that is backward. . . . In "advanced" Europe, the *sole advanced* class is the proletariat. As for the living bourgeoisie, it is prepared to go to any length of savagery, brutality and crime in order to uphold dying capitalist slavery' ('Backward Europe and Advanced Asia' [*Collected Works*, Volume 19, p. 99]).

The naturalist movement of the 1880s and 1890s still had a certain connection to the workers' movement – however loose, vacillating and unclear this may have been – and owed everything positive that it achieved to precisely this connection. Expressionism, however, could no longer make the same connection. This was above all the fault of the expressionists themselves, whose bourgeoisification, even in their oppositional strivings, was so advanced that they could only raise even their 'social' questions to the level of a subjective idealism, or a mystical objective idealism, and could find no understanding of the social forces acting in the real world. This development, the objective foundation of which was parasitism as the general tendency of the epoch, the ever stronger subordination of the petty bourgeoisie to capital, the increasing concentration and monopolization of the 'free' intellectuals' field of activity (press and publishing), and the growing importance of a parasitic rentier stratum as the decisive audience for 'progressive' literature and art, was effected quite naturally in interaction with the prevailing tendencies in the German workers' movement. Here we stress only those aspects most important for this connection, in particular revisionism. Whereas in the era of naturalism the effect of the workers' movement on the world outlook of the naturalist writers led in the direction of materialism, even if this was for the most part mechanical and vulgarized, revisionism accomplished a return to the subjective idealism of Kant (Bernstein, Conrad Schmidt, Staudinger, Max Adler), or else Mach (Friedrich Adler). It lay in the very nature of things that revisionism had closer connections with the left bourgeois intelligentsia than did its adversary, and was reinforced moreover by all kinds of circumstances (academic connections, for example via the Marburg school); in particular, it was reinforced by the fact that the struggle against revisionism in Germany was precisely at its weakest at the level of world outlook – here in particular we can see the effect of the lack of ideological clarity and political and organizational uniformity on the part of the left wing of the workers' movement. In the pre-war era this had as good as no influence on bourgeois opposition movements, and was also very much inhibited ideologically in criticizing these effectively and hence influencing them from the standpoint of revolutionary Marxism. On top of this, there was a further important distinction between the situation with naturalism and with expressionism, in that the former got to know the workers' movement in the period of the illegal struggle against the anti-socialist law, which was – all things considered – a heroic one, growing up with the experience of the 'great commotion', whereas for the latter the already very marked bourgeoisification of the labour aristocracy and labour bureaucracy was not without influence. This influence was reinforced by the international anarchosyndicalist critique of this tendency by Sorel, which was particularly influential among the intelligentsia, Sorel's effect getting under way at precisely this time (Michels's book on the sociology of political parties was part of the same phenomenon). Once again, the weakness of the revolutionary wing of the workers' movement meant that it was unable to exert any significant counter-effect.

The result of these circumstances was that the oppositional cutting edge of expressionism was far less sharp than that of naturalism. In contrast to naturalism's depiction of poverty, which concealed a social criticism and an anti-capitalist world outlook, for all its confusion, expressionism only managed a quite abstract opposition against 'middle-classness' [*Bürgerlichkeit*], an opposition which already betrayed its middle-class basis, and hence the common basis of world outlook that it shared with the middle-classness it was allegedly combating, by the way that it completely divorced the concept of middle-classness, right from the start, from any class connection. Here we shall simply introduce a few typical quotations, taken in fact from the period of the war and immediately after, i.e. from a period in which the politicization of even expressionism was far sharper than it had been in the pre-war era. Rudolf Leonhard,[7] for example, wrote: 'There are (at least today) only two classes: the middle class [*Bürger*], to which almost the whole aristocracy belong, as only a few of them are really aristocratic, as well as almost the entire proletariat, and on the other hand the non-middle-class [*Unbürger*] . . . who cannot be defined in any other way, though they are in fact very well defined by this' ('*Tätiger Geist*', *Ziel-Jahrbuch II*, Munich and Berlin, 1918, p. 375). Again: 'The question is to defeat the middle class, both bourgeois and proletarian, on all fronts, above all in the fields of middle-classness [*Bürgertum*]' (ibid., p. 115). We can also quote Blüher,[8] the later fascist: 'This time, however, the bourgeois can be found at all levels of society' (ibid., p. 13). The most extreme formulation is perhaps that of Werfel[9]: 'The poet is in no position to understand political abstraction; he lies if he claims to believe in nations and classes' (*Das Ziel*, I, 1916, p. 96). Since the social criticism is directed against 'middle-classness' in general, and since it disdainfully rejects the economic problem of exploitation (not to mention the specific problem of imperialism), it comes into neighbourly proximity to the philosophical 'interpretations' and 'critiques' of capitalism from the purely bourgeois aspect (Simmel's 'philosophy of money', Rathenau), as well as to the romantic movements against capitalism. What is specific to the expressionist social critics is simply that they remain even more firmly trapped on the ideological surface: their 'anti-middle-class' stance always had a bohemian character in the pre-war period.

As an opposition from a confused anarchistic and bohemian stand-point, expressionism was naturally more or less vigorously directed against the political right. And many expressionists and other writers who stood close to them took up a more or less explicit left-wing position in politics (Heinrich Mann is an exceptional case). But however honest the subjective intention behind this may well have been in many cases, the abstract distortion of basic questions, and especially the abstract 'anti-middle-classness', was a tendency that, precisely because it separated the critique of middle-classness from both the economic understanding of the capitalist system and from adhesion to the liberation struggle of the proletariat, could easily collapse into its opposite extreme: into a critique of 'middle-classness' from the right, the same demagogic critique of capitalism to which fascism later owed at least part of its mass basis. What is important in this connection is more the fact that there are certain common ideological tendencies, than why, whether and to what degree various particular writers or ideologists of fascism began their career as expressionists (e.g. Hanns Johst[10]).

For expressionism is undoubtedly only one of the many tendencies in bourgeois ideology that grow later into fascism, and its role in the ideological preparation for fascism is no greater – if also no less – than that of many other simultaneous tendencies. Fascism, as the general ideology of the most reactionary bourgeoisie in the post-war era, inherits all the tendencies of the imperialist epoch in as much as these express decadent and parasitic features; and this also includes all those that are sham-revolutionary or sham-oppositional. Naturally, this inheritance involves a transformation and reconstruction; what in earlier imperialist ideologies was still vacillating or just confused, is now transformed into something openly reactionary. But anyone who gives the devil of imperialist parasitism even his little finger – and this is done by all those who adhere to the pseudo-critical, abstractly distorting and mythologizing variety of imperialist sham oppositions – ends up by giving his whole hand.

This division is deeply rooted in the very essence of expressionist anti-middle-classness. And this abstract impoverishment in content not only marks the developmental tendency of expressionism, and hence its ultimate fate, it is right from the start its central and irresolvable problem of style, for this extraordinary poverty of content stands in crying contrast to the pretension of its delivery, to the exaggerated and over-intense subjective emotionalism of its presentation. This is the central stylistic problem of expressionism, which we shall deal with below.

What we have to do first, however, is show how the world outlook of expressionism is in fact the same world outlook of subjective idealism as that of German imperialism's 'official' philosophy. Striking proof of this is given in an essay by Kurt Hiller, from a right-wing philosophical position. Hiller takes as his starting-point the extreme relativist theories of F. Somlo and G. Radbruch, and only 'overcomes' relativism for his part by the following *salto mortale*:

> Thus whereas the relativist 'solves' a legislative problem in a thousand ways, on the basis of a thousand different moralities, the voluntarist solves it unambiguously on the basis of his own morality. . . . The voluntarist in no way inquires whether (his) values are 'justified' or not – he simply applies them (loc. cit., pp. 117–18).

It is no wonder, then, that Hiller finds 'the motto for the ethics and political philosophy of the future' in Nietzsche's 'will to power' (ibid., p. 122), just as later, writing under the editorship of the 'socialist' Ludwig Rubiner, Wilhelm Herzog was to say of Nietzsche: 'Not a socialist, but still one of the boldest of world revolutionaries' (*Die Gemeinschaft*, p. 64). Given this world outlook – intended as objective, as the overcoming of relativism and agnosticism, but in reality remaining relativistic and agnostic – the task of art and literature follows accordingly. Kurt Pinthus, one of the leading expressionist theorists, says of this:

> We felt ever more clearly the impossibility of a humanity that had made itself completely dependent on its own creation, on its science, technology, statistics, trade and industry, on an ossified social order, and bourgeois and conventional customs. This recognition meant the beginning of a struggle against both the epoch and its reality. We began to resolve the surrounding reality into the unreality it is, to penetrate through the phenomena to the essence, and to surround and demolish the enemy by assault on the mind. We sought first of all to distance ourselves from our environment by ironic superiority, by grotesquely jumbling its phenomena, *floating easily through the viscous labyrinth* (Lichtenstein, Blass), *or rising into the visionary with the cynicism of the music-hall* (van Hoddis)[11] (Preface to the anthology *Menschheitsdämmerung*, Berlin, 1920, p. x. My emphasis: G.L.).

What is important for the expressionists' world outlook here is in particular the way in which they penetrate from the 'appearance' to the 'essence'. We see how Pinthus sums up the ten years of expressionist theory and practice: 'We began to dissolve the surrounding reality into a non-reality. . . .' But this is not just a subjective idealist resolution of the question, i.e. the shift from the question of transforming reality itself (genuine revolution) to transforming ideas about reality, it is also a mental escape from reality. And this no matter how 'revolutionary' the guise in which the flight is masked, no matter how honestly certain expressionists might have subjectively taken this masquerade for revolutionary action.

In the pre-war period this ideology of flight was expressed much more clearly. Wilhelm Worringer, whose profound connection with the expressionist movement and its world outlook we have already seen from his 'funeral oration', expressed this quite unambiguously in his *Abstraktion und Einfühlung* ('Abstraction and Empathy', Munich, 1909), a book of fundamental importance for expressionist theory. Here 'abstraction' (i.e. the art of the 'essence') stands in sharp opposition to 'empathy', by which Worringer means in particular the naturalist and impressionist art of his immediate past and present. Worringer's polemic is only superficially concerned with art history: the 'retrieval' of primitive, Egyptian, Gothic and Baroque art in opposition to the one-sided preference for the art of ancient Greece and the Renaissance. His book owes its striking effect rather to the fact that Worringer makes the position he is really defending very clear, and it is in this connection that the renaissance of primitivism, of Baroque, etc., is so highly characteristic of the new art that he propagates. This is also clearly shown in the way that, as a representative theorist of the 'empathy' he is attacking (i.e. in his view, the 'classical' tendency), he does not pick on an art theorist of the classical period itself, but rather the modern aesthetician Theodor Lipps, whose theory in fact amounts to a justification of psychological impressionism. With Worringer, therefore, we find the same phenomenon in the field of the theory of art as we meet with time and again in the theory and practice of the new art itself: the problems and attempted solutions of the bourgeoisie's revolutionary period are totally forgotten, and as far as these works are taken into consideration, they are simply equated with certain modern phenomena of decline (in this case, the old realism, which objectively was socially critical, is equated with psychologistic impressionism).

The opposing tendency, 'abstraction', is naturally tackled in the same way. Worringer seeks to characterize Egyptian art, and gives a very clear and exact description and confirmation of the escapist character of his own expressionist tendencies and the world outlook on which they are based. I shall again quote simply a few important passages. Worringer takes as his starting-point 'agoraphobia', anxiety 'in the face of the wide, unconnected and confused world of appearances'. 'Humanity's development in a rationalistic direction has repressed that instinctive anxiety, conditioned by the lost position of man within the universe.' Only Oriental culture has preserved this correct recognition. Worringer sums this up by saying:

> The less humanity has become spiritually reconciled with the phenomenon of the external world, and the less it has acquired a relation of trust towards it, the more powerful is that dynamic from which the highest abstract beauty is attained . . . with primitive man the instinct for the 'thing in itself' is also most strongly developed (in Worringer's case this always means the un-knowable thing in itself: G.L.). The increasing command of the external world, and habit, involve a blunting and obscuring of this instinct. Only after the human spirit has gone through the whole course of rationalist knowledge, in a development of millennia, does *the feeling for the 'thing in itself' again awake in him, as the final resignation of his essence.* What was previously instinct is now the final product of reason. *Hurled down from the arrogance of knowledge, man faces the world just as lost and helpless as did primitive man* . . . (ibid., pp. 16 and 18; my emphases: G.L.).

On the surface, Worringer's clear ideology of escape seems sharply to contradict the 'activist' positions of Hiller and Pinthus – which are also quite different from each other on the surface. But this is simply a superficial contradiction: the same class tendencies, and hence the same tendencies in world outlook, lead this escapist ideology to take different and contradictory forms. Pinthus, who of course takes the 'thing-in-itself' as unknowable just as much as does Worringer (cf. *Die Erhebung*, p. 411), involuntarily concedes this himself by characterizing the pre-war expressionism as an ironic defence against reality, stressing its 'cynicism of the music-hall' – in methods that are no more than the typical gestures of superiority always found in bohemian literature, which itself takes flight before the real struggle with reality, and disguises its perplexity and embarrassment in the face of real and important problems (Pinthus's 'labyrinth'; others refer to 'chaos') in ironic attacks on symptoms. In Hiller's case, the escape again lies in the way that he conceals the class antagonisms in the field of law, which he discusses, in the superficial ideological form of relativism, so as to avoid taking up a position towards them, and 'overcomes' relativism rather by putting the arbitrary subjective 'decision' in place of the former inability to decide (a typical concealing and obscurantist ideology of the declining bourgeoisie, or rather of a section of the bourgeoisie that no longer dares appeal to an open defence of its class interests). This gesture of 'decision' covers up Hiller's flight from a decision between the bourgeoisie and the proletariat, whether the concealment is deliberate or not.

The outward gestures and forms of expression are different. But the class content, the helplessness in the face of the problems of imperialism (which of course are idealistically distorted here into 'eternal human problems'), the flight from their solution, are all the same.

2. EXPRESSIONISM AND THE IDEOLOGY OF THE USPD [GERMAN INDEPENDENT SOCIALIST PARTY]

The World War and its ending form the high point of expressionism. In this period it attained an importance that went beyond the literary field in the narrow sense – the first literary movement to do so in Germany since the beginnings of naturalism. This seems at first sight to contradict what we have maintained about the ideology of expressionism, but only at first sight. For we did indeed grant that expressionism was a literary opposition movement, even if, as a result of the circumstances that we explained, it stood ideologically on the same terrain as its adversary (imperialism). We shall now see that this common ground was never really abandoned, even at the time of the most violent, and subjectively most sincere, opposition. The passionate struggle of the expressionists against the war was objectively only a mock battle, even when their literary works suffered prosecution in wartime Germany. It was a struggle against war in general, and not against the imperialist war, just as the expressionists struggled against 'middle-classness' in general, and not against the imperialist bourgeoisie, and as in the further course of development of war and revolution they directed themselves against 'violence' in general and not against the concrete counter-revolutionary violence of the bourgeoisie. This form of extreme abstraction, extreme idealistic distortion and evaporation, in which all appearances are reduced to an 'essence', follows organically and necessarily from the preconditions of class and world outlook sketched out above. Appearances – 'bourgeoisie', 'war', 'violence', all in the abstract – were conceived right from the start in an external and ideological fashion, and not in terms of their actual being, while the penetration to the 'essence' led merely to an abstraction that was subjective and arbitrary in form, and hollow and empty in content. 'Bourgeois', for example, was taken to mean what appears common to the most varied ideological forms of appearance of bourgeois life, from a subjective standpoint: divorced from any actual economic and social determination in space and time.

This form of abstraction is not just originally determined by class, as we have seen, it also acquires a very definite and concrete class content precisely by way of its abstract emptiness. Since the abstraction is not in fact a penetration to the social roots of the phenomena, but rather an *abstracting from* them – conscious or unconscious, intentional or unintentional – an ideology of *diversion* from the key point of the class struggle is first of all created, which necessarily collapses into reaction as the battle hots up. We have already seen the general outlines of the 'anti-middle-class' ideology. Its emotional roots undoubtedly lie in a romantic anti-capitalism, but since this only proceeds from the most superficial ideological symptoms of capitalism, since on its way to the 'essence' it turns directly and vigorously away from the economic, and since in this way it also finds similar symptoms in the proletariat (bourgeoisification of the labour aristocracy and labour bureaucracy), it is not too hard for it to decree in place of the class antagonism between proletariat and bourgeoisie an 'eternal' or 'philosophy-of-history'-based antithesis between 'middle-class' and 'non-middle-class' man. The next and positive step is of course the demand for this 'non-middle-class' elite to take the leadership of society into their own hands. This idea is put forward with grotesque candour in Kurt Hiller's essay *'Ein deutsches Herrenhaus'* ['A German House of Lords'] (*Ziel-Jahrbuch II*, 1918) which presents a scenario in which the 'league' of this 'intellectual' elite influences public opinion to such an extent, by way of 'high-class conferences and extravagant public meetings', that only one 'last step' remains: 'The executive of the league . . . is appointed by the German constitution as an upper house' (pp. 410–15). This utopia deserves mention not just on account of its foolishness, but precisely because the ideological threads are clearly visible that draw a professedly 'extreme left' section of the intelligentsia towards fascism: the path from 'mentally overcoming' the class division in society, and class antagonisms, to the rule of the 'elite', the path from Nietzsche to fascism via Sorel and Pareto. What this involves is not the personal development of certain individuals – Sorel himself never became a fascist – but rather the course of development of the ideology, which by the most diverse left and right steps leads necessarily to fascism, the affinity between this 'extreme left' conception and the chiefly intellectual 'leagues' that stand close to fascism being the most striking point.

The expressionists' attitude to the war followed the same methodological course in theory and practice: from certain symptoms, to the subjectively and arbitrarily abstracted 'essence'. This time, however, the movement of thought reflected an oppositional process in which the broadest masses were involved, its political expression in the course of the war being the USPD. It lies in the very nature of the case that the symptoms here reached an altogether different force and tangibility from those that the expressionists had criticized before the war under the rubric of 'middle-classness'. The expressionists now depicted in verse and prose the full terrors of the war, the hopelessness of the trenches, the horrors of 'technical' mass murder, the brutality of the war machine, all in the most grisly of colours, revealing all its atrocities. And this revelation was now not just something static, it served a struggle, the struggle against 'war'. This is the precise point at which the inner affinity with the USPD takes effect. There were many among the leaders of the Social Democrat party, right from the beginning, who had strong tactical reservations about the party's unconditional subordination to all the aims and methods of German imperialism. The rejection of the war by ever greater sections of the masses gradually forced them to take a more decisive position. Yet they naturally came no further than the idea, and political formulation, of the spontaneous yearning for peace of the broad masses, not penetrating through to an understanding of the causes of the war and thus to a recognition of its imperialist character, and in no way seeking to give the resistance to the war a socialist stamp.

The USPD arose out of the earlier 'Marxist centre' at the very time when the masses of workers were pressing ever more forcibly in the direction of revolutionary action, even if spontaneously, confusedly, and without a clear understanding either of the way ahead, or of their goals. Its express ideological intention was to divert the masses from the path of revolution. The theory of the USPD was the direct continuation of the theory of the 'centre', in that it was concerned on the one hand not to lose touch with the discontent of the masses, nor to come into conflict with their feelings, while on the other hand, and above all, it was anxious not to cut the cord that still connected it with overt opportunism, which in the war situation developed into social-chauvinism. The preservation of this connection, which remained in existence unchanged in the theory and tactics of the USPD even after its organizational break with the SPD itself, shows that in class terms the USPD, too, had not completely broken with the imperialist bourgeoisie, that its 'opposition' to the overt support for the imperialist war on the part of the right wing, its 'struggle' against the Cunows and Südekums, objectively still formed an essential component of the SPD's war policy. Lenin recognized this connection right from the start, and expressed it as such. He discussed the essays by the social-chauvinist 'Monitor' in the *Preussische Jahrbücher* in the following terms:

'Monitor' held that the SPD's attitude during the war was unobjectionable, i.e. from the standpoint of the bourgeoisie. It was performing, in other words, an unobjectionable service for the bourgeoisie and against the proletariat. The 'regeneration' of the SPD as a national-liberal labour party was making powerful progress. Yet:

> Monitor thinks that it would be very dangerous for the bourgeoisie if the Social-Democrats were to move *still further to the right*. 'It must preserve its character as a labour party with socialist ideals; for the day it gives this up a new party will arise and adopt the programme the old party had disavowed, giving it a still more radical formulation' (*Preussische Jahrbücher*, 1915, no. 4, pp. 50–1). Monitor hit the nail on the head. That is just what the British Liberals and the French Radicals have always wanted – phrases with a revolutionary ring to deceive the masses . . . ('Opportunism and the Collapse of the Second International' [*Collected Works*, Vol. 22, p. 114]).

But the USPD could only fulfil this task because it shared the spontaneous mass sentiment against the war, and by a pseudo-tactic of struggle against the war it prevented the true proletarian class instinct expressed in this mass sentiment from developing into clear revolutionary class consciousness.

> The left-wing Social Democrats in Germany say that imperialism and the wars it engenders are not accidental, but an inevitable product of capitalism, which has brought about the domination of finance capital. It is therefore necessary to go over to the revolutionary mass struggle, as the period of comparatively peaceful development has ended. The 'right'-wing Social Democrats brazenly declare: since imperialism is 'necessary', we too must be imperialists. Kautsky, in the role of the 'Centre', tries to reconcile these two views (Lenin, 'The Collapse of the Second International' [*Collected Works*, Vol. 21, p. 224]).

This is not the place to analyse the theory and history of the USPD in detail. All that is required here is to show how the refined social-chauvinists, the Kautskys, Hilferdings and Max Adlers, all took the greatest pains, as the elevated theorists they were, to retouch the overall picture of the war so as to brush away imperialism, to present the war as a 'misfortune', an 'accident' or a 'mistake' made by certain individuals or small strata, simply so as not to be forced to call for civil war as the only effective weapon against it, but rather to persuade the masses that there was a way back to the status quo, the lost 'paradise' of peace that had existed before the war (even in the form of the Kautskyan utopia of 'ultra-imperialism'), so as not to be forced to make a genuine break with the SPD leadership and hence with the bourgeoisie (which was precisely why they broke with it *in appearance*). A theory was therefore put forward to lead the masses astray from the revolutionary path, which diverted them from the correct practice by acknowledging the superficial appearances and their spontaneous reflexes of thought and feeling, but prevented any understanding of these that rose above the level of this spontaneity. Its generalization of these surface appearances, the investigation of their nature and origin, was undertaken only in a purely formal manner; it did not get down to their real nature and roots in imperialism. The formal generality that thus emerged (opposition to war in general – support for peace in general) acquired a specific class content precisely through this formalism, its clearest expression being Kautsky's celebrated formulation that the International was simply an instrument of peace, and that the struggle of socialists in the war must be directed towards the re-establishment of peace. The USPD ideology corresponded, therefore, to the spontaneous anti-war sentiment of the disillusioned petty-bourgeois and backward workers; it did not require them to go beyond their spontaneous feelings and ideas in theory, and held out to them in practice a hope that seemed easier to realize, with less friction, and more 'legally', than civil war. It linked up, therefore, with all the petty-bourgeois prejudices and all the consequences of the bourgeoisification of social-democracy resulting from its opportunist policies, strengthening and reinforcing these precisely by seemingly going beyond them, by its apparent and abstract opposition to the superficial appearances. In this way it sought to guide the mass movement back onto bourgeois lines, a mass movement which spontaneously (though *only* spontaneously) was marked by the striving to escape the boundaries of middle-classness and the subordination of the workers' movement to the imperialist class aims of the bourgeoisie. The overt delivery of the workers' movement to the imperialist bourgeoisie would have come to grief in practice against the resistance of the masses, if the spontaneous resistance of the masses had been illuminated by genuine class consciousness, if the Spartacist League had not been incapable, for both external and internal reasons, of striking a really decisive blow at the USPD ideology among the mass of working people.

The methodological connection between expressionism and the USPD ideology is already apparent, I believe, from these few observations. Its social basis is that the expressionists became the literary mouthpiece of precisely that section of the mass movement that was guided by the USPD in the direction I have described. The expressionists, moreover, were far more closely connected with the petty-bourgeois wing of this movement than with its proletarian section, as a result of their social being, which had the result that the spontaneous, unclear, but instinctive strivings in the direction of proletarian revolutionary action were weaker in their case than they were among the proletarian supporters of the USPD. On the other hand, however, the method of abstraction analysed above, which diverts from the real battlefield of the class struggle, was also a spontaneous manifestation of the expressionists' own class position; their continued use of this method in their world outlook and creative method was thus not just a political manoeuvre, treachery or a betrayal.[12] The objective affinity of method, which at some points amounted to actual identity, was due to the fact that both tendencies, USPD and expressionism, while remaining on the class foundation of the bourgeoisie, sought to avoid a confrontation with the underlying causes by their attacks on symptoms. Within this affinity, however, there was the distinction that the expressionists who, naïvely, and out of genuine conviction, retained the backward, petty-bourgeois values, imagined – both in their world outlook and in their creative method – that at the level of form they had reached the topmost peaks of abstraction, the purest essence of the phenomena, and necessarily fell into the same exaggerated and empty, even if subjectively honest, pathos, that characterizes this era of war and revolution.

They reached this peak of abstraction by counterposing 'war' in general to 'man' in general. Kurt Pinthus, for example, wrote: 'But – and this is the only way that political literature can also be art – the best and most passionate of these writers struggle not against the external conditions of humanity, but rather against the condition of deformed, tormented and misled man himself' (*Menschheitsdämmerung*, p. xiii). In this way, the question of the struggle against war was shifted from the battlefield of the class struggle onto the private realm of morality. A false world outlook and a wrong morality are the real cause of the atrocious human condition of the present. Max Picard,[13] again, counterposed the impressionistic and expressionistic world outlooks: Through impressionism man absolved himself of responsibility. . . .

Instead of conscience towards things, all that was needed was knowledge of their connections' ('Expressionismus', in the anthology *Die Erhebung*, pp. 329–30). He continued: 'This concern only for connections is what made possible the long war. Everything is already contained in all things, war is already in all things, war can be derived from all things, war can disappear and come back again. And so back and forth. Mars, as *individual* to be encountered and grasped, no longer exists; he dies each day into a thousand things, and comes to life again each day out of a thousand things' (ibid., p. 331). Here we see the 'pure' concept at the summit of idealist distortion: the mythological figure of Mars is more tangible for Picard, more capable of taking 'responsibility', than is the real complex of facts of the imperialist war. The true theorist of expressionism, Kurt Pinthus, drives this abstraction yet further, if that is possible. He maintains that 'all created and mechanical systems and organizations gain power over those who create them and develop a vile social and economic order' ('Speech on the Future', ibid., p. 402). The laws that are put forward here Pinthus calls 'determinants': 'If we are to speak for the future, this means we must proclaim a struggle against these determinants, call for their overcoming, preach *anti-determinism*' (ibid., p. 403; my emphasis: G.L.).

The process of overcoming these 'determinants', according to Pinthus and all other expressionists, thus takes place in the human head. The overcoming of a concept in thought is synonymous for them with the abolition of the reality to which the concept refers. This extreme subjective idealist 'radicalism' connects very closely with the USPD ideology at two points. First, in the way that the real cause of events is sought not in the objective economic foundations, but rather in 'inadequate understanding', in the 'mistakes' made by individuals and groups. Pinthus expressly says that 'not the determinants are to blame, but we ourselves', in the very same sense that, according to Kautsky, imperialism really goes against the interest of the greater part of the bourgeoisie itself, who are simply 'misled' by a minority; or as the Austro-Marxists made military and diplomatic cliques responsible for the war, and seriously investigated what 'mistakes' this or that person might have avoided, with a view to escaping further war, which they alleged did not necessarily arise from the capitalist system as such. Secondly, the subjective 'radicalism' of the expressionists agreed with the USPD ideology in as much as human education was now logically viewed as the central problem of the social revolution. It is well known how the neo-Kantian Max Adler gave this question a central role, with great emphasis, and sought to persuade the workers – with all the sham-radical phrases that he knew how to use – that the education of the 'new man' who would create and build socialism had to precede the seizure of power, the revolution. Here again the expressionist and the USPD ideology meet up. And once more, of course, with the difference, despite the agreement in content, that what with Max Adler was a betrayal of Marxism, a twisting of Marxism into its direct opposite, follows in the case of the expressionists spontaneously from their class position.

Pinthus traces the domination of human life by the 'determinants' to the fact that 'our education is designed completely in terms of historical causation'. 'And in this way human life . . . is made completely dependent on determinants that lie outside its spirit' (ibid., p. 402). In a positive formulation: 'We could see ever more clearly that man can only be saved by man, and not by the environment' (*Menschheitsdämmerung*, p. xi).

Viewed from this standpoint, the expressionists' attitude to the question of violence, and their affinity with the USPD, is clear both in content and form. The abstractly idealist conception of the rigid antithesis between 'man' and 'violence' (state, war, capitalism) receives clear expression on all sides. 'Today violence is battling against the spirit', said Ludwig Rubiner (loc. cit., p. 275), and his drama *Die Gewaltlosen* shows very clearly all the implications of this conception of 'violence'. No other violence can or may be opposed to 'death' and 'soullessness', i.e. no violence on the part of the oppressed; this would only reproduce the old situation with a simple change of sign.

Karl Otten, therefore, preached to the unemployed:

> You want to erect the same god
> With newspaper, money and war
> Who now torments mankind with bloody face
> With fire and slaughter, stock-exchange, order and victory.
>
> ('Arbeiter' ('Worker'), in *Menschheitsdämmerung*, p. 183)

The same idea is expressed still more clearly by René Schickele:

> I renounce:
> Any kind of violence,
> Any compulsion,
> And even the compulsion
> To be good to others.
> I know: . . .
> Violence turns
> What began well
> Into evil
>
> ('Abschwur', ('Renunciation'), ibid., p. 273)

The intention behind these expressionist writings is very 'radical'. Far more 'radical' and 'revolutionary', they allege, than the revolutionary workers who confront the violence of imperialistic capitalism with the violence of the revolutionary proletariat. They do not consider for a moment that through this very abstract − and so uncompromising! − confrontation they end up precisely where they serve the class interest of the bourgeoisie, as the revolutionary situation comes to a head. Kautsky and his fellow-thinkers seek to confuse the workers about the clear Marxist conception of the proletarian dictatorship, by rigidly counterposing 'dictatorship' in general to 'democracy' in general, by seeking to dismiss by sophistic arguments the difference between the dictatorship of the bourgeoisie, which is the essential class content of every bourgeois democracy, and proletarian democracy, which is 'a thousand times more democratic than any bourgeois democracy' (Lenin). And this abstract counterposing of dictatorship in general and democracy in general serves precisely to brush under the carpet the inescapable necessity of revolutionary violence during the transition period. As Lenin wrote:

> And note how he [Kautsky] inadvertently betrayed his cloven hoof when he wrote: '*peacefully, i.e. in a democratic way*'!
>
> In defining dictatorship, Kautsky tried his utmost to conceal from the reader the fundamental feature of this concept, namely, revolutionary *violence*. But now the truth is out: it is a question of the contrast between *peaceful* and *violent revolutions*.
>
> That is the crux of the matter. Kautsky has to resort to all these subterfuges, sophistries and falsifications only to *excuse* himself from *violent* revolution, and to conceal his renunciation of it, his desertion to the side of the liberal labour policy, i.e. to the side of the bourgeoisie ('The Proletarian Revolution and the Renegade Kautsky' [*Collected Works*, Vol. 28, pp. 238–9]).

It is characteristic that Max Weber, who at this time was extremely influential among the left bourgeois intelligentsia, put the question in a similar manner to Werfel: violence, or the Sermon on the Mount. Either accept the state, with all the violence that Weber completely recognizes as part of the bourgeois state, i.e. either pursue a bourgeois politics in the framework of the bourgeois state, or else 'turn the other cheek', be 'holier', and follow the way of Francis of Assisi or Tolstoy. Any attempt to escape from this dilemma Weber considered madness, hopeless confusion. The expressionists, for their part, vacillated between the ideologies of Kautsky and Weber, though it necessarily followed from their class position that most of them stood closer to the Weberian dilemma – even without being aware of it as such.

The direction in which this reactionary and utopian sham radicalism leads, and how clearly it flows into a counter-revolutionary preaching of tolerating the violence of the capitalist class, can be seen very clearly in Franz Werfel's poem 'Revolutionsaufruf' ('Revolutionary Appeal') (in *Menschheitsdämmerung*, p. 215). Here Werfel says:

> Just let the powers that be trample all over you,
> Let the forces of evil stab you unceasingly,
> See how fiery justice rises from your ashes.

In Werfel's case, this is not just a poetic mood. In a longer essay, 'The Christian Message. An Open Letter to Kurt Hiller', he takes up the struggle, quite consistently, against 'politicization' (even in the expressionists' sense), and for Christianity. 'What is the aim of political activism?', he asks:

> It is to remedy evil with evil's own means (the activist is resolved on becoming a trade-union secretary). He seeks to attain his goal in the old way. He wants for example to use the organization that he has learned from the present regime for social welfare. And this is where the dangerous error lies. . . . Social unrest is unrest against one social order, in the interest of another order of the same kind, simply with a different label (*Das Ziel*, II, pp. 215–18).

These formulations are important because they are the necessary and logical consequences of the expressionist theory as analysed above. Kurt Hiller, who, as we saw, shares the same social premises and world outlook as Werfel, seeks in his reply (ibid., pp. 229 ff.) to justify 'activism' against Werfel's objections. He finds himself, however, very much on the defensive, his arguments subdued and embarrassed. He speaks of all kinds of things (for instance, the question whether it is ethical to kill flies), but has no word of an answer to the key point of Werfel's attack, which is extremely consistent. This is in no way accidental, for Hiller's sham-revolutionary 'activist' theory of the dominance of the 'spirit' (cf. his 'House of Lords project' in the same volume [see above, p. 92]) simply draws purely verbal and inconsistent conclusions from the same social premises and world outlook that Werfel thinks through to the end. He has therefore to be very cautious in his efforts to persuade Werfel to desist from the logic of his argument, and is in no position to refute him.

We have seen how the anti-violence ideology stretches from the sham-revolutionary phrase through to open counter-revolutionary capitulation before the bourgeoisie's white terror. The ideological affinity with the USPD's theory of violence is scarcely in need of further proof. But we must emphasize once again that here, too, the expressionists wrote from the spontaneity of their petty-bourgeois class position, whereas the leadership of the USPD were involved in a deliberate political manoeuvre designed to rescue the threatened rule of the bourgeoisie. In this respect the similarity to the USPD is still closer than it was with the anti-war struggle. At that time the expressionists were carried along by a mass upsurge that at times took them far above the 'realpolitical' goals of the USPD, in however unclear a manner. Later on, however, they expressed the division and vacillation of the petty bourgeoisie in the face of the approaching proletarian revolution. Fear of revolutionary 'chaos' has necessarily to gain the upper hand. When Hasenclever[14] described the revolution, his main concern was not the class enemy — with which he was very quick to 'fraternize' — but rather this 'chaos':

> Lightless embers. Night on the barricades.
> Violence is in the air, everything is permitted.
> The thieves' lantern slinks in the suburban shop.
> Looting raises its ugly head.
> You fighters for freedom, establish your freedom,
> Before the unfaithful betray your work . . .
> Wars will not abolish violence . . .

('Der politischer Dichter' ['The Political Poet'] in *Menschheitsdämmerung*, p. 166: there follows a hymn to the League of Nations)

Werfel's overt panic is more honest and consistent than Hiller's activism, which indeed is 'active' only in leading the revolution onto the path of the 'spirit', i.e. pressing it into a constricted bourgeois framework. And these efforts are so close to the strategy of the USPD that the boundaries between the two often disappear, both materially and sometimes even personally (Toller in Munich).[15] The bitter struggles of the first ten years of revolution, and the initial defeats of the revolution in Germany, were to shatter ever more clearly the sham distinctions between revolutionary phrase and whimpering capitulation. And so expressionism came to an end as the dominant literary tendency in Germany — at the same moment in time, and this by no accident, as the dissolution of the USPD.

3. EXPRESSIONISM'S CREATIVE METHOD

The creative method of expressionism is still more evidently and directly connected with its world outlook than was the case with earlier movements. This is not a function of the relatively greater devotion to theory that characterizes expressionism – this theory being contradictory and confused – but rather of the principally programmatic character of the expressionists' actual works. In the very period of its strength, expressionism sought to give its works the same manifesto-type quality that always marked its theory. The same manner of viewing and dealing with reality prevailed at this level too.

The attitude the expressionists adopted towards reality, and this means both their philosophical attitude to objective reality and their practical attitude to society, has already been characterized above as subjective idealism, by detailed quotation and analysis, a subjective idealism, however, that stakes a claim to objectivity. In referring once again to the formulations of Worringer, Pinthus and Picard, we add here a further passage from Max Picard in which the application of the expressionists' epistemological method (penetration to the 'essence') to creative practice becomes clearly visible.

> The expressionist [says Picard] . . . is emotional in that it seems as if he has never taken part in the midst of things and their movement, but had to hurl himself into them with a great leap from afar, and because with this leap of emotion things can be captured from the vortex of chaos. Emotion alone, however, is not enough to fix a thing snatched in this way. *It is still necessary to transform a thing, as if it had never stood in relation to other things in the chaos, so that it is no longer recognized by them and can no longer react on them. Abstraction and stereotyping are necessary, so that what has been achieved does not slip back again into the chaos.* In this way, so much passion is pressed into a thing that it almost breaks apart, and the thing can only concern itself with maintaining the tension of its own break-up; it can then no longer reach out to anything else (*Die Erhebung*, p. 333; my emphasis: G.L.).

The connection with Worringer's 'abstraction' is immediately visible here. Three points need to be made. Firstly, that reality is conceived right from the start as 'chaos', i.e. as something unknowable, ungraspable, which exists without laws; secondly, that the method needed to grasp the 'essence' (here called the 'thing') must be isolation, tearing apart, the destruction of all connections, the lawless tangle of which is precisely what makes up the 'chaos'; and thirdly, that the 'method' used for grasping the 'essence' in this way is passion, something that is presented right from the start as irrational, and counterposed rigidly and exclusively to reason and understanding.

If we now consider these three aspects of their creative method somewhat more closely, it begins to become clear why reality had to appear to the expressionists as 'chaos'. They stood in a romantic opposition to capitalism, yet purely in an ideological sense, not even seeking any insight into its economic laws. Reality consequently appeared to them as so 'meaningless' and 'soulless' that not only was it unrewarding to engage in it, it was in fact degrading. The task of the writer was tyrannically to introject a meaning into this 'meaninglessness'. As Pinthus put it, writing is 'not ethically indifferent and accidental like history, but rather the portrayal of a self-conscious spirit that develops, wills and forms itself' (ibid., p. 414). But if this trumpeting arrogance is to be concretely portrayed, we find very frequently, and in fact precisely in those cases where the writer's efforts are honest, a typical petty-bourgeois helplessness and sense of loss in the workings of capitalism, the impotent remonstration of the petty bourgeois against being ground down and trampled on by capitalism. Georg Kaiser's finest drama, *From Morning Till Midnight*, depicts this situation in a very lively and perceptive way, and is especially penetrating about the hollowness and vacuousness of such a 'revolt'. His poor cashier, who embezzles and absconds for no apparent reason, finds he can do nothing with this supposed 'freedom' (and with the monetary preconditions behind it). He has already been beaten down and turned into a 'cog' in the same mechanism, if in a slightly different position, long before fate catches up with him. Kaiser's other plays, and the comedies of Sternheim, show that what is involved here is less the weakness of the hero than that of the writer himself.[16] It is simply that this weakness is openly expressed in the better and more honest plays of Kaiser's, whereas Sternheim, for example, seeks to conceal it beneath a supercilious air of superiority that presents itself as very fashionable and bohemian. The same is true in expressionist poetry. Werfel, writing how 'we are all strangers on the earth', simply expresses rather flabbily and sentimentally, but at least openly, what in Ehrenstein's[17] verse comes out as violently bombastic and tortured:

And though the engines brashly roar
And airplanes soar up in the sky
Man lacks the constant, world-shaking power.

He is like mucus, spat on a rail . . .
The rushing torrents drown helplessly in the sea.
The Sioux Indians in their war-dances are unaware of Goethe
And the pitiless eternal Sirius does not feel the passion of Christ.
Suns and atoms, bodies in space,
Rise and fall without the tug of feeling
Rigidly unaware of one another.

('Ich bin des Lebens und des Todes müde'
['I am tired of life and death'] in *Menschheitsdämmerung*, p. 37)

It is plain to anyone that these feelings are in no way new. They are an age-old component of the poetry of the urban petty bourgeoisie. What is new in expressionism, from the point of view of content, is simply the quantitative intensification of this sense of loss and despair. And this again is a necessary product of the position of the petty bourgeoisie in the imperialist era. As far as form is concerned, the intensification of content brings about a qualitative change. The movements that preceded expressionism, in particular naturalism, genuinely sought to portray the hopeless entanglement of the petty bourgeois in the capitalist mechanism, his impotent subordination to the capitalist system – even if they did so inadequately, for the naturalists themselves failed to recognize the social basis and the economic driving forces, and thus could not portray them; they, too, clung to surface phenomena (for example marriage and the family in their psychological reflections), even when they tried to portray these in some kind of social connection (still necessarily external and superficial). It was characteristic that naturalism was superseded by intensifying rather than making good its defects. Impressionism brought an extraordinary refinement *vis-à-vis* naturalism in the portrayal of the outward surface of life and the psychological impulses unleashed at this level, but in a way that was still further divorced from its social basis, making the portrayal of objective causes still more impossible. (It should be stressed here, if this is not superfluous, that this technical obstacle to realism is the result and not the cause.) Symbolism then decisively separated the emotional symptoms even from the externally and superficially conceived social environment, portraying a helplessness in general, a sense of loss in general, etc.

What was new in the creative method of expressionism lay in the way that on the one hand it accelerated this process of abstraction, while on the other hand it transformed its formal orientation. The impressionists and symbolists, as open and honest subjectivists, subjectivized their creative method more and more, i.e. they mentally abstracted the material to be depicted from its real foundations. Yet they still preserved the general structure of immediate reality: the stimuli that provoked these impressions were still ascribed priority over the subject impressed by them, this priority being at least externally dynamic; they confronted the subject as an external world. This was of course only in the world they portrayed. Their theory already conceived these impressions as products of the creative subject, at least in their 'how' aspect; their 'what' and 'why' still remained in places an unknowable thing-in-itself. (Here there are the most diverse transitional forms between the later naturalism and these new creative methods.) The reversal that expressionism seeks to effect was that of transferring the process of creation – which existed in the mind of the modern writer – into the structure of the work itself; i.e. the expressionist depicts the 'essence' already sufficiently known to us, and – this is the decisive question of style – only this 'essence'. We have repeatedly pointed out how this 'essence' had nothing in common with the objective summary and emphasis of the general, permanent, recurring and typical features of objective reality. The expressionist precisely abstracted away from these typical characteristics, in as much as he proceeded, like the impressionists and symbolists, from the subjective reflex in experience, and emphasized precisely what in this appears – from the subject's standpoint – as essential, in as much as he ignored the 'little', 'petty', 'inessential' aspects (i.e. precisely the concrete social determinations) and uprooted his 'essence' from its causal connection in time and space. This 'essence' is then presented by the expressionist as the poetic reality, as the act of creation that simultaneously reveals the 'essence' of reality as attainable by us.

He does this in poetry by nakedly exposing this creative process itself, this distilling out of the subjective aspects, this abstracting away from the objective reality; by gathering together as a literary form his own inability to arrange and master the objective reality in thought, making this into the chaos of the world itself and simultaneously the sovereign act of the writer. He does this in the objective forms (such as drama, for instance), by presenting only this experiential centre as reality, and grouping everything else around this centre, seen only from this standpoint. He thus stands in contrast to the realist writers who conceived drama as the objective struggle of opposing social forces. He finds himself in closer affinity, however, with the impressionists and symbolists, who similarly stopped portraying the contradictions of objective reality, replacing them more and more with the contradiction between subject and reality. It is simply that with these latter (e.g. Maeterlinck) objective reality actually disappears, giving way to the impression it makes on the subject, such as abstract fear, etc., whereas the expressionist dramatists place the writer himself on the stage as central character, and portray all the other actors only from his point of view – exclusively as what they are for this central character (the expressionist 'essence').

In this way, a double and insoluble dissonance arises. On the one hand, these characters become in their form mere silhouettes, who must however claim on the stage to be real living beings. On the other hand, the writer is forced to express the problem abstracted in this way in its unconcealed hollowness and vacuity; he cannot rest content with his emotional reflexes, for all their emptiness, in the way that the symbolist can. We therefore get such gems of wisdom as the following:

> *The Son:* And what am I to do?
>
> *The Friend:* Destroy the tyranny of the family, this medieval abcess; this witches' sabbath and torture chamber with brimstone! Abolish the laws – re-establish freedom, men's highest good.
>
> *The Son:* At the point of the earth's axis I burn again with enthusiasm.
>
> *The Friend:* Then you should realize that the struggle against the father is what revenge against the prince was a hundred years ago. Today *we* are right! At that time the crowned heads fleeced and enslaved their subjects, stole their money, locked their minds in dungeons. Today we are singing the *Marseillaise*! Any father can still freely have his son starve and drudge, and prevent him from doing great things. This is simply the old song against injustice and cruelty. They insist on the privileges of the state and nature. Away with them both! Tyranny disappeared a century ago – let's help the growth of a new nature! (Hasenclever, *Der Sohn*, Act 4, Scene 2).

We have quoted this representative expressionist drama at some length in order to show quite clearly how the content of the conflict here is basically in no way different from the typical family conflict of the naturalists (from Hauptmann's *Friedensfest* to Hirschfeld's *The Mothers*). In both cases a phenomenon that results from the capitalist social order is presented, with the writers understanding it as such. But while the naturalists, with the almost photographic fidelity of their superficial presentation, kept at least certain (uncomprehended) features of the mode of appearance of this conflict, the expressionist abstraction from reality only serves up as the 'essence' a childish nonsense. Of course, this nonsense is not accidental: it shows close affinity in content with the romantic and reactionary 'youth movements'. And through this creative method, which copies the processes with which this subjectivism has striven impotently to master the reality in thought as faithfully and as superficially as the naturalist photographed his uncomprehended impressions, this 'essence' is supposed to be discovered, demonstrated and exposed by literary work.

This is an exaggerated subjectivism, appearing here with the empty gesture of objectivity. In this way there arises a sham activity of the creative subject, in which the expressionist theory sees the principle that distinguishes expressionism as something radically new in relation to all former art (by which it always means the impressionism that immediately preceded it). The theorists of expressionism overlook the fact that class content and basic world outlook remain the same, and exaggerate the distinction in form into a rigid and exclusive antithesis. The continuity of development is only apparent, only inscribed on the surface. The process of impoverishment of content, in particular, continues in expressionism with unchanged direction, only at a greater pace. The very method of isolation by which the expressionists believe they can grasp the 'essence' involves a decisive step forward in this direction, for it means the deliberate ignoring of the determinations whose richness, linkage, entwining, interaction, sub- and superordination, in a dynamic system, are what form the foundation of all portrayal of reality. Worringer's abstraction, Picard's 'removal from connections', and Pinthus's 'essence', thus all mean a deliberate impoverishment in the content of the reality portrayed. What is 'new' in expressionism, and comes out of the struggle against the inessential superficial determinations of impressionism, thus increases the emptiness and lack of content, for in reality the superficiality of the immediately grasped determinations can only be overcome by research into the real, underlying and essential determinations. A 'pure essence' divorced from all determinations is necessarily empty.

There are *no* 'pure' phenomena, nor can there be, either in Nature or in society – that is what Marxist dialectics teaches us, for dialectics shows that the very concept of purity indicates a certain narrowness, a one-sidedness of human cognition, which cannot embrace an object in all its totality and complexity (Lenin, 'The Collapse of the Second International' [*Collected Works*, Vol. 21, p. 236]).

This thesis of Lenin's is also of extreme importance for our argument, in that it underlines yet again the connection between the ideology and creative method of expressionism and the USPD and ultra-left in the war and post-war period (Pfemfert and *Aktion*).[18] The ideological emptying of the concept of revolution – 'pure' capitalism, 'pure' socialist revolution – is most closely connected with opportunist politics in both right and left variants. The complete emptying of content of the concept of revolution by the expressionists is of course the most extreme point of these efforts, in which different political shadings may be eclectically mixed together. A sham movement towards content and objectivity, 'struggling' against the preceding clearly subjective idealist and agnostic tendencies, overcoming them only apparently, in a formal manner, both ideologically and artistically; a sham movement, which in actual fact strengthens the subjectivist tendencies, empties out content, and which objectively, therefore, is and can only be a linear continuation and intensification of the pre-imperialist bourgeois tendencies, since its class basis, despite the changed conditions, remains the same.

The atrophy of content as the necessary result of expressionism's deliberate creative method is to be seen on all sides in the tendency to the deliberate elimination of all concrete determinations. Picard deduces, for instance, from his attempt to 'reduce the sphere of chaos', that expressionism does not want to know 'how a thing arose, does not even want to see what a thing is, but only that it is'. Causality is to be eliminated, since it increases 'the number of things' in the chaos by 'patterns of transformation between cause and effect' (*Die Erhebung*, p. 337). The expressionists, therefore, place themselves again here in that great series of ideologists of the imperialist era who, in the interest of rescuing old theoretical ideas, or with the purpose of introducing a new mythology of causality, deny the objective linkage between objects and processes in the external world. This series stretches from Nietzsche and Mach through to Spengler, Spann and Rosenberg. Herwarth Walden[19] draws from these premises, which, as we have seen, are indeed general premises of the expressionist world view and not just the opinions of particular theorists, conclusions that involve linguistics as well. He combats the sentence for the sake of the word. 'Why should only the sentence be understandable, and not also the word?', he asks. If all determinations are rejected on principle as 'disruptive', then of course in language, too, what must prevail is not the living context with all its ramifications, but rather the isolated word, abstracted and applied outside any context. Word and sentence are counterposed just as rigidly and exclusively as thing and connection were in philosophy. The attempt to reproduce the interconnection of reality in words in an all-round way must necessarily appear from this standpoint, that of the 'personal' caprice of the writer, as a violation of the word. 'Because writers like to dominate, they make the sentence prevail over the word. But the word rules. The word tears up the sentence, and poetry is piecework. Only words connect. Sentences happen only accidentally' (Introduction to the anthology *Expressionistische Dichtung*, Berlin, 1932, pp. 11–12).

Here we can see the internal contradictions of expressionism as contradictions of its creative method. Firstly, its extreme subjectivism is revealed – a subjectivism that borders on solipsism. Walden is only logical in saying of his premises: 'The expressionist picture of verbal art offers the image without relationship to the world of experience. Illogicality makes the non-sensuous concept perceptibly palpable' (ibid., pp. 12 and 16). Similarly Otto Flake:[20] 'It is a half measure to select a "theme" . . . What is called real, the environment and the facts outside of me, exist in fact only in my brain, in as much as I acknowledge them and want them to be so . . .' ('Souveränität', in *Die Erhebung*, p. 342). The grasping of the essence, the supposedly 'purest form' of objectivity, collapses into the 'non-objective' art of absolute caprice. The impressionist lack of content, as seen in the accumulation of inessential and only subjectively significant superficial features, now undergoes a formal – though only formal – intensification: the purely subjective 'expression', emptied of content and separated from the objective reality, can only produce in its totality an empty series of 'eruptions', a rigid combination of sham movements. For it is unavoidable – and this is the second point – that expressionism should raise the question of totality. Its internal contradiction, from the standpoint of class basis and world outlook, shows itself in the expressionist creative method in the contradiction that, while on the one hand it has to lay claim to a total portrayal (simply on account of the social and political position it adopted during the war and after), on the other hand this creative method does not permit the portrayal of a living and dynamic world. The totality, therefore, can only be brought in via an external surrogate, and is purely formal and empty in the works of expressionism. 'Simultaneism',[21] for example, is such an empty and formal external means designed to substitute, for the missing internal all-round context, an external juxtaposition of words grouped by association. But this means a gaping contradiction between content and form. And the sham solution that expressionism invents shows the same antagonism in its most intense form. The nothingness of the content – and this is the third point – is disguised in a self-trumpeting emotionalism in the use of language. The early expressionism of the pre-war period, and even its vegetative epigones after the ebb of the first revolutionary wave, could display this division quite openly, with destructive self-irony, thus apparently overcoming it artistically, but this was ruled out for expressionism in its heyday. These writers were forced, by their attitude towards war and revolution, to present themselves with great excitement and self-assurance as 'leaders', and to offer the empty subjectivity of their vacuous and irrational 'concepts' as proclamations, appeals and directions. Their language, divorced from the objectivity of external reality, thus ossified into a hollow 'monumentality', and their inadequate ability to penetrate the content had to be replaced and concealed by the hysterical exaggeration of pictures and images thrown together without any internal connection. This language bears the clear marks of its class content, the helplessness, dressed up as 'leadership', of a rootless and decomposing petty-bourgeois intelligentsia, caught in the midst of world-historical, even if still not fully matured, class struggles between proletariat and bourgeoisie. And in and through this division, this language adequately expresses the real class content of expressionism, by unveiling precisely the nullity of the imagined contents, involuntarily but all the more nakedly. An empty dynamism as its principle – 'the dynamic as principle is itself to become the human quality, what is revolutionary in man is to be perpetuated over and above the transient' (Wolfenstein)[22] – the 'eternal' revolution, i.e. a revolution divorced from the class struggle, finds corresponding expression in this language. This dynamism is not that of the genuine revolutionary, it is forced on these petty-bourgeois writers from outside, by historical events, and is therefore hysterically exaggerated. It goes without saying, of course, that once the external stimulus dies down, the hysterical exaggeration also subsides: with the relative stabilization, the petty-bourgeois intelligentsia found their way once again to a peaceful and self-possessed emptiness, the 'new objectivism'. Those few who did not just imagine themselves to be revolutionaries, who, however unclearly, were genuinely striving towards the proletarian revolution and not the 'eternal revolution of humanity', jettisoned their expressionist baggage as they clarified their attitude towards the revolution. Expressionism was left behind in the course of development.

The very partial and problematic interest with which expressionism is honoured by fascism can certainly not suffice to awaken expressionism from this death. The fact that the fascists, with a certain justification, see expressionism as a heritage that they can use, only seals its tomb the more firmly. Goebbels accepts expressionism, and also the validity of the 'new objectivism' (which is again instructive), but he rejects naturalism, which 'gets distorted into environmental description and Marxist ideology', i.e. he maintains artistic continuity only with the art of post-war imperialism. He justifies this in the following interesting way: 'Expressionism had healthy beginnings, for the epoch did have something expressionist about it.' If words do have any meaning, and with Goebbels this is not always the case, this means that he thinks of the expressionist abstracting away from reality, the expressionist 'essence', in other words expressionist distortion, as a method of portraying reality, as an adaptable means for fascist propaganda. The upside-down justification that reality had something expressionist about it, shows the way in which myth-making idealism has subsequently proceeded. The expressionists themselves took their creative method only as a stylizing grasp of the 'essence'; the mendacious demagogue Goebbels identifies this method with the reality itself.

It goes without saying that this 'resurrection' of expressionism is only partial. Expressionism can never win back its dominant position of the years 1916 to 1920. On the other hand, Goebbels couples expressionism with the 'new objectivism' as 'steely romanticism'. On the other hand, the fascist Professor Schardt, for example, gives it an extremely elevated pedigree. Any kind of 'naturalism', i.e. any genuine grasp and reflection of reality, is rejected by Schardt as 'un-German'. The expressionist pedigree, on the other hand, with its 'Gothic and Faustian yearning for the infinite', begins with Walther von der Vogelweide, the Naumberg school of sculpture and Grünewald, and leads on through to Stefan George, Nolde and Barlach. What is specifically expressionist is reduced here to a mere moment in this eclectic search for a style, its diverse elements being held together only by the common intention of the fascists, their flight from portrayal of reality, though a flight that pompously disguises itself as a 'Faustian' self-elevation over the ordinary, 'un-German' reality.

It is not accidental that fascism has accepted expressionism as a part of its inheritance. Even in the field of literature, fascism has failed to produce anything genuinely new. It brings together all the parasitic and putrefying tendencies of monopoly capitalism into an eclectic and demagogic 'unity', all that is new being the way in which this collation is effected, and in particular the way it is exploited in order to create a mass basis for a monopoly capitalism threatened by crisis and revolution. New also is the radicalism with which all knowledge of objective reality is rejected, and the irrational and mystical tendencies of the imperialist epoch are intensified to the point of nonsense. It is evident that this must lead in the literary field to the radical rejection of any realism. Even that naturalism which was so lame and superficial in comparison with the revolutionary period of the bourgeoisie has to be condemned as 'un-German', and where the fascist theory and practice of literature still does permit a kind of realism, this is in the pseudo-realist, half or completely apologetic traditions of late German romanticism. Only the realism of the 'new objectivism' is so openly apologetic, and leads so clearly away from the artistic reproduction of reality, that it can find a place in the fascist inheritance. Expressionism, however, as we have shown, links up with this turning away from reality, both in its world outlook and also in its creative method. As a literary form of expression of developed imperialism, expressionism stands on an irrational and mythological foundation; its creative method leads in the direction of the emotive yet empty declamatory manifesto, the proclamation of a sham activism. It has therefore a whole series of essential features that fascist literary theory could accept without having to force them into its mould. Naturally the conscious tendencies of expressionism are different from this, indeed sometimes even the direct opposite. And for this reason it can only be incorporated in the fascist 'synthesis' as a subordinate element. But its abstracting away from reality, and its lack of content, facilitate such an incorporation and 'Gleichschaltung' to an extraordinary degree.

This acceptance of expressionism is of course also still much contested. The general battles between different tendencies within National Socialism can be seen also in the field of literary theory. Alfred Rosenberg calls the supporters of expressionism artistic followers of Otto Strasser, while Nazi students rage against the 'Sturm-und-Drang tendency in painting of crazed dilettantes and philistines', against 'beards and velvet collars', against the 'Greco-Romano-Wilhelmine academicism of suburban painters dressed up as National Socialists', etc.

However violently these discussions swing to and fro, their importance should not be overrated. Rosenberg may well speak of a 'war on two fronts: against decadence and against regression', but in actual fact the theory and practice of national socialism is a unity of decadence and regression. The expressionists certainly wanted anything but a regression. But since they could not free their world outlook from the basis of imperialist parasitism, since they shared uncritically and without resistance in the ideological decay of the imperialist bourgeoisie, even being sometimes its pioneers, their creative method needed no distortion to be pressed into the service of fascist demagogy, of the unity of decadence and regression. Expressionism forms a legitimate part of the general 'November legacy' of national socialism. For despite its rhetorical gestures, it was unable to rise above the horizon of the 1918 Weimar republic. Just as fascism is the necessary result of the November betrayal of the German working class and the revolution by the SPD and USPD, it can also take up this November legacy in the literary field.

1934

Note, 1953: That the National Socialists later condemned expressionism as a 'decadent art' in no way affects the historical correctness of the above analysis, G.L.

Marx and the Problem of Ideological Decay [1938]*

'People who are weak cannot be sincere' – La Rochefoucauld

Marx was thirteen years old when Hegel died, and fourteen on the death of Goethe. The decisive years of his youth fell in the period between the July revolution of 1830 and the February revolution of 1848. His first major phase of political and journalistic activity coincided with the period leading up to the revolution and the ideological leadership of revolutionary democracy by its proletarian wing.

One of the key questions for the ideological preparation of Germany for the revolution of 1848 was the debate around the decomposition of Hegelianism. This process marked the end of the last great philosophy of bourgeois society.

At the same time, it became an important component in the rise of dialectical materialism. The construction of the new science of historical materialism, however, also involved a critical debate with the rise and break-up of classical economics, the greatest and most typical new science of bourgeois society. As the critical historian of classical economics, Marx discovered the history of this dissolution and was the first to write it. His summary characterization of classical economics at its watershed in the years 1820–1830 is at the same time a weighty and many-sided presentation and criticism of the ideological decay of the bourgeoisie.

This decay set in with the bourgeoisie's seizure of political power, with the shift in class struggle that brought the conflict between bourgeoisie and proletariat to the centre of the historical stage. This struggle, wrote Marx, 'sounded the knell of scientific bourgeois economics. It was thenceforth no longer a question, whether this or that theorem was true, but whether it was useful to capital or harmful, expedient or inexpedient. In place of disinterested inquirers, there were hired prize-fighters; in place of genuine scientific research, the bad con-

* First published in *Internationale Literatur*, no. 7, 1938, pp. 103–43.

science and the evil intent of apologetic' [*Capital*, Vol. 1, Moscow, 1961, p. 19].

This critique was preceded in time not only by that directed against the Hegelian epigones of the 1840s, but also by the splendid and comprehensive critique of the political decay of the bourgeois parties in the revolution of 1848. In Germany the bourgeois parties betrayed the broad interests of the bourgeois-democratic revolution, in which the interest of the people was represented, to the Hohenzollern dynasty, while in France they betrayed the interests of democracy to Louis Bonaparte.

Directly linked to this critique, after the defeat of the revolution, came Marx's critique of the social-scientific reflections of this betrayal. Marx concluded his judgement on Guizot with the words: '*Les capacités de la bourgeoisie s'en vont*', and in the *Eighteenth Brumaire* he condensed the grounds for this verdict into an epigram: 'The bourgeoisie had a true insight into the fact that all the weapons which it had forged against feudalism turned their points against itself, that all the means of education which it had produced rebelled against its own civilization, that all the gods which it had created had fallen away from it' [*Collected Works*, Vol. 11, pp. 141–2].

1

We can see present in Marx, therefore, a comprehensive and systematic critique of the great turn of political ideology into apologetics, a process of decay that affected the whole of bourgeois thought. It is quite impossible to discuss this critique fully here, or even to enumerate its aspects completely. For this we should need a history of bourgeois ideology in the nineteenth century compiled on the basis of Marxist research. In the present essay, therefore, we shall simply emphasize a few important perspectives, deliberately selected from the standpoint of the connection with literature of those great social, political and ideological tendencies that called this turn into being.

We begin with the flight from reality, the flight into the realm of 'pure' ideology, the liquidation of the spontaneous materialism and spontaneous dialectics of the representatives of the 'heroic period' of bourgeois development. The thinking of the apologists was no longer fertilized by the contradictions of social development; it sought on the contrary to adjust these in accordance with the economic and political needs of the bourgeoisie.

Directly after the revolution of 1848, Marx and Engels criticized a pamphlet by Guizot on the differences between the English and French revolutions. Before 1848 Guizot had been one of those major French historians who exposed the role of the class struggle in the emergence of bourgeois society. After 1848 he sought to prove at any price that the preservation of the July monarchy was a command of historical reason, and 1848 simply one great mistake.

In order to demonstrate this reactionary thesis, Guizot stood the whole of both French and English history on its head, and forgot everything that he himself achieved in a long career of historical research. Instead of using the differences between English and French agricultural development in their relationship to the rise of capitalism as the key to investigate the differences between the English and French revolutions, he took as his starting-point the exclusive historical legitimacy of the July monarchy, as a historical *a priori*. He projected into English development the prevalence of a religious and conservative element, thus quite ignoring the historical reality, i.e. in particular the bourgeois character of landed property in England and the special development of philosophical materialism and the Enlightenment.

The following results are thereby reached. On the one hand: 'For M. Guizot, English history ends with the consolidation of the constitutional monarchy.... Where M. Guizot sees only placid tranquillity and idyllic peace, the most violent conflicts, the most thorough-going revolutions, were actually developing' [*Collected Works*, Vol. 11, p. 255]. On the other hand, parallel with this brushing aside of historical facts and the real moving powers of history, there emerged a definite mystification: 'M. Guizot has recourse to religious phrases, to the armed intervention of God. Thus, for instance, the spirit of the Lord suddenly descends upon the army and prevents Cromwell from proclaiming himself king, etc., etc.' [ibid.]. Under the influence of the 1848 revolution, therefore, one of the founders of modern historical science was turned into a mystifying apologist for the class compromise between the bourgeoisie and the survivals of feudalism.

This liquidation of all earlier attempts by significant bourgeois ideologists to grasp the genuine dynamic forces of society fearlessly, and untroubled by the contradictory reality they discovered, this flight into an ideologically adjusted, superficially conceived, subjectively and mystically distorted pseudo-history, is the general tendency of this ideological decay. Just as the liberal and democratic parties in France took flight in the face of the June insurrection of the Paris proletariat, and hid themselves under the wings of the Hohenzollerns, Bonapartes and company, so the ideologists of the bourgeoisie also took flight, and preferred to concoct the most blatant and absurd mysticisms rather than look the fact of the class struggle between bourgeoisie and proletariat straight in the face and grasp the causes and nature of this class struggle scientifically.

From the methodological standpoint, this turn is expressed in the way these theorists, as we already saw with Guizot, concerned themselves ever less directly with reality itself, but instead concentrated on formal and verbal debates with past doctrines.

It goes without saying that such debate with one's forerunners plays an important role in every science, and with the classic figures of economics and philosophy it also assumed great importance. For them, however, debate of this kind was only one occasion among many for getting to grips with the reality in a deeper and more all-round way. Only with those eclectics who glorify the existing conditions does scientific doctrine get so far divorced from the life it is supposed to reflect, and it gets all the more divorced, the stronger pressure the apologist feels to falsify the reality.

This self-exclusion from the life of society practised by eclectic pseudo-science tends more and more to transform scientific assertions into mere phrases. This is the same verbal emptiness in relation to both past and present that Marx satirized in the case of the French 'Radicals' of the 1848 revolution. In the great years of 1789 to 1793 the relationship of the revolutionaries to classical antiquity, even extending to matters of dress, was a progressive element in the revolution, driving it forward. But when the 'Mountain' of 1848 decked itself out in the words and gestures of its predecessor of 1793, this was no more than a caricature: here its words and gestures stood in sharp opposition to its real actions.

I should like to give two examples of this turn in bourgeois science, one economic and the other philosophical.

Marx gives the following characterization of James Mill, with whom this development began, although Mill himself still had certain elements of the genuine scientist about him:

His raw material is no longer reality, but the new theoretical form in which the master [Ricardo] has sublimated it. It is in part the *theoretical disagreement of opponents of the new theory* and in part the *often paradoxical relationship of this theory to reality* which drive him to seek *to refute* his opponents and *explain away* reality . . . On the one hand, Mill wants to present bourgeois production as the absolute form of production and seeks therefore to prove that its real contradictions are only apparent ones. On the other hand, [he seeks] to present the Ricardian theory as the absolute theoretical form of this mode of production and to disprove the theoretical contradictions, both the ones pointed out by others and the ones he himself cannot help seeing. . . . It is simply an attempt to present that which does not exist as in fact existing. But it is in this *direct* form that Mill seeks to solve the problem. Thus no solution of the matter is possible here, only a sophistic explaining away of the difficulty, that is, only *scholasticism* [*Theories of Surplus-Value*, Part 3, London, 1972, pp. 84, 85, 87].

Since the dissolution of Hegelianism in Germany, however different the social and ideological development of this country was from the English, was a process whose social roots were ultimately related to the break-up of the Ricardian school, the facts of the matter here, and Marx's judgement of them, necessarily show a certain methodological similarity. This is how Marx sums up his critique of the philosophical and historical conception of the radical young Hegelians with particular reference to Bruno Bauer: 'The abstract and nebulous expression into which a real collision is distorted by Hegel is held by this "critical" mind to be the real collision itself' [*The German Ideology, Collected Works*, Vol, 5, p. 99]. This general method of the turn to apologetics in bourgeois thought is most clearly shown when it is confronted with the contradiction of social progress. The contradictory character of progress is a general problem of class society's development.

The universally developed individuals, whose social relations are their own collective relations and as such are subject to their own collective control, are the product not of nature, but of history. The degree and the universality to which the capacities are developed which make this individuality possible presuppose a mode of production based on exchange values. This mode of production brings about the general alienation of the individual from himself and from others, but at the same time it actually creates that universality and diversity with which his relations and abilities are endowed. At earlier stages of history the single individual appears more complete precisely because he has not yet elaborated this wealth of relationships and opposed them to himself as autonomous social forces. It is as absurd to feel nostalgia for that primordial wealth as it is to deem it essential to cling to the [present] level of total poverty. The bourgeois outlook has never overcome its antagonism to that romantic view, and because of this the latter will accompany the bourgeoisie as its justifiable antithesis to its dying day [*Grundrisse*, Harmondsworth, 1973, p. 162; translation modified].

What Marx is demonstrating here is the necessary antithesis between the bourgeois defence of progress and the romantic critique of capitalism. In the final flowering of bourgeois science, this antithesis was present in the work of the most important economists, Ricardo and Sismondi. With the turn towards apologetics, the Ricardian line became distorted and debased into a direct and vulgar apology for capitalism. From the romantic critique of capitalism there developed a more complicated and pretentious, but no less mendacious and eclectic apologia for bourgeois society, as an indirect apologia, its defence from its 'bad side'.

The methodological starting-point of the former tendency, the outright and direct apologia for capitalism, we find again with James Mill. As Marx characterizes this method: 'Where the economic relation – and therefore also the categories expressing it – includes contradictions, opposites, and likewise the unity of the opposites, he emphasizes the aspect of the unity of the contradictions and denies the *contradictions*. He transforms the unity of opposites into the direct identity of opposites' [loc. cit., p. 88].

It was in this way that Mill opened the flood-gates for the most blatant apologetics of vulgar economics. From his still partly serious research work, the way led rapidly downwards into the thoughtless glorification of the 'harmony' of capitalism, to Say, Bastiat, and Roscher. Economics came to be ever more restricted to a mere reproduction of surface phenomena. The spontaneous process of scientific decay went hand in hand with the deliberate and venal apologetics of capitalist economics.

> The more the vulgar economists in fact content themselves with translating common notions into doctrinaire language, the more they imagine that their writings are plain, *in accordance with nature* and the public interest, and free from all theoretical hair-splitting. Therefore, the more alienated the form in which they conceive the manifestations of capitalist production, the closer they approach the nature of common notions, and the more they are, as a consequence, in their natural element. This, moreover, renders a substantial service to apologetics [ibid., p. 503].

This is the line taken by simple and direct apologetics, the ideological line that debases bourgeois ideology into a cowardly and compromising liberalism.

What is more complicated, and for us today more dangerous, is the other extremely one-sided attitude to social progress, for it is out of the vulgarized and decadent conception that romantic anti-capitalism very soon arrived at, already in fact with Malthus, that the barbaric social demagogy of fascism eventually developed, as the capitalist system gradually putrefied.

Malthus sought to apologize for capitalism in the context of the discords of this economic system. It is instructive, therefore, to compare his conception with those of Ricardo and Sismondi, so as to see the contrast between his form of apologetics and those of the last two classic figures of political economy.

Ricardo supports production for production's sake. This means, as Marx puts it, 'the development of human productive forces, in other words the *development of the richness of human nature as an end in itself*'. Ricardo therefore took up a fearless and honest position against any class that in any way inhibited this progress, i.e. even against the bourgeoisie, when necessary. And when he openly and cynically equates the proletariat of capitalist society with machinery, draught animals and commodities, the cynicism here lies purely in the situation itself. He can do so, says Marx, 'because they really are mere commodities in bourgeois production. This is stoic, objective, scientific. In so far as it does not involve *sinning* against his science, Ricardo is always a philanthropist, just as he was in *practice* too' [*Theories of Surplus-Value*, Part 2, London, 1969, pp. 117–19].

Malthus's defence of capitalist society follows a diametrically opposite path. Marx summarizes its main points as follows:

Malthus also wishes to see the freest possible development of capitalist production, however only insofar as the condition of this development is the poverty of its main basis, the working classes, but at the same time he wants it to adapt itself to the 'consumption needs' of the aristocracy and its branches in State and Church, to serve as the material basis for the antiquated claims of the representatives of interests inherited from feudalism and the absolute monarchy. Malthus wants bourgeois production as long as it is not revolutionary, constitutes no historical factor of development but merely creates a broader and more comfortable material basis for the 'old' society [*Theories of Surplus-Value*, Part 3, London, 1972, p. 52].

Malthus also links up with the romantic critique of capitalism, by stressing its discordances. So, too, does Sismondi *vis-à-vis* Ricardo; he emphasizes the rights of individual human beings, which are materially and morally destroyed by capitalist development. However one-sided, and in the broader historical sense unjustified, this view may have been, and however much Sismondi was forced to retreat ideologically into the past, he does have the credit of having discovered 'the contradictions in capitalist production'. 'He forcefully *criticizes* the contradictions of bourgeois production but does not *understand* them, and consequently does not understand the process whereby they can be resolved' [ibid., pp. 55–6].

For all the severity of his criticism of these romantic views of Sismondi, Marx nevertheless maintains that there was present here a suspicion of the merely historical and transitory character of capitalist society. With Sismondi, the romantic critique of capitalism, the discovery of its necessary contradictions and discords is thus the important achievement of a fearless and honest thinker.

Both the content and direction in which Malthus displays the discordances of capitalism are completely opposite to this.

> Malthus is interested not in concealing the contradictions of bourgeois production, but on the contrary, in emphasizing them, on the one hand, in order to prove that the poverty of the working classes is necessary (as it is, indeed, for this mode of production) and, on the other hand, to demonstrate to the capitalists the necessity for a well-fed Church and State hierarchy in order to create an adequate demand for the commodities they produce [ibid., p. 57].

With Malthus, therefore, this decay of the romantic critique of capitalism appears very early on in its most repulsive and meanest forms, as an expression of the ideology of the most reactionary section of the English bourgeoisie in the very violent class struggles of the early nineteenth century. Malthus is thus a precursor of the most extreme degeneration of bourgeois ideology, as became the general rule only later under the influence of the international events of 1848.

This crisis reduced one of the most talented and shining representatives of anti-capitalism, Thomas Carlyle, to a decadent cripple, a mendacious apologist for capitalism. Before this crisis, Carlyle was a courageous, profound and ingenious critic of the terrors of capitalist civilization. Just as the Frenchman Linguet in the eighteenth century, or in the nineteenth century – from different standpoints of class and world outlook – Balzac and Fourier, all exposed fearlessly the contradictions of capitalism, so Carlyle too, in his works prior to 1848, waged an untiring campaign of exposure against the prevalent capitalism, against those who praised it for its unproblematic progressiveness, and against the mendacious theory that this progress served the interest of the working people.

The storms of the 1848 revolution, however, brought about what Marx and Engels called 'the decline of literary genius in historical struggles which have reached a point of crisis' [*Collected Works*, Vol. 10, p. 301].

In the events of 1848, Carlyle saw not the weakness, division and cowardice of bourgeois democracy in its defence of the great historic interests of the working people, but simply chaos, delirium and universal catastrophe. He assessed the bankruptcy of bourgeois democracy in 1848, really a function of its betrayal of the people, as the bankruptcy of democracy in general. He demanded 'order' in place of 'chaos', placing himself on the side of the reactionary bandits who defeated the 1848 revolution. He viewed the rule of the 'noble' in society, and a correspondingly hierarchical system, as an 'eternal law of nature'.

But who were these 'noble' people? In fact, the 'leaders' of industry. Carlyle's critique of capitalism suffered even in his militant period – like Sismondi's very different but similarly romantic critique – from the fact that he saw the road leading to the rescue of civilization from barbarism not in the future, but rather in the past.

The ideological result of the panic induced in him by the revolution was that Carlyle's former 'hero' was now replaced by the 'captains of industry', his romantic anti-capitalism transformed into a philistine apology for the capitalist system.

It already corresponded in content to the mendacious baseness of the common-or-garden terrified philistine, distinguished only by the now quite superficial brilliance of his language, and his formal paradoxes. And even this distinction does not redound to his credit. For his very brilliance gives his philistinism a mendacious and demagogic power of seduction. 'The "*New Era*" in which genius rules', said Marx, 'is thus distinguished from the old era principally by the fact that the whip imagines it possesses genius' [ibid., p. 309]. Carlyle, previously honest and highly gifted, descends to the spiritual and moral level of a Malthus.

In England, the philosophy that defended bourgeois progress saw its uncelebrated demise already before this time. (In Germany, the break-up of Hegelian philosophy marked this step in the development.) In Hobbes and Locke, Helvétius and Holbach, the bourgeois philosophy of progress had found its brilliant and courageous representatives. They had certainly suffered from illusions as regards this progress, and given them the form of a philosophical system; but since these illusions had been necessary from the standpoint of world history, their philosophical expression could and necessarily did lead to the discovery of important elements of the real historical development, in a profound and ingenious manner. Capitalism's defence of universal progress is in their case, and in the case of their followers, inseparable from this defence, a fearless exposure of all the now visible contradictions and atrocities of bourgeois society.

The ignominious demise of this great and glorious line of philosophical development was represented by the theorist of utilitarianism, Jeremy Bentham. But whereas romantic anti-capitalism degenerated into a gaudy and mendacious demagogy, the decadence of the philosophy of progress was far more overt: a vapid and unconcealed philistinism. Marx depicts this demise precisely by emphasizing the relationship of Bentham to his glorious forerunners:

> He simply reproduced in his dull way what Helvétius and other Frenchmen had said with esprit in the 18th century. . . . With the dryest naïveté he takes the modern shopkeeper, especially the English shopkeeper, as the normal man. Whatever is useful to this queer normal man, and to his world, is absolutely useful. This yard-measure, then, he applies to past, present and future. The Christian religion, e.g., is 'useful', 'because it forbids in the name of religion the same faults that the penal code condemns in the name of the law'. (The reader will recall the atheistic boldness of philosophers from Hobbes through to Helvétius. G.L.). . . . Had I the courage of my friend, Heinrich Heine, I should call Mr Jeremy a genius in the way of bourgeois stupidity [*Capital*, Volume 1, Moscow, 1961, pp. 609–10, note].

In Bentham, therefore, we have embodied the capitalist philistine, in all his stark sobriety, without any illusion of romantic glory. It will be clear to the reader, however, after the above analyses, that the social kernel of romantic anti-capitalism's decorative pomp is likewise the cowardly and spineless philistine of capitalist society. This profound inner insight must be particularly emphasized in as much as here the Marxist method in exposing ideological decadence can most clearly be seen. Behind the pompous facade of great, profound or even 'revolutionary' sounding phrases, the Marxist exposure unveils time and again the fearful and ugly mug of the capitalist philistine. The form in which this capitalist philistinism appears in science is eclecticism, the elevation of the philistine 'on the one hand, on the other hand' to a scientific 'method', the denial of the contradictions of life, or – what comes to the same thing – the superficial, immediate and uncomprehending rigid counterposing of contradictory determinations. The more embellished this eclecticism, the hollower it generally is inside. The more 'critical' and 'revolutionary' its guise, the greater the ideological danger it presents for the working masses who initially revolt in a state of ideological unclarity.

In this era of great crisis for bourgeois ideology, Marx criticized this change of direction in all fields, history, economics, sociology and philosophy, in detail and devastatingly. As for the later and still more debased development, only in exceptional cases did Marx and Engels consider it worthy of detailed analysis (*Anti-Dühring*). They generally spoke with summary contempt, and quite correctly so, of those eclectic and watery broths that were now cooked up for the ideological stupefaction of the masses. Would-be clever opportunists and opponents of dialectical materialism have objected to this summary judgement, and reproached Engels for an ignorance of more recent development in science because he did not take issue, for example, with Riehl or Cohen. Today we hear similar reproaches in relation to Nietzsche or Bergson, Husserl or Heidegger. They have as little justification as the criticisms of thirty years ago which Lenin refuted with brilliant irony in his *Materialism and Empirio-Criticism*.

If the thinking reader surveys Marx's own criticism of decadent ideology, he will without trouble find in the eclectic mixture of immediacy and scholastics served up by Mill the key to the real understanding of many modern thinkers who are bruited about as so profound.

2

It is a social necessity that ideological decadence does not throw up any fundamentally new problems. Its basic questions are, just like those of the classical period of bourgeois ideology, answers to the problems posed by the social developments of capitalism. The difference is 'simply' that the earlier ideologists offered honest and scientific answers, even if these were incomplete and contradictory, whereas the ideologists of the period of decadence are too craven to utter what is, and conceal this flight either as 'objective scientificity' or as romantic partiality. In both cases the answer is essentially uncritical, and remains on the surface of phenomena, trapped in immediacy and eclectically pinning together contradictory fragments of ideas. In his *Materialism and Empirio-Criticism* Lenin brilliantly showed how Mach, Avenarius and others only repeated, cravenly and contortedly, what the idealist reactionary of a former age, Berkeley, had uttered aloud.

At the root of both periods of bourgeois ideology, therefore, there objectively lies the central problem of the development of capitalism. We have already seen in the preceding discussions how the problem of the contradictory character of progress was arbitrarily broken down and trivialized by the ideologists of the period of decay. We shall now turn to another key complex of problems in capitalist society, the social division of labour.

The social division of labour is much older than capitalist society, but as a result of the ever stronger dominance of the commodity relation its effects acquire an extent and profundity that turns into something qualitatively new. The first underlying fact of the social division of labour is the separation between town and country. According to Marx, this is 'the most crass expression of the subjection of the individual under the division of labour, under a definite activity forced upon him – a subjection which makes one man into a *restricted town-animal*, another into a *restricted country-animal*, and daily creates anew the conflict between their interests' [*The German Ideology, Collected Works*, Vol. 5, p. 64]. (My emphases: G.L.)

The other equally basic fact of the social division of labour, the division between physical and mental labour, continuously deepens this conflict especially in capitalist development. The development of capitalism also differentiates mental labour into different and separate spheres, with competing material and mental special interests arising between them, and the formation of a corresponding specific kind of specialists. (Consider, for example, the specific psychology of lawyers, technicians, etc.)

What is specific to capitalist development – and this is particularly indicated by Engels in *Anti-Dühring* – is that here even the ruling classes are subjected to the division of labour. Whereas the more primitive forms of exploitation, especially those of the Greco-Roman slave economy, created a ruling class that essentially remained untouched by the division of labour, under capitalism this extends, as Engels wittily and convincingly shows, even to those members of the ruling classes whose 'speciality' consists in doing nothing.

The capitalist division of labour thus does not just subject to itself all fields of material and mental activity, it drives deep into the soul of every single person, and brings about far-reaching deformations, which subsequently appear in various forms in the various modes of ideological expression. The subjection without a struggle to the effects of this division of labour, the uncontradicted acceptance of these spiritual and moral deformations, and indeed even their deepening and embellishment by decadent thought and literature, forms one of the most essential features of the period of decay.

This question, however, should not be viewed in a superficial way. From a superficial standpoint, the period of decay is marked by a continuous romantic bewailing of specialization: a decorative and romantic glorification of the great figures of past epochs, whose life and activity still exhibited a comprehensive universalism, and repeated emphasis and criticism of the disadvantages of an all too narrow specialization. The basic tone in all this glorification and complaint is that an ever narrowing specialization is the 'fate' of our epoch, a fate that no one can escape.

What is most usually adduced as an argument for this view is that the scope of modern science has reached such a level that the individual's labour-power can no longer permit him to master the entire field of human knowledge, or at least wide regions of this, without abandoning the scientific level for mere dilettantism. And indeed, if we consider those 'comprehensive syntheses' that the post-war era in particular has delivered us, i.e. those of Spengler, Leopold Ziegler, Keyserling, etc., this argument seems well justified. These really are pure dilettantes, building their 'synthetic' houses of cards on the basis of hollow analogies.

But no matter how convincing this argument might seem at first sight, it is still incorrect. The fact that modern bourgeois social science has not outgrown a narrow-minded specialism is correct, but the reasons for this lie entirely elsewhere. They do not lie in the extensive scope of human knowledge, but rather in the type and direction of development of the modern social sciences. In these, the decay of bourgeois ideology has reached such a pass that they can no longer understand one another, and that study of one no longer furthers a deeper understanding of the others. This narrow-minded specialism has become the method of the social sciences.

This can be seen very clearly from the example of a scholar of our own time who, even though meticulous in his scientific work, and having acquired a broad and many-sided knowledge, still failed to raise his thought above the level of this narrow specialism: Max Weber. Weber was an economist, sociologist, historian, philosopher and political theorist. In all these fields he gained a level of knowledge that went far beyond the average, and was, on top of this, at home also in all fields of art and its history. And yet we cannot find in him even the shadow of a genuine universalism.

Why not? To answer this we have to cast a short glance at how the particular sciences with whose aid Weber sought a general understanding of social history were disposed. First of all, the new science of the era of decay, sociology as a special science, arose because the bourgeois ideologists wanted to view the laws and history of social development separate from the economy. The objectively apologetic tendency in this development is only too obvious. After the rise of Marxist economics it became impossible to ignore the class struggle as the fundamental fact of social development, if one studied social relationships on the basis of economics. In order to evade this necessity, sociology came into being as a separate science of its own, and the further it developed its particular method, becoming ever more formalist, the more did it replace investigation of real causal connections in social life with formalist analyses and empty analogies.

Parallel with this development we had the flight of economics itself from analysis of the overall process of production and reproduction into analysis of isolated and superficial phenomena of circulation. The 'marginal utility theory' of the imperialist period is the acme of this abstracting and formalistic evacuation of the real contents of economics. Whereas in the classic period the prevailing effort was directed towards understanding the connection between social and economic problems, the era of decay built up an artificial, pseudo-scientific and pseudo-methodological barrier between the two, an artificial separation that exists only in the imagination. There was a corresponding development in the science of history. Here, too, before the era of decay, economics and sociology were separated only methodologically and secondarily in concrete investigations, so deeply and closely was history tied up with the development of production and the inner forward movement of the social formation. In the period of decay, this connection is also broken in an artificial way that objectively serves the purpose of apologetics. Just as sociology is supposed to be a science with its own laws, yet without economic or historical content, so history is supposedly limited to the presentation of the 'uniqueness' of a particular series of events, without the law-like character of social life being brought into account.

It is clear that on such a foundation of world outlook and methodology the work of the economist, the sociologist and the historian have no longer anything to do with one another, and can no longer provide each other with any concrete help or assistance. So if Max Weber managed to be both sociologist, economist and historian, and subsequently brought this sociology, economics and historiography together (uncritically) into a 'synthesis', this meant that he necessarily maintained the division of labour between these sciences even in his own head. The mere fact that a man has mastered them does not mean that they can be dialectically interconnected and lead to knowledge of the real relationships of social development.

It might sound somewhat surprising that a man with such a many-sided education as Max Weber maintained so uncritical a relationship to the sciences that he simply accepted them as they were immediately offered to him by the development of the era of decay. This uncritical tendency, however, is particularly reinforced in Weber's case by the fact that he was also a philosopher. As an adherent of the neo-Kantian school, he had precisely learned to give this methodological division and separation a philosophical sanction; this philosophy 'deepened' his conviction that he was faced here with an 'eternal structure' of human understanding.

Neo-Kantian philosophy also taught Max Weber something else, i.e. the fundamental lack of connection between thinking and acting, theory and practice. Firstly, this theory taught a complete relativism: the formal equality of all social phenomena, the equal inner value of all historical forces. The Weberian scientific doctrine, as a logical conclusion of neo-Kantianism, demands an absolute theoretical reservation of judgement *vis-à-vis* the phenomena of society and history.

Ethical behaviour, for Weber, accordingly arises from a mystical decision of the 'free will', and has nothing to do with knowledge of the facts. Weber expresses this idea, this eclectic amalgam of extreme relativism in knowledge and complete mysticism in behaviour, as follows:

Here (i.e in practical behaviour: G.L.) we are precisely confronted with the struggle of different gods with one another, and this is so for all time. It is like the old world, still not disenchanted of its gods and daemons, only in a different sense; just as the ancient Greek first gave a sacrifice to Aphrodite, then to Apollo, and particularly to all the gods of his own city, so it is still today, only without the mythical garb of that behaviour, which however was in itself quite transparent. These gods and their struggles may well be governed by fate, but certainly not by any 'science' [*Gesammelte Aufsätze zur Wissenschaftslehre*, Tübingen, 1922, pp. 545 ff.].

It is clear that Max Weber could not attain any genuine universalism with such views, but at most the personal union of a group of narrow-minded specialists in one man – himself. And the apologetic and escapist character of this entrapment of a highly talented, hard working and subjectively honest ideologist in the confines of the scientific division of labour of decaying capitalism, can easily be unravelled in its social causes if we read the little that Weber wrote about socialism. In a lecture, Weber 'refuted' socialist economics on the grounds that the 'right to the full proceeds of labour' was an unattainable utopia. This great scholar, who would have died of shame if he had given a wrong date for an event in ancient Chinese history, was evidently quite unaware of the refutation of this Lassallean theory by Marx. He descends here to the level of the professional anti-Marxist, to the level of the philistine terrified by the 'equality-mongering' of the socialists.

Here it is already clearly apparent how the capitalist division of labour penetrates and deforms the soul of individual men, how it makes a man who stands both intellectually and morally above the average into ultimately no more than a narrow-minded philistine. This domination of human consciousness by the capitalist division of labour, this fixation of the apparent autonomy acquired by the superficial moments of capitalist life, this intellectual separation between theory and practice, also separates understanding from emotion in the people who capitulate to capitalist life unresistingly.

Here we see the reflection in an individual human being of the fact that in capitalist society specialized professional activities acquire apparent autonomy from the overall process. But while Marxism sees this living contradiction as a result of 'social production and private appropriation', the apparent antithesis on the surface is fixed by the science of the period of decay as an 'eternal human destiny'.

In this way, the average citizen perceives his profession as making him a tiny cog in a tremendous machine, with no inkling of its overall movement. And if this connection, this necessary social character in individual activity is simply denied, anarchist-fashion, the division still remains, simply with a pretentiously negative and pseudo-philosophical foundation. In both cases society appears as an incomprehensible, mythical power, whose fatalistic objectivity, devoid of any humanity, threatens the individual.

This evacuation from social activity of its entire content has the necessary ideological consequence for the individuals affected that their private life now seems to be led outside this mythologized society. 'My home is my castle' is the form of life of every capitalist philistine. The 'little man', humiliated yet ambitious in his job, lets all his suppressed and perverted instincts for power run riot in his own home.

But the objective connection between social phenomena cannot be done away with by any distorted reflection, no matter how stubborn its ideological fixation. In this ideologically fenced-off and narrow circle of private life, the social still comes to claim its own. Love, marriage and family are objective social categories, 'forms of being' and 'determinations of existence' of human life.

The distorted reflection in the soul of the philistine once again reproduces here the false antithesis between dead objectivity and vacuous subjectivity. On the one hand, these forms again grow into a fetishized and mystified 'fate', while on the other hand the emotional life of the philistine, which has become rootless and cannot be externalized in his behaviour, flees still further into a 'pure internality'. It is ultimately a matter of indifference, here too, whether the real conflict that arises here is glossed over and the conventional money marriage of the bourgeois decked out with the hypocritical veneer of a mendaciously pretended individual love, or whether the romantic revolt sees only an empty shell in any realization of human feelings, the deadening principle and 'fate' of necessary disillusion, and takes refuge in complete isolation. In both cases, the contradictions of capitalist life are reproduced distorted and uncomprehended, in a one-sided philistine manner.

The reader will recall how Marx, in analysing the individual's subordination to the capitalist division of labour, emphasizes precisely the confined and animal-like character of this subordination. This is now reproduced in any person who does not concretely and really rebel against these social forces. From the ideological point of view, this confinement is expressed in the fashionable conflict of the world outlooks of the last few decades, the conflict between rationalism and irrationalism. The impossibility of settling this conflict in bourgeois thought stems precisely from the fact that it has such deep roots in capitalist life, as dominated by the division of labour.

The ideologists of today deck out this irrationalism in the most seductive colours of a 'primordial and profound truth'. In actual fact, a continuous line runs through from the confined superstition of the peasant, via the skittles and card games of the philistine, through to the 'meaningless refinements' of emotional life, whose rootlessness is lamented by Niels Lyhne.[1] Rationalism is a feeble and shameful capitulation before the objective necessities of capitalist society. Irrationalism is a protest against it which is just as impotent, just as feeble, just as empty and thoughtless.

Irrationalism as a world outlook fixes on this evacuation from the human soul of all social contents, and rigidly counterposes it to the equally mystified evacuation of the world of the understanding. In this way, irrationalism not only becomes the philosophical expression of the ever growing lack of culture in human emotional life, it also helps to promote this. It increasingly appeals, parallel with the decay of capitalism and the sharpening of class struggles in the period of acute capitalist crisis, to the worst instincts in man, to the animal and bestial side that capitalist oppression causes to be dammed up under pressure. If the mendacious and demagogic slogans of fascism about 'blood and soil' were able to find so rapid a reception and seduce such large sections of the petty bourgeoisie, then the philosophy and literature of the decadent period, which awakened these instincts in its readers — very often, of course, without even an inkling of how they might be used, often indeed vigorously rejecting such consequences — is in large measure responsible, for it helped in fact to cultivate these feelings.

The social connection between the over-refinement of vacuous individuality and this unleashed bestiality might strike many readers as paradoxical, caught as they are in the prejudices of our time. But they can readily be shown in the whole intellectual and literary production of the decadent period. Take for example one of the gentlest and most sensitive poets of the immediate past, Rainer Maria Rilke. A basic feature of Rilke's, both as a poet and a human being, was his terrified retreat from the soulless brutality of capitalist life. In one of his letters, he presents the attitude of children towards the crazy ways of adults, the child's withdrawal from this senseless activity into a neglected corner by himself, as the model for the poet's own attitude towards reality. And Rilke's poems express this sense of loneliness with an often fascinating linguistic power.

But let us look at a poem of this kind somewhat more closely. In his 'Book of Images' Rilke draws the portrait of the Swedish king Charles XII, as a legendary incarnation of this lonely melancholy amidst the bustle of a military life. The legendary king spends his youthful years alone, he rides alone in the fierceness of battle, and only at the close of battle does a certain warmth light up in his eyes.

The basic theme of this poem is the mood of lonesome melancholy. The poet identifies himself with this in his work, and it is for this that he demands our sympathy. But what did this fine and lonely melancholy look like in reality? Here Rilke depicts a poetic moment from the life of his hero:

And, when some sadness overcame,
he'd sometimes make a maiden tame,
and search out, by whose ring she came,
and whom she'd given hers,
and hunt to death the man she'd name
with a hundred harriers.

[*Selected Works*, translated by J. B. Leishmann,
vol. 2, London, 1960, p. 120]

This idea could have come from Goering, but no one would think of hymning the fat marshal with Rilke's entrancing song of sadness. What is outrageous in this poem is not the mere fact of a bestial brutality, but rather that Rilke, without even being aware of it, leads us into this bestiality via the profound sympathy he arouses with the lonesome melancholy and spiritual refinement of his hero, not even noticing that he is speaking about something bestial in a bestial tone. For him, this is simply an isolated episode, woven into the stylized tapestry of episodes that drift through the soul of the legendary hero without troubling either himself or the poet. All that is real for Rilke is the melancholy feeling of his hero.

The outbreaks of bestial rage on the part of ordinary petty bourgeois express the same condition of life and a similar sentiment as this verse. But in human terms, a large section of these average philistines are still superior to Rilke, for they have at least an inkling that such bestiality is incompatible with genuine human existence. The irrationalist and exclusive cult of vacuous refinement has made the gentle poet Rilke insensitive to this distinction.

3

This path of ideological development is socially necessary, but it is by no means necessary in the fatalistic sense for every individual. Such fatalism only appears in vulgar sociology, not in Marxism. Here, on the contrary, the connection between individual and class is presented in the full complexity of the dialectic of reality. We can summarize this conception as far as our present problem is concerned by saying that Marxism simply shows the impossibility for the individuals who make up a class of 'overcoming the barriers of class existence *en masse*, without superseding them. Only in accidental cases can the individual dispense with them.' The word 'accidental' should of course be understood here in the sense of the objective dialectic of accident and necessity.

The complicated, uneven and non-fatalistic relationship between individual ideologists and the fate of their class is to be seen in the way that it is only on the surface that society appears bound by ossified laws whose reflection in a distorted form is the mark of the ideology of the era of decay. In reality, social development is a living and moving unity of contradictions, and the continuous production and reproduction of these contradictions. The result of this is that no ideologist whatsoever, no matter from what class he originates, is trapped hermetically and solipsistically in the existence and consciousness of his own class, except in the conception of vulgar sociology. In reality, he is always faced with the entire society.

This living and moving unity of antithesis in the development of the whole society, this contradictory unity of the whole society, is a basic tenet of Marxist social doctrine. In Marx's own words:

The propertied class and the class of the proletariat present the same human self-estrangement. But the former class feels at ease and strengthened in this self-estrangement, it recognizes estrangement as *its own power* and has in it the *semblance* of a human existence. The latter feels annihilated in estrangement: it sees in it its own powerlessness and the reality of an inhuman existence. It is, to use an expression of Hegel, in its abasement the *indignation* at that abasement, an indignation to which it is necessarily driven by the contradiction between its human *nature* and its condition of life, which is the outright, resolute and comprehensive negation of that nature [*The Holy Family, Collected Works*, Vol. 4, p. 36].

It is particularly important for our conception here that the antithesis in question is not simply that between bourgeoisie and proletariat, but presents itself as an internal contradiction within each of the two classes. The bourgeoisie possesses only the semblance of a human existence. A living contradiction must necessarily arise between semblance and reality, for every individual of the bourgeois class, and it is to a great extent dependent on the individual himself whether he pacifies this contradiction using the means of ideological deception that his class constantly presses onto him, or whether this contradiction remains alive within him and leads to him tearing up the deceptive integuments of bourgeois ideology, either completely or at least in part. It goes without saying that bourgeois class consciousness wins out in the overwhelming majority of cases. But even here, its dominance is not automatic, not without contradiction, and certainly never without a struggle.

We have already shown how this illusory character of a truly human existence extends to all aspects of bourgeois life. The revolt of the bourgeois against this illusion thus in no way necessarily involves right from the start any tendency towards a break with his own class – let alone a conscious tendency. Partial revolts of this kind arise continuously and on a massive scale in the course of life itself, though it needs a great intellectual and moral power, particularly in conditions of general decay, for an individual genuinely to break through them and expose this semblance of human existence for what it is. The entire apparatus of apologetically romantic criticism of capitalism is designed precisely to lead such revolts astray, and lead those among the rebels who are intellectually and morally weaker back among the white sheep of capitalism, via the detour of a 'very radical' ideology. Somewhat schematically, we can list as follows the possibilities of development open to individuals from the bourgeois class:

First, simple subjection to the apologetic decadence of class ideology (in which case we make no distinction between direct and indirect, superior and ordinary forms of apologetics);

second, a complete break with the class, as made by those individuals with the highest intellectual and moral level. This is a phenomenon which, as already foreseen in the *Communist Manifesto*, assumes the proportions of an important social phenomenon in times of revolutionary crisis;

third, the tragic collapse of highly talented people in the face of the contradictions of social development, the intensification of class antitheses with which they are neither intellectually nor morally able to cope. We have already seen the example of Carlyle, and in our own days the fate of Gerhart Hauptmann shows the same social features;

fourth, the collision that honest ideologists come into with their own class, as a result of their experiencing the great contradictions of the epoch, following up this experience boldly and giving it fearless expression. This collision and conflict with the bourgeois class may in certain circumstances remain for a long time unconscious and latent, and need in no way always end up with a conscious move over to the proletariat. The significance of the situation that thus arises depends on how deeply the individual in question experiences the contradictions of the epoch and actually thinks them through, and to what degree he finds it possible, both mentally and in external behaviour, to pursue this course to its logical conclusion. This is also to a great extent an intellectual and moral problem.

But of course it is not only an individual intellectual and moral problem. For quite apart from the infinite variety of possible variations in the material and intellectual position of the individual, including circumstances that have either a favourable or unfavourable effect on this development, the possibilities offered by the different fields of ideological activity also differ greatly in this respect.

The situation is least favourable in the social sciences. Here the power of apologetic traditions is at its strongest, and the ideological sensitivity of the bourgeoisie greatest. Here, accordingly, any penetrating mental grasp of the contradictions of real life leads almost unavoidably to a rapid and radical break with the class. Any honest and genuinely scientific work in the field of social science that goes beyond the mere collection and arrangement of new data must inevitably come rapidly up against these barriers. Any open confession of a consistent philosophical materialism, any recognition of the theory of surplus-value in economics, with all its consequences, any conception of history that can see the driving force of development in the class struggle, and see capitalism as a transitional social form, etc., lead to an immediate and radical break with the bourgeoisie. Since moral choice operates with such extraordinary rigour in this field, it is no wonder that even talented representatives of bourgeois ideology capitulate before the various traditions of apologetics, and confine themselves to an external originality in ideological expression, or to a mere collection of data.

The situation in the natural sciences is far more complicated. The bourgeoisie is forced at the price of its very existence to carry forward the development of technology, and hence also of the natural sciences, thus at least to provide a relatively broad scope for the development of the pure sciences. The natural sciences can thus experience a substantial upswing even in the period of decay. The problem of the real dialectic in nature crops up time and again, bursting the rigid framework of the mechanical and metaphysical world outlook. Most important theoretical discoveries arise continuously. But it becomes extraordinarily hard, in the conditions of the decay period – in fact almost impossible – to advance from these newly discovered facts and theories in natural science to their philosophical generalization, to the genuine philosophical elucidation of their basic concepts. The philosophical terrorism of the present-day bourgeoisie frightens off the spontaneous materialism of important natural scientists and prevents them from thinking through and expressing the materialist conclusions that follow from their own discoveries in more than a half-hearted, vacillating and inhibited manner. On the other hand, the predominance of decadent philosophy leads constantly to the collapse of these dialectical problems into a reactionary philosophical relativism and idealism. In Lenin's *Materialism and Empirio-Criticism* this problematic is exhaustively depicted.

What is important for us here is the general cultural and ideological condition of the period of decay. We have therefore to stress two related phenomena that cast a sharp light on the contrast between the present situation and earlier epochs:

First, the fact that philosophy does not promote the genuine development of the natural sciences, and in particular the elucidation of their method and basic concepts, but rather inhibits this. We need only recall the period prior to this present decadence, in which from Nicholas of Cusa through to Hegel, from Galileo through to the great natural scientists of the first half of the nineteenth century, philosophy and natural science continuously cross-fertilized one another, the most important philosophical generalizations being the work of natural scientists themselves, while major philosophers similarly promoted the immediate work of mathematics and the natural sciences, in direct pursuit of their methodological analyses;

second, a sharp contrast can be seen in the broad cultural and ideological effect of the popularized teaching of natural science. In the period of the rise of the bourgeoisie, the great discoveries of natural science, from Copernicus to Darwin, were important elements of a general and socially effective revolutionizing of the consciousness of the masses. Today, the great discoveries of the modern natural sciences in the capitalist countries have their effect almost invariably only via a filtering by reactionary philosophy. In as much as they are popularized and penetrate into the consciousness of the masses, this happens in the form of a relativistic-idealist distortion, the struggle against causal thinking, the replacement of causality by statistical probability, and the 'disappearance' of matter – all this is deployed on the widest possible scale to spread a nihilistic relativism and an obscurantist mysticism.

Art and literature occupy a particular and in many ways more favourable position in this development. Of course, the unpropitious character of the present age for this field, too, should not be overlooked. For the contrast with earlier periods which we have already emphasized has highly disadvantageous effects on the development of artists and writers as well. We need only think of the great progressive effect on Goethe and Balzac of the theory of evolution, as opposed to the devastating influences of Nietzsche, Freud or Spengler on the writers of our own time.

Intrinsically, however, the room for manoeuvre within which even the most fearless artistic fidelity can operate without leading to a complete and open break with the bourgeoisie, to the necessity of a move over to the proletariat, is incomparably greater here than in the social sciences. Literature is the immediate portrayal of individual human beings and individual destinies, which only join up with the social relations of the epoch at a later stage, and need by no means necessarily exhibit a direct linkage to the conflict between bourgeoisie and proletariat.

The Marxist position, stressed earlier, of the problem of the internal contradictions in the existence of the bourgeoisie, comes into effect here, and creates a wider and more fruitful scope for the development of writers and literature. For as long as these contradictions have not become so deep and so blatant that they are unmistakably visible to everyone on the immediate surface, at which point it becomes impossible for the bourgeoisie to allay them or distort their significance, the attempt is made time and again to press literary works of this kind into the bourgeoisie's service. Here we have repeatedly spoken of the complex mechanism of indirect and even sham-revolutionary apologetics. This mechanism includes not only the attempt to exploit all kinds of social ambiguities, every failure of a writer to follow his ideas through to their logical conclusion, for the bourgeoisie's own ends. This is how the Russian bourgeoisie operated with Tolstoy after the revolution of 1905 – to give an example of the first importance. Through this ideological policy, which has become extremely dangerous, indeed quite fatal, for many writers who were intellectually or morally somewhat weak, certain Epicurean 'intermundia', as it were, have come into being in the society of capitalist decay, which have made it possible for some important writers to struggle successfully against the tide of the general development, with its general decadence and prevailing anti-realism.

But this recognition of a particular space opened for the development of important realist writers in the period of general decadence should not be misconstrued as meaning that the determination of literature mentioned above – i.e. that it immediately depicts only individual human beings and their fate, and only in the last analysis do the great social contradictions openly present themselves – involves a general abstinence on the part of these important realists from the central social conflicts of their time. Quite the contrary. The further these writers push forward in their recognition of social reality, the more vigorously these key problems stand before their eyes, both in terms of their world outlook and their literary technique. Zola, perhaps, expressed this feeling most acutely: 'Each time that I immerse myself in a particular material, I come up against socialism.' But in various ways, which differ according to the individual personality, social circumstances and concrete class struggles, so do Tolstoy and Ibsen, Anatole France and Romain Rolland, Shaw and Barbusse, Thomas and Heinrich Mann, all come up against the complex of these central contradictions.

4

The complex and by no means fatalistic dialectic of the necessity of this ideological decay thus indicates an individual escape route, albeit a hard one, for the major realists who hail from the bourgeois class.

We can see, therefore, that here again the question is not a radically new one, but is simply that of the intensification and coming to a head of those problems that determined the fate of literature in earlier times as well. In short, the question is still that of the 'triumph of realism', which Engels, in his analysis of Balzac, identified so acutely as the triumph of realistic portrayal, of the correct and profound reflection of reality which rose above Balzac's own individual and class prejudices. And when Marx subjected Eugène Sue, in *The Holy Family*, to a devastating criticism all along the line, he did not forget to point out that the portrayal of Fleur de Marie in the first half of Sue's novel is genuinely realistic.

In spite of her frailty, Fleur de Marie at once gives proof of vitality, energy, cheerfulness, resilience of character – qualities which alone explain her human development in her *inhuman* situation. . . . So far we have seen Fleur de Marie in her original . . . form. Eugène Sue has risen above the horizon of his narrow world outlook. He has slapped bourgeois prejudice in the face [*Collected Works*, Vol. 4, pp. 68 and 70].

The particular conditions that underlie the 'triumph of realism' in the period of decay must therefore be investigated somewhat more closely.

This victory was no miracle, but rather the necessary outcome of a very complex dialectical process and the fertile interaction between writer and reality. True, with the onset of the period of decay, this interaction becomes ever more difficult, placing ever greater demands on the intellectual and moral personality of the individual writer. Anyone who is so far entangled in apologetics that he has more or less consciously participated in the adjustment of reality according to the needs of the ruling class is inevitably lost as a writer, even if with talented and instinctively realist writers this process often takes place only slowly, and is marked by struggle and contradiction.

Closer and more detailed investigation is needed into the situation of those writers who do not succumb to this capitulation to apologetics, and who thus attempt to impress on their works their own view of the world, irrespective of whether this is one of acceptance or rejection. This formal, abstract and Kantian conception of literary honesty is however far from sufficient to explain the problem. Subjective honesty may well be an inescapable precondition for the triumph of realism, but it only provides the abstract possibility of this, not yet the concrete.

Nor is the mere appeal to world outlook sufficient either. We know that the relationship between world outlook and literary work is extraordinarily complex. There are cases in which a politically and socially reactionary world outlook fails to prevent the development of a real masterpiece of realism, and there are also cases in which precisely the politically progressive character of a bourgeois writer assumes forms that obstruct the development of realism in his portrayal. In other words, the question is whether the elaboration of reality that is summed up in the writer's world view opens a path for him leading to the unconfined treatment of reality, or else erects a barrier between him and reality, blocking his full devotion to the wealth of social life.

It is clear how the entire world outlook of the period of decay, remaining stuck as it does on the unconsidered ideological surface, with its tendency towards flight from the major problems of social life, and its self-important but sorry eclecticism, is very suited to make more difficult the writer's attainment of an unconfirmed and profound treatment of reality. The prejudices that the writer has to overcome in himself undoubtedly grow greater with the general development of ideological decay, both in quantity and in quality. The inhibiting effect of these tendencies in world outlook is still further reinforced by the way that the aesthetics of the period of decay ever more strongly presents anti-realist tendencies as the essence of art, so that in this way, too, an unfavourable and misleading effect is exerted on the writer's development.

Given conditions that are so unfavourable, both socially and ideologically, the honesty of a writer must rise decisively above the level of subjective formality, maintaining a certain social and ideological content, and through the force of this content bringing about a movement of receptiveness and openness towards reality, awakening a deep inner reliance on the reality thus perceived, if the writer's fearlessness is to lead him to the literary reproduction of the world thus seen.

We might remind the reader here of the motto of the present essay. In *Faust*, Goethe expressed a related idea in a more profound, comprehensive and positive sense:

> And yet choice spirits, fit the depths to see,
> Grasp infinite faith in an infinity.
>
> [*Faust*, Part Two, translated by Philip Wayne, Harmondsworth, 1975, p. 72.]

But inasmuch as we have spoken here of content and direction, these terms have so far remained all too abstract. What is involved here can in no way be reduced simply to a conception of the world that is correct in terms of social science. This would be to demand of writers that their world outlook should be that of dialectical materialism. The connection we arrive at here is a double one, its aspects closely related and in constant interaction. The mental world picture that the bourgeois writer takes over in the period of decay is principally based on a falsification of reality and its relationships, whether this is deliberate or not. The spontaneous realism of any writer continuously exposes and demolishes this world picture, through the conflict between it and the reality. What is decisive here is not the extent to which the writer draws the necessary and correct conclusions from this antithesis, even in thought. It is rather a question of whether, in the case of such conflict, he gives priority to the correctly perceived and experienced reality, or else to the world outlook with which he has grown up.

This conflict is already latent in every perception, every experience of reality. The prejudices of the period of decay divert people's attention from perception of the really important phenomena of the epoch. Even if these phenomena are experienced, these prejudices operate in the direction of a misleading 'deepening', and away from investigation of the real underlying causes of the phenomenon in question. In every writer of the period who is of any consequence for realism, therefore, a constant battle develops against the prejudices of ideological decadence. Indeed the battle is a double one: a battle to overcome these prejudices in the treatment and assessment of reality itself, and a battle to overcome them in the writer's own mental life, in his attitude to his own inner experiences and mental processes. What is of particular importance here is that for the majority of writers of our time this literary overcoming of the mental, emotional and moral prejudices of the period of decay generally takes place without a basic change in the mental apparatus of world outlook characteristic of the present decadence.

The two things stand in continuous interaction. But as long as the writer in his portrayals does not break through the psychological illusion of the capitalist division of labour that we have already depicted, as long as he takes the fetishized antithesis of the era of decay between feeling, experience and understanding at face value, both for himself and for his writing, as long as he does not grasp, in his experience as a writer, and in the way that it actually creates human beings, the hidden, conflictual and contradictory unity of the two things, then he cannot attain that level of emotional culture which is essential to any really significant realist literature.

The great educative effect of Maxim Gorky consists not least in this struggle for culture in human emotional life, in which Gorky quite correctly saw the decisive requirement for a new literary upswing. For as long as Gorky operated as a revolutionary writer in a capitalist environment, he waged an incessant polemic against that emotional barbarism that decadence has produced in all fields of human activity, including that of literature. And after the victory of socialism in the Soviet Union, Gorky focused his attention on the way that the battle against this barbarism made more rapid and decisive progress among the advanced masses of the people than it did among the writers, who were slower in overcoming the ideological residues of capitalism and its era of decay than were their readers, so that they remained behind their readers, and behind life itself, in emotional culture.

In a letter to Vsevolod Ivanov, Gorky vigorously emphasized this superiority of emotional culture on the part of the working-class vanguard. He saw precisely this as the basis for a great future resurgence, when this emotional culture would be correspondingly broadened and deepened in content.

Their emotional world [wrote Gorky about these workers], an emotion that precedes the understanding of the world by intellectual logic – will naturally lead them on to appropriate the logic of the ideas that lie in the essence of things. Our writers are less cultured from the emotional standpoint, if not actually uncultured, and this is still the case when they have read Lenin's books. They are familiar with the ideas, but in their case these ideas hang in a void, without any emotional foundation. This is in my opinion the distinction between the writer and the reader in our present age. And it is in terms of this distinction that I explain to myself the entire weakness of our present-day literature.

This passage from Gorky is of still greater importance and actuality for capitalist reality. For the bourgeois writer has neither an intellectually correct world outlook to draw on, nor a connection with a circle of readers whose emotional and socio-political vitality can help him develop and press forward in the direction of a genuine emotional culture. In capitalist reality, his general condition is to be enclosed in himself. He has to find his way through the thicket of inhibiting prejudices using only his own devices. (The fact that the major realist portrayals almost always find a wide and enthusiastic readership even in the era of decay is highly significant. But under capitalist conditions, this broad and popular effect of the major works of realism does not change the fact that the writer has to seek and find his way to such portrayal against the general tide.)

Just as is the case with any major appeal for genuine culture, that of Gorky does not involve anything radically new. He restates the best traditions of human development in the particular conditions of the construction of socialist culture. For what he refers to here as the culture of the emotions, is something that progressive eras in the past already possessed – in their own manner, and within their necessary social limits – something that has only got lost in bourgeois development in its period of decay. In order to bring this situation clearly to light, we can quote here a remark that Vauvenargues made about Boileau. The reason for selecting this precise quotation from the infinite number of similar expressions on the part of earlier writers is that the fashionable decadent philosophy always slanders the Enlightenment as an age of one-sided 'understanding' which neglected the 'emotional life', and depicts Boileau in particular as a dry and dogmatic representative of this 'understanding'. Vauvenargues, however, says:

Boileau demonstrates, both by his example and by his precepts, how all the fine qualities of good works spring from the living expression and depiction of the true. But this so pertinent expression belongs less to reflection, which is subject to error, than to a very intimate and very faithful feeling for nature. For Boileau, understanding was not something separate from emotion; this is precisely where his instinct lay.

This unity of the emotional and the rational life, this permeation of the emotions by the culture of understanding, this re-emotionalizing of the highest ideas – a principle which is common to both the Enlightenment figure of Vauvenargues and the socialist humanist Gorky – has been torn to shreds and destroyed in the intervening period.

This is at the root of the low level of modern bourgeois literature, not only in the sense of the ideas actually presented in such works, but also in the sense of the spiritual level of the people portrayed in them. It is at the root of the crudeness and animal bestiality that marks the portrayal of emotional life in the bourgeois literature of the period of decay. Hence also the ever decreasing respect that modern bourgeois literature enjoys from the few serious and cultured people of this era. And hence, too, the tremendous and inspiring success of the few genuinely realist works, those that are based on a genuine culture of emotions and ideas, that our age has produced.

The declining social respect for modern bourgeois literature is essentially a function of the way that the feeling grows ever stronger, in people who are deeply committed and bound up with real life, that it is a useless waste of time to spend it on this literature. They can get nothing new and fundamental out of it; modern bourgeois literature only depicts, in a formally promising manner, what every average person already knows about life.

What then really is new and fundamental? The human being. 'To be radical', wrote Marx in his early *Critique of Hegel's Philosophy of Law*, 'is to grasp the root of the matter. But for man the root is man himself' [*Collected Works*, Vol. 3, p. 182]. The tremendous social power of literature consists in the fact that it depicts the human being directly and with the full richness of his inward and outward life, in a concrete fashion not equalled by any other field of reflection of objective reality. Literature is able to portray the contradictions, struggles and conflicts of social life in the same way as these appear in the mind and life of actual human beings, and portray the connections between these collisions in the same way as they focus themselves within the human being. This is a great and important field of discovery and investigation of reality. Here, literature can supply – and I mean of course genuinely deep and realistic literature – experiences and knowledge that are completely new, unexpected and fundamental even for those people with the profoundest understanding of social relationships. This was stressed by Marx time and again with reference to Shakespeare and Balzac, and by Lenin with reference to Tolstoy and Gorky.

The breakthrough to an understanding of this kind, to such a literary experience of human beings, is the triumph of realism in literature. It is evident that a writer can only attain significance in this sense if he has managed to overcome the distortions of prejudice in his own case, a prejudice which the ideology of the decadent epoch spreads over man and his world, individual and society, the inward and outward life of the human personality, in the most diverse of forms.

But self-knowledge and knowledge of the world cannot be mutually divorced. It is impossible for someone to overcome the decadent illusion in himself without a knowledge and experience of the deeper connections of life, without breaking through the brittle and encrusted surface that conceals these connections under capitalism, conceals the deeper and contradictory unity, this ossification being fixed ideologically by the ideology of the decadent epoch and mystified into something conclusive and final. The depth of the literary vision, of the realist approach to reality, is always passion – no matter how the writer might formulate his world outlook intellectually – the passion not to accept anything as naked, cut and dried, dead experience, but to resolve the human world into a living inter-relationship between human beings. Whenever the prejudices of class society are too strong in a writer for him to do this, and he abandons this literary resolution of society into human relationships, then the writer ceases to be a realist.

It is precisely here that any writer, and particularly the writer of the decadent epoch, necessarily gets caught up in himself, for the confusing and fetishizing illusion is embedded in his own feelings, experiences and ideas, and evokes their rigid separation and mutual autonomization in his own mind as well. But precisely here, too, the problem is no more one of simple 'introspection', a purely internal self-dissection, than social criticism, on the other hand, is purely 'objective'. It is only in the living interaction of these two lines of self-examination that a real penetration to the sources of life can develop. As Marx so pertinently expressed it: 'The real spiritual wealth of the individual depends completely on the wealth of his real relationships.'

The result of this central position of the real human being in literature, this 'microcosmic' and 'anthropological' form that is specific to literature, is that even in the era of general decay a certain genuine and significant realism is possible, though so too is a rapid acceleration of all the phenomena of decline that are characteristic of the epoch. The two things both follow from the important place that the real, living human being assumes in literature, from this immediacy in the portrayal of the real human being. For if such immediacy becomes the real focus of the living conflicts of the epoch, then something great, new and fundamental comes into being, something which only realist literature is in a position to express. While if on the other hand this immediacy remains caught up in the decadent and fetishized mystification of present-day capitalist life, then it becomes simply a springboard for the empty and pretentious estrangement of literature from life, for the evacuation from literature of all content: literature becomes a mere playground for formal experiments.

5

This characteristic of literature leads to the problem of the social morality of the realist writer, the artistic significance of his honesty, strength and fearlessness.

This means above all, as we have seen, the self-critical dissolution of the capitalist illusion in the writer's own psyche. Examination of his own mental impulses and experiences in terms of their origin and development, and of their conversion into human praxis. If decadent literature takes ever greater pains to eliminate plot and story from the literary aesthetic as 'obsolete', this is precisely a self-defence of the decadent tendencies. For the portrayal of a story, a real plot, leads inevitably to testing feelings and experiences against the external world, weighing the living interaction with social reality and finding this light or heavy, genuine or false, whereas the psychologistic or surrealistic introspection of the decadents (whether in the manner of Bourget or of Joyce) simply offers the superficial internal life a completely unrestricted field, entirely free from any criticism. The danger that arises from this false subjectivism, the uninhibited living-out of the writer's internality, is that he stands facing a world of free experiment in which he can mingle uninhibitedly as he will. His characters then fail to obtain any independent and autonomous life of their own. The immanent dialectic of their fates, therefore, cannot lead the writer anywhere beyond his original intent and prejudices, and cannot refute these prejudices through the fearless portrayal of the real developmental process in actual life. And we know that the essence of apologetics consists precisely in this adjustment of reality. The less the writer arbitrarily dominates his characters and plot, the greater are the prospects that realism will prevail.

What is involved here is a very complex and dialectical aspect of the literary depiction of reality. The aesthetic of the Enlightenment oversimplified this relationship by its mechanical theory of reflection; though the practice of many writers who expressed such views did of course go far beyond the limits of their theory – for example, Diderot. Classical German philosophy, on the other hand, rightly stressed the dialectical contribution of the creative subject, though always on condition that this creative subjectivity must be directed towards the reproduction of the essence of reality. The first artistic theory of the era of decay was the German romantics' concept of 'irony', in which this creative subjectivity was already absolutized, with the subjectivity of the work of art already degenerated into an arbitrary play with the self-created characters.

Marx, in his critique of Eugène Sue, recognized from the start this apologetic effect of the intervention of the writer into the world of his characters:

> Eugène Sue's personages . . . must express, as the result of *their* thoughts, as the conscious motive of their actions, his own intention as a writer, which causes him to make them behave in a certain way and no other [loc. cit., p. 182].

It goes without saying that the modern decadents have only deep contempt for the primitive and relatively candid apologetic methods of a Sue. They and their theoretical defenders 'simply' forget that by the very nature of things any adjustment of reality – no matter how crude or refined – amounts to the same thing, and that the unrestrained and false subjectivism that they practise in literature necessarily opens up the possibility of such adjustment, and indeed seduces the writer towards it. The very working of capitalism takes good care that this weakening of the writer's resistance is turned to good use.

The writer's control of his own feelings and experiences by their impact on the objective reality of social life has a profound effect on his choice of material. For unconstrained subjectivity, the choice is pure caprice: this 'all-powerful' subjectivity can be introduced into any theme whatsoever, and any choice of theme arises simply from such an arbitrary introduction of subjective experiences into a material that in itself has nothing to do with this. (The modern subjectivist philosophy, which replaces the depiction of reality by 'introjection', and replaces causal connections by analogies, reinforces this tendency by its own influence on the writers' world outlook.)

For the genuine realists, on the other hand, their theme is both produced and supplied by socio-historical development. Gottfried Keller already expressed this idea very pertinently in a letter to Hettner:

All literary material takes the form of a remarkable, or rather very natural, circle. There is no such thing as individual sovereign originality and novelty in the sense of the geniuses of caprice and the imagined subjectivists. What is new in the good sense is simply that which proceeds from the dialectic of the movement of culture.

A genuine literary subjectivity, in other words, one that is rich and developed both humanly and artistically, arises only through such a utilization of the ego in this way, by bursting the (Machist) barriers of merely subjective ego experiences. This presupposes a rich experience of life, an intensive examination of one's own experiences in their conflicts with the objective forces of social life. We repeat, however, that the literary touchstone for the authenticity and depth of this literary subjectivity can consist only in the creation and elaboration of a genuine plot.

A literary subjectivity of this kind is thus already rich and developed, because a genuine love of life and human beings arises in it as the result of its own contact with life. And the broader and deeper the horrors of declining capitalism develop, the more contradictory, harder and more paradoxical this love is.

This problem, too, affects the entire history of class societies, and in particular the period of capitalism. It is simply that it comes particularly to a head in the era of the general crisis of the capitalist system. Schiller already saw very clearly how there were two types of attitude that the writer could asume towards life.

> Poets are always caretakers of nature, by their very concept. Where they can no longer completely play this role, and have experienced already in themselves the destructive influence of arbitrary and artificial forms, having even had to struggle with these, then they appear as witnesses and avengers of nature.

In both cases, love of life and of human beings are involved. Recall, for example, the terrible era of primitive accumulation in England. The great realist Defoe depicted the life of people caught up in this mechanism in his marvellous *Moll Flanders*, with a broad and deep realism. This realism was directly inspired by his great love for human beings; the contradictory but ultimately heroic indestructibility of his heroine could only arise out of this love, which none of the cruelties of society could destroy. Swift may well appear to be the complete antipode to this model, and many of his readers complain about his harshness and coldness, particularly in the fearsome and disconsolate last part of *Gulliver's Travels*. But if this masterpiece is read carefully and with sympathy, then it is impossible not to be aware of the ardent love of life and of humanity that was necessary for Swift to perceive the way in which people were ground down both outwardly and inwardly by primitive accumulation: human beings as repulsive and stinking animals, in contrast to the wise and benevolent horses of the final part, these being the marvellously satirical embodiment of genuine humanity.

Without such a love for humanity and life in general, something that necessarily involves the deepest hatred for a society, classes and their representatives who humiliate and deform human beings, it is impossible for any genuinely major realism to develop today in the capitalist world. This love and its complementary hate lead the writer to expose the wealth of relationships in human life, and the mortified world of capitalism, as an incessant battle against these mortifying powers. Even if his portrayal shows that the human beings of today are pitiful fragments and caricatures of true humanity, the writer must have experienced in himself what the possibilities of such true humanity are, its fullness and richness, so as to bear witness to and to kindle from this human fragmentation a feeling of struggle against the world that produces this every day and every hour.

But those writers who have not seen and experienced this process, who depict the given world of capitalism simply as it directly appears to them – even if they take a socio-political position against it – are capitulating before the 'fatalism' of this development *precisely as writers*. The mode of portrayal of the literature of the era of decay, the portrayal of the finished products of the capitalist deformation of man with an elegiac or outraged sentiment simply tacked on afterwards, is nothing more than the literary fixation of the surface phenomena plus commentaries that do not and cannot touch on the essence of the matter. For all the external diversity of materials and mode of presentation, we find in this juxtaposition of false – because dead – objectivity and false – because empty – subjectivity, the old Marxian characterization of the ideology of decadence: immediacy plus scholasticism.

6

For many people, this equation of scholasticism with sentiment may at first sound somewhat paradoxical. As in all these questions, however, it is necessary to keep to criteria that elucidate the essence of the matter, rather than such as are merely formal. The essence of the matter is that scholasticism in the ideology of the decadent epoch is a system of ideas that is exceedingly complex, working with very intricate and cleverly thought out characteristics which lack only one little thing: that they do not relate to things as they actually are. The emotional discernment and experiential refinement in the literary depiction of reality in terms of subjective sentiment shares all these 'merits' and defects of scholasticism in theory. It accompanies and surrounds people and events to whose decisive changes of fate it is intrinsically unrelated, whose fundamental objective problems it does not illuminate, but on the contrary, the more differentiated and intricate these are, the more it confuses and obscures them.

We have already brought to the centre of our discussion the portrayal of the human being, from the standpoint of the general aesthetic of literature. We can now add that this mode of portrayal is spontaneously, from its own logic, a vigorous exposé of the inhumanity of capitalism, and the more so, the further this inhumanity is developed and generalized in the course of the system's general crisis. The writer who portrays real human beings need in no way be completely aware, indeed he need not be aware at all, that a portrayal of such real human beings in their real social conflicts is already the beginning of a rebellion against the prevailing system. Comparisons are always somewhat askew, and in what follows, the reader can therefore make the customary reservations required. But it has often been said that the hydra of revolution already lurks in every strike. Lenin of course struggled vigorously against ideas that proclaimed a spontaneous and necessary growth of the revolution out of any strike whatsoever. He always stressed the necessity for consciousness, for the ideological generalization of the discontent and anger of the workers that finds spontaneous expression in strikes. But if the linear and necessary connection between the two things was rightly contested by Lenin, he certainly did not deny that in strikes we have an important part of the objective and subjective conditions which, when consciously developed further, and raised to a higher ideological level, make the workers into genuine revolutionaries. In the same complex and dialectical sense, the writer who portrays real people in real conflicts, in spontaneous and in most cases unconscious contradiction to capitalist society, exposes from a particular point of view, once again very often spontaneously and unconsciously, the inhumanity of this system. If we follow the development of such major realists as for example Anatole France or Thomas Mann, it is instructive to observe how the uneven and contradictory process of developing consciousness of this spontaneous rebellion against capitalism emerges from the necessities of literary portrayal itself.

Taken superficially, only the requirements of true literary art come into conflict here with the enmity towards art that Marx repeatedly emphasized as characteristic of the capitalist system. But as in all cases, so this antithesis between the requirements of artistic harmony and beauty and the general ugliness of the capitalist epoch can be related back to the great and substantial problems of the mass struggle.

In the entire course of development of the literary theory and practice of the era of decay, we can see how from the bourgeois side the portrayal of real people in real conflicts becomes ever more attenuated, so that this portrayal adapts itself to the level of human existence that is still compatible with the rising inhumanity of capitalism. To put it more precisely: the theory of the decadent epoch demands of art not the portrayal of real human existence under capitalism, but on the contrary that semblance of an existence which Marx referred to in the passage quoted above [p. 133]. It demands of writers the portrayal of this semblance as the only possible and genuine existence for human beings.

Inasmuch as major realists, whatever their world outlook, and whatever material they may use, portray the real dialectic of illusion and genuine existence in the human condition, inasmuch as they expose the illusion as illusion by the portrayal of actual existence, they come spontaneously into conflict with the capitalist system, and with the ideology of its era of decay.

This question is simple and illuminating if we consider the official literature of the era of decay, recognized as such either by aesthetic theory or in a *de facto* sense. There arises here, on the basis of this direct adaptation to capitalist ideology, a mendacious 'harmony', a literary reasoning away of the real contradictions of the capitalist system. Writers of the Gustav Freytag[2] type, for example, portray, as it were, a 'humanity' which corresponds to the conflicts of actual capitalism as much as apologetic vulgar economics corresponds to capitalism's contradictions. And it is evident without further commentary that this adaptation, as it develops further, leads to an ever lower level of literature designed simply to maintain the system, a so-called literature for the broad masses.

This process is more complex and less easily perceptible, though it is therefore all the more important, in the case of the talented and subjectively honest writers of the era of decay. With them, their entrapment on the surface, the lack of a criticism of capitalist inhumanity, in terms of

genuine *literary* portrayal, assumes the most diverse and seductive formulations, which are generally honestly believed in by those affected,
and which then lead to the writers in question to cling to the surface
phenomena – now deliberately, in the belief that this is particularly
'revolutionary', either in a literary or even in a political and social sense
– and to renounce what is really the most genuine and profound literary
revolt against capitalist inhumanity. Here we can only indicate some of
the main tendencies in this ideology that diverts writers from the
struggle against the capitalist system.

One of the most important and influential theories has been the view
that literature is a kind of science. This arose under the influence of
positivism, in parallel – and this by no means accidentally – with the rise
of modern sociology, separated in its method from economics. This
'scientific' conception of social life, which saw human beings as a
mechanical product of environment and inheritance, expelled from
literature precisely the most profound conflicts of human life. In its
mechanistic view, these were disparaged as romantically exaggerated
conflicts confined to the individual, which reduce the objective worth of
literature, now exhalted to the position of a science. (Think for example
of Taine's criticisms of Balzac, and particularly those of Zola.) Genuine
portrayal of the human being is now replaced by a wealth of superficial
detail. Instead of the great eruptions of the human spirit against the
inhuman aspects of social development, we have flat depictions of what
is elementary and animal in man, and instead of human greatness or
weakness in conflicts with society, we have flat descriptions of external
atrocities.

As the decadent epoch further progresses, this false objectivity of a
'scientificity' that stifles literature is repeated at an ever higher level.
German naturalism already shows a tremendous decline in its level of
human portrayal, in comparison with Flaubert or Zola. And the revival
of 'scientific objectivity' in the post-war period, with the 'new objectivism', often already uses this objectivity for more or less overtly
apologetic ends. The objectivity here is very often a clear and overt
attenuation of the conflictual character of human life, a capitulation
before the inhumanity of post-war capitalism that is scarcely any longer
concealed.

In literature and literary theory there are of course very many reactions against this mortifying objectivity. But inasmuch as abstract objectivity is counterposed to an equally abstract subjectivity, the result is
the same, merely with the signs changed. Whether it is a question of the

fetishized powers of external life, or exclusively of the spirit, in both cases the conflicts of real human life are eliminated from the literary work. Those tendencies that react against 'scientificity' in literature may well appeal to the actual life of human internality, but they abstract from human social relations, which they describe in abstract opposition to naturalism as 'superficial' and attack, correspondingly fetishizing in a now overtly mystical fashion the so-called 'eternal powers' of life. We thus get once again an abstractly superficial and distorted reflection of the conflicts in human life, for the real struggle between man and society, a struggle within society, is lacking. Lacking, too, are the objective determinations of human life, through which alone the soul acquires and develops its riches; all preconditions for a genuinely profound portrayal of humanity – with conscious and deliberate artistic purpose – are thrown out of the window.

This situation, too, we can only elucidate with a few indications. In the first dramas of Maeterlinck, which at one time had a major effect on people, death, for example, was always artificially separated from all concrete social relations and the individual conflicts of life, so as to portray it as an 'eternal problem' of the human condition. What was the result? Simply animal fear at the mere fact of death, which at times was very strikingly depicted from a technical point of view; from a literary standpoint, however, a mere abstraction. Let us consider on the other hand a great realist such as Tolstoy, who also considered death as a central problem. Tolstoy, however, time and again portrayed death in connection with the individual and social life of particular human beings. For this reason, death always appears in his work in a quite different form, rich and complex, even if the purely animal fear of death and of the hour of dying plays a major role in many cases. We need only refer to the death of Nikolai Levin in *Anna Karenina*, or of Andrei Bolkonsky in *War and Peace*, or to *The Death of Ivan Ilyich*. In each case, this moment appears as a mere moment in a very rich individual and social connection. And on top of this, dying, for Tolstoy, obtains a further profound and socially critical significance, exposing the individual and social life of the individual in question. The more meaningful this life was, the more harmoniously related to human social existence, the less terror does death have. The dread of death in the abstract, as fetishized by Maeterlinck, appears in Tolstoy's work as the tragic self-judgement on himself of a person who was condemned by class society to a meaningless and unworthy life, one that stifled humanity in his own life. Finally, we must concern ourselves briefly with a very widespread literary prejudice about genuine human portrayal. Very many writers, and even readers too, say that the broad form of human portrayal as developed by the classical realists does not tally with the 'pace of modern life'. This prejudice has no better foundation than that of the impossibility of overcoming the specialization of the capitalist division of labour, which we have already discussed in the case of Max Weber.

By taking the 'pace of modern life' as criterion for portrayal, very many present-day writers (including some Soviet ones) come up with a level of understanding and presentation of human beings that corresponds more or less to the observation of human personality that is possible from brief acquaintance on a railway journey.

This tendency is also given various kinds of theoretical support. It is reinforced by the subjectivist tendencies in present-day philosophy, which dissolve the objective world into perceptions and deny not only the objectivity of the external world, but consequently also that of the human personality. 'The ego is unsalvageable' (Mach); or to quote Nietzsche as a consistent theorist of decadence, and a worthy forerunner of Mach, who saw the literary portrayal of humanity and the creation of characters as something merely superficial:

> this *very imperfect* attitude of ours towards man is matched by the poet, inasmuch as he makes into man (in this sense 'creates') outlines as *superficial* as our knowledge of man is superficial. . . . Art starts from the natural *ignorance* of man about his interior condition (in body and Character) . . . ['Human, All Too Human', para. 160, *Complete Works*, ed. O. Levy, Vol. 9, London, 1909, pp. 163–4].

But what is this celebrated 'pace of life'? It is nothing more than the inhumanity of capitalism, which seeks to reduce the relationships between human beings to those of mutual exploitation, to cheating and the struggle not to be cheated, so that accordingly capitalism develops at this abstractly superficial level, where everything human is eliminated, a practical cunning in those involved, a flatly utilitarian understanding of human behaviour, the very essence of which is precisely the complete ignoring of everything human.

It goes without saying that many writers who work on the basis of this 'pace of life' and its artistic consequences (e.g. Dos Passos) have precisely the opposite intent. They see themselves as honest and bitter opponents of the capitalist system. But this socio-political intention of opposition comes through in their writing only at a superficial level, only in this abstractly political and abstractly social tendency. The outcome in such cases is an abstractly revolutionary utilitarianism. The portrayal of human beings, the appearance of their individual specificity, is thus reduced to their abstract function in the class struggle, in the same way as is done by those writers who capitulate to the capitalist world, either directly and normally, or in the indirect anarchistic manner, with whom portrayal of human beings is reduced to their function in the capitalist 'struggle for existence'. The inhumanity of capitalism makes its appearance in the portrayal of this 'pace of life' as a fatalistic *a priori* of our age.

It is quite immaterial whether this mode of depiction is presented purely ascetically, in a way that explicitly rejects all particulars, or whether it is decked out with (naturalistic or surrealistic) detail. For the real dialectical contradiction in human social life, that which is decisive for the literary portrayal of human existence, is completely eliminated here – i.e. what Marx formulated in the phrase that individuals belong to a class 'only as average individuals', so that their individual life is linked in a contradictory way with their own class, these contradictions being the material that the great realists used to develop and illuminate the objective conflicts in concrete human life. What in actual life is the result of complex struggles, the real relationship of the individual to the class and through this to the society as a whole, appears here simply as a naked result, in which, just as in the treatment of economic life by vulgar economics, all social determinations simply vanish, economic life therefore being presented as abstract, empty and meaningless. It is the abstract surface of the capitalist economy that celebrates its literary triumph in this kind of portrayal – even if the individual writers in question see themselves politically as the most resolute opponents of the capitalist system.

We said that the essential question was not that of particulars. But the role these play is far from unimportant. For if this reduction of human beings to the utilitarianism of capitalist inhumanity, to the mode of appearance of the capitalist surface, is not just depicted nakedly and ascetically, in an abstractly overt manner, but is actually poetically celebrated, then something far worse very often arises. Marx wrote of the economics of Adam Müller: 'It is made up of current prejudices, skimmed from the most superficial semblance of things. This incorrect and trite content is then "exalted" and rendered sublime through a mystifying mode of expression' [*Capital*, Volume 3, Moscow, 1962, p. 389; translation modified]. For this kind of embellishment, which generally consists of an over-refined irrationalism and an appeal to the 'original' (the animal or bestial), increases still further the decadent character of such literature. It objectively adds to the general decadent tendency an idealization of this decay, a deepening and poetic embellishment of the decay and hence an apology for it, even if this is in many cases not the intention.

Even the ascetic acceptance of this phenomenon as identical with reality means abandonment of the literary battle against capitalist inhumanity. And in this further case, we have on top of this capitulation an embellishment that emphasizes the disharmonic, however unintentional and however modern it may sound.

7

The Marxian critique of ideological decay is designed to bring out the real philistinism that lies concealed behind the rhetorical superficiality. Thus Marx characterized Stirner's work as essentially 'the unity of sentimentality and bragging', and his philosophy in general as follows: 'The philosophy of rebellion, which has just been presented to us in the form of bad antitheses and withered flowers of eloquence, is in the final analysis only a boastful apology for the parvenu system' [*The German Ideology, Collected Works*, Vol. 5, p. 382].

At a later date, Lenin gave a profound and correct political characterization of all anarchistic and kindred tendencies when he stated that these are all modes of expression of the petty bourgeoisie driven mad by the crises of capitalism.

What is philistine and petty-bourgeois here is being taken in by mere words, intoxicated by phrases, instead of a fearless comparison of subjective convictions with objective reality. The phrase in this sense is a political, scientific or literary expression which does not reflect the real movement, which in no way takes the trouble to recognize and express it, and which therefore, even if it does occasionally touch on the reality, becomes ever more tangential to the real curve of development.

In the field of literature, this characteristic of the phrase must be especially emphasized. For even the stutterings of naturalism and impressionism, the silence of Maeterlinck, the inarticulateness of Dada and the ascetic objectivity of the 'New Objectivism', are from the standpoint of content, considered in relation to reality, only phrases. And just as it is this actual content that makes the phrase a phrase, so it is his actual behaviour towards reality that makes the ideologist a petty-bourgeois philistine or a victor over philistinism. It is this actual movement that decides, not the costume or mask, nor the spiritual level considered in isolation, nor yet the amount of knowledge or 'mastery' of form.

Petty-bourgeois philistinism can be mentally overcome only through a genuine understanding of the great conflicts and crises of social development. The philistine confronts these conflicts without any understanding, even if he is drawn into them, and even if he plays a passionate part in them. What this means for literary practice, if we bear in mind the central task of literature as already put forward, i.e. the portrayal of real human beings, is the need to know what is true, what is false, what is objective, what is subjective, what is important, what is unimportant, what is great, what is petty, what is human, what is inhuman, what is tragic, and what is ridiculous.

This knowledge is a reflection of the dialectical relationships of objective reality. Problems of assessment and evaluation constantly crop up even in the ideology of the era of decay. But these are always fundamentally subjective in character. It is from the subject's standpoint that reality is supposedly 'revalued' (Nietzsche).

The shift from knowledge of these real relationships into the field of subjectivity was recognized and criticized by Marx already in the period of the 1848 revolution, as a symptom of objective capitulation to the reactionary forces in history. It is precisely if the tendencies towards objective progress in life are not recognized, particularly if these are more or less consciously ignored and subjective desires put in their place as the motive forces of reality, that ideological decadence arises. Precisely because the objective movement of history contradicts bourgeois ideology, so does even the most 'radical' and 'profound' introduction of such purely subjective moments collapse with objective necessity into support for the reactionary bourgeoisie.

In connection with the debates on Poland in the Frankfurt parliament, Marx criticized the whole range of phenomenal forms assumed by the betrayal of the democratic revolution. What is important for us here is not his critique of the common-or-garden apologists for Polish partition. It was far more significant that two well-known writers of that time who both had a left-wing orientation, Arnold Ruge and Wilhelm Jordan, appeared with a theory that, starting out from a 'profound' recognition of Poland's tragic fate, led on to a justification of the reactionary and undemocratic German policy. Understanding of the tragic necessity of Poland's demise, said Jordan and Ruge, must awaken a deep sympathy in us for the Polish people, but this same understanding forbids us intervening in the tragic history of Poland. Understanding of the Polish people's tragedy, therefore, meant in the last analysis sanctioning the status quo, the division of Poland between the three reactionary powers of mid-nineteenth century Europe.

Marx's exposure of the petty-bourgeois philistinism of this conception proceeded naturally enough from an analysis of the actual situation. The facts were that when Poland was first partitioned, it was the internal conflicts within the country's aristocratic democracy, and the rise of the great nobles, that necessarily led to the nation's political disappearance. But since 1815 the rule of the aristocracy as a whole had become as outmoded and undermined as that of the aristocratic democracy had in 1772. The same historical necessity, therefore, that had brought about the demise of the aristocratic democracy and with it of the Polish nation in general, had now placed on the agenda the democratic revolution, the peasants' revolution and the consequent restoration of the Polish nation.

The 'profound' conception of this tragedy held by Ruge and Jordan was thus a betrayal of the interests of international and German democracy, as these stood in 1848, a capitulation to the interests of the Prussian, Austrian and Russian autocracies. The 'profundity' of this conception was a mere phrase, having nothing to do with the objective historical development; those who proclaimed it were petty-bourgeois philistines who took phrases for reality, found themselves lost in a development they did not understand, and unwittingly served the interests of European reaction.

Marx's critique is also of particular interest for us here in as much as he touches in the context of a political debate on the central point of the decadent tendencies in tragedy: i.e. the inclination to replace the objective portrayal of world-historical conflict by the subjective insight of the tragic hero into the tragic necessity of his fate. The major transitional forms of this development express this tendency with mounting decisiveness. It is an important moment in the 'further development' of the Hegelian theory of tragedy by F. T. Vischer, and plays an ever more decisive role in Grillparzer's work after 1848 (*A Conflict Between Brothers in the House of Hapsburg*), as well as that of Hebbel (*Agnes Bernauer, Gyges and his Ring*). Having now sunk a long way from this intellectual and literary level, this view of tragedy has become an ever more fundamental element in the lack of real plot, lack of dramatic conflict and psychologism of modern drama.

We have already shown how decisive for a writer is a correct evaluation of his characters and their conflicts, and this means the very opposite of a subjective evaluation. The great sureness shown by earlier writers in their portrayal of human beings, in the depiction of their relationships and in the development of their conflicts, is based on the way that they managed to put forward genuinely objective, socially objective standards that proceeded from a deep understanding of reality.

It goes without saying that these standards bear the marks of their time, of the social conditions in which they were discovered and deployed in literature. Like all other human knowledge, they contain a relative element. But only modern science of the era of decay, which always ignores the dialectic of the absolute and the relative, overlooks for the sake of this relative element the objective and absolute core in these correct and profound discoveries of standards for judging human beings, their actions and their destinies. Vulgar sociology coarsens this relativism and brings it to a head through a pseudo-Marxist 'class analysis'. In vulgar sociology, everything is presented as 'class-dependent' in a mechanically fatalistic sense, and this gives rise to a completely relativistic view which puts everything on the same level. Everything is equally necessary, even the most repulsive apologetics for declining capitalism. It is an apology for apologetics.

The modern relativistic sentiment also protests against the objectivity of such standards of value from the standpoint of the complexity of life. It is said that the phenomena of life are so intricate and contradictory that the application to them of any standard must have a coarsening effect that violates their real refinements and transitional forms. This seems to clarify things at first, but it is fundamentally false. The great writers of former times understood the complexity of their characters and situations, with the contradictions and entangled transitional forms of real life, far better than the relativists of today. Don Quixote, Falstaff and Tristram Shandy's Uncle Toby are complex and contradictory characters, who get into highly complex and contradictory situations, so that the impression we get of them leads time and again from the comic to the noble and touching. But Cervantes, Shakespeare and Lawrence Sterne all knew very well precisely when, at what point, and to what extent their heroes were ridiculous or tragic, evoking affection or sympathy. And in complete contrast to the view of the modern relativists, these writers could depict the finest transitional forms transparently and clearly, with all their nuances that illuminate and enrich what is fundamental, precisely because they saw and assessed the correct meaning of every feeling and every action objectively.

This sureness of portrayal – and the flexibility and elasticity that is necessarily bound up with it – are lost as a result of the subjectivism and relativism of the decadent period. And this is where the bold, but of course far from always successful, battle of the major realists against the ideologically unfavourable conditions of the era of decay makes its appearance. This battle is exceedingly complex but, by analysing it, it is possible to attain a correct and not merely schematic view of the relationship between world outlook and literary production, and see the possibilities and dangers of the 'triumph of realism' in the era of decay in a more concrete fashion than we have so far presented them.

We can take as our example here Henrik Ibsen, certainly a major writer. In his play *The Wild Duck*, which he himself saw as a new departure in his work, he reached the very threshold of a magnificent and exemplary comedy of the self-destruction of bourgeois ideals, the exposure of the mechanism of hypocrisy and self-deception in declining capitalist society. Towards the end of the play, there is an important conversation between the representatives of two opposing standpoints: Gregers Werle, the Don Quixote of traditional bourgeois ideals, the 'ideal demands', and the cynic Relling, who defends hypocrisy and self-deception as a vital necessity for people. In this dialogue, Relling refers to the fact that he had told the degenerate theology student Molvik that he was 'demoniac':

GREGERS: Isn't he demoniac, then?

RELLING: What the devil does it mean to be demoniac? It's just a piece of nonsense I hit upon to keep the life going in him. If I hadn't done it, the poor simple creature would have collapsed years ago under his self-contempt and despair . . .

RELLING: While I remember it, young Mr Werle – don't use that exotic word 'ideals'. We have a good enough native word: 'lies'.

GREGERS: Do you mean that the two things are related?

RELLING: Yes. Like typhus and typhoid fever.

GREGERS: Dr Relling, I shan't give up until I have rescued Hjalmar from your clutches.

RELLING: All the worse for him. Take the saving lie from the average man, and you take his happiness away too.

[Ibsen, *Three Plays*, translated by Una Ellis-Fermor, Harmondsworth, 1950, pp. 243–4.]

This is a bold and profound exposure of capitalist philistinism in its various shadings. (And in how many would-be 'demonic' modern

writers are we not struck by the cynical truth of what Relling says here!)
If it had been possible for Ibsen to pursue his argument to its logical
conclusion, both artistically and in terms of world outlook, he would
have been the greatest playwright of his time, a worthy successor to the
classic writers of comic drama. What then is the barrier? Before *The
Wild Duck* Ibsen had vigorously scourged the hypocrisy of bourgeois
society, and time and again pointed out that the proclaimed ideals of the
ascendant bourgeois class had now become hypocritical lies, no longer
having anything in common with bourgeois practice. He accordingly
portrayed the tragic conflicts that arose from the collision between ideal
and reality. Although this problematic is somewhat too narrow to
expose the deepest contradictions of bourgeois society, yet major and
irresolvably tragic contradictions of love, marriage and family in
bourgeois society do appear in his work, particularly in *A Doll's House*
and *Ghosts*. Ibsen's literary practice here goes beyond his world
outlook and the questions this raises for him. If Nora and Mrs Alving
take their ideals seriously and even tragically, it is this that becomes the
pivot of the tragic conflicts in Ibsen's own eyes; in his actual portrayal,
this moral seriousness is simply the occasion and stimulus. These
women possess such moral vigour and consistency that their actions
burst the shell of the bourgeois family, expose its deep and corroded
hypocrisy, and tragically show up its social and human contradictions.
Here Ibsen portrays the reality more broadly and objectively than his
own world outlook would suggest.

In *The Wild Duck*, Ibsen stands on the threshold of a modern,
bourgeois-philistine *Don Quixote*. Gregers Werle represents with equal
conviction and hopelessness the ideals of the heroic period of bourgeois
development, caught up in the midst of capitalist philistinism, just as
Don Quixote honourably and hopelessly represented the ideals of a dis-
appearing knighthood during the rise of bourgeois society. These 'ideal
demands' of Ibsen's directed at the degenerate petty bourgeois of
capitalist society, dissolve as deeply into the realm of the ludicrous as
did the knightly ideals of Don Quixote in his time. In Ibsen's case, this
ridiculousness is intensified still further and becomes a really splendid
comedy. What Gregers demands from genuine marriage, i.e. ruthless
candour and honesty, is put into practice by his father, a deceitful old
capitalist, with whom he had broken relations for that very reason, and
by Mrs Sorby, a shrewd hussy and careerist. The 'ideal demand' of
reciprocal truthfulness and honesty as the foundation of marriage is
cynically realized by these two cunning cheats as the basis of the

peaceful continuation of their former lives. The old ideals are thus not only debased by the inability to realize them, by being distorted by degenerate people into lies and hypocrisy, but Ibsen also shows how the cynical big capitalists can exploit these ideals for their own brutally egoistic ends. In this world of cynicism and hypocrisy, bourgeois idealism perishes in the same tragi-comic fashion as did the knightly ideals in the tragi-comic adventures of the knight of the sad countenance. Ibsen was very close to writing a great comedy of his time.

And yet however close, he failed to achieve this. As Marx said of the historic function of great comedy:

> The gods of Greece, already tragically wounded to death in Aeschylus's *Prometheus Bound*, had to re-die a comic death in Lucian's *Dialogues*. Why this course of history? So that humanity should part with its past *cheerfully* ['Contribution to the Critique of Hegel's Philosophy of Law. Introduction', *Collected Works*, Vol. 3, p. 179].

This was the historical task of the Falstaff comedies, and of *The Marriage of Figaro*.

This cheerful parting from the past is something that Ibsen failed to achieve. *The Wild Duck* already suffers from this. The character of Gregers Werle has neither the enchanting comedy nor the tremendous nobility of Don Quixote. And the reason for this is that Cervantes was both aware that the ideals of his hero had passed into history, and dissolved into its mists, and equally aware of the human purity, subjective honesty and heroism of Don Quixote. He recognized both these aspects correctly, and assessed them correctly too. Ibsen, on the other hand, despite his own profound and exposing criticism, clings desperately to the contents of Gregers Werle's proclamations. He seeks not only to rescue Werle's subjective purity and honesty, but the content of his attempts as well. Here Ibsen's own portrayal gives rise to the most frightful dialectical contradictions, as well as the most splendid comic situations. But he cannot altogether use these in his play, as he assesses his hero incorrectly, partly overrating him and partly underrating him, partly elevating him beyond his actual merits, and partly unjustly debasing him.

In the further course of his work, after the fading of his ideals – ideals which *The Wild Duck* still objectively presents, despite its mistakes – Ibsen subsequently sought to create heroes who met the demands raised by Gregers Werle and yet are not susceptible to Relling's criticism. In this way he got caught in a false aristocratism. He sought to create a man who would be superior to the average, a man who rose above the old contradictions, and yet – in closest connection with his inability to criticize the content and real historical situation of Gregers Werle's ideals – he was forced to portray this new man in terms of the old material, simply with artificial elevation and intensification.

Ibsen was far too realistic, consistent and fearless a writer not to understand and also portray what was mean, repulsive and even ridiculous in his new heroes, in Rosmer, Hedda Gabler and Solness. But he forces himself despite this to present them as tragic heroes who rise above the average level. The division in human standards apparent in *The Wild Duck* is accordingly continuously intensified. These characters are still more strongly both under- and overrated by their author. This undifferentiated and unelucidated juxtaposition of mutually exclusive judgements forces Ibsen to create characters who stand constantly on tiptoe so as to seem taller than they really are, whose 'tragic nobility' is artificially and inorganically stretched upward by use of symbolist devices, even while their painfully produced and hence never really convincing stature is continuously subjected to bitter mockery by the writer himself.

It is no accident, then, that Ibsen's deliberate resort to symbolism commences precisely in *The Wild Duck*. This symbolism is the artistic means for reconciling at least in appearance what is in actual fact irreconcilable, for artificially concealing the contradiction that is unresolved in life, misunderstood, perceived in a distorted fashion and reproduced still most distortedly. Precisely in the case of such a major realist as Ibsen, we can see how symbolism failed to overcome the artistic contradictions of the realist attempts of the late nineteenth century, and was actually the literary expression of the fact that these writers had been unable to deal with these contradictions in human, ideological or artistic terms. They fled into symbolism and were ruined in it. For symbolism in no way offers any solution for the contradictions of this realism, but means on the contrary the perpetuation of these contradictions at an artistically lower level that is still further from grasping reality.

Ibsen's tragic transition, from a realism still combined with naturalistic elements, to a contradictory emptiness of symbolism is extraordinarily instructive for our present investigation. For it shows how little these processes are fundamentally artistic in nature. They represent in fact crises in the world outlook of the writers concerned. And the literary expression of these crises of world outlook is precisely the loss of a standard for the portrayal of human beings, their actions and destinies, of what these human beings socially and morally represent, what is the meaning of their fate in the reality of social life, and what form their relationships with other people actually take.

In Ibsen's case we still see the tragic seriousness of this crisis. Not simply on account of his great talent and literary honesty, but on account of the objective socio-historical significance of the problems with which he wrestled, and which he did not manage, in a tragic and crisis-bound way, to overcome. As the literature of the decadent era further developed, the figure of the maddened petty bourgeois comes ever more to the fore, inflating his philistinism into eccentric and isolated heroics, and capitulating before every modern superstition of a 'cosmic' tragic destiny.

No one should think we are exaggerating here. It would of course go beyond the framework of the present essay if we sought to analyse this development of drama after Ibsen in any detail. We shall therefore only take one characteristic example. It is well known how in the decades immediately prior to the war August Strindberg played a leading role as a playwright and was in many respects placed far above Ibsen. His later works were very important for the rise and development of symbolism as a theatrical movement, as well as for its further growth into expressionism.

Here I shall just take a short passage from one of the most celebrated and 'profound' dramas of this period of Strindberg's. In the first part of the trilogy *To Damascus*, his two heroes, the Stranger and the Lady, meet up at a crossroads. They immediately fall in love. The Stranger is supposed to collect a letter from the post office, but he fails to do so, as it could only contain bad news. They go on an excursion and have a frightening experience. Here we restrict ourselves to one particular aspect, i.e. that the Stranger's lack of money plays a major role in the whole series of humiliations that he and his lover have to undergo, a role which Strindberg constantly emphasizes. In the final scene of this first part, they meet up again at the same street corner after many adventures. And now we have the following dialogue, after the Lady has reminded her friend of the uncollected letter:

LADY: Go and fetch it. And believe it may contain something good.
STRANGER [*ironically*]: Good?
LADY: Believe it. Try to imagine it.
STRANGER [*goes into the post-office*]: I'll try.

The LADY *walks up and down, waiting. The* STRANGER *comes out with a letter.*

LADY: Well?
STRANGER: I am ashamed. It was money.
LADY: You see. All this misery, all these tears – for nothing.

[*The Plays of August Strindberg*, translated by Michael Meyer,
vol. 2, London, 1975, p. 109.]

In scenes such as this we see quite unconcealedly what it is that the false profundity of modern literature, the literature of decadence, actually presents. The highly praised stature of the late Strindberg is supposed to consist in the way that he powerfully portrayed the 'mysterious forces' of human life. The real content of these 'mysterious forces', however, as the reader can see for himself, is nothing more than a self-inflated and hence mendacious 'objectification' of petty-bourgeois superstition.

It goes without saying, of course, that even this superstition has its social roots: the uncertainty of life under capitalism, which Lenin repeatedly emphasized as being the source of the persistence and resurgence of religious ideologies under capitalism. But the pretentious and often fundamentally unrealistic mode of portrayal of the late Strindberg does not disclose this real source of the experiences he portrays. On the contrary, it serves only to give these underived, unexplained and unelucidated experiences a false air of profundity and mystery. Strindberg does nothing more than give literary objectivity to the normal conceptions of the petty-bourgeois philistine, which he regards with complete lack of critical distance, deepening these in such a way as to create the illusion that genuinely mysterious powers existed to correspond with the superstitious fear of the philistine. In this way, he reaches a spiritual level of grasping reality that is objectively still below that of the superstitious philistine, who generally believes far less in the mystified objectivity of his conceptions than does the celebrated 'avant-garde' writer.

And yet Strindberg, both as an individual and in terms of his literary talent, still stands far above those dramatists of decadence who achieved their celebrity contemporarily with him or somewhat later, such as Wedekind, Kaiser and Hasenclever.

The example of Strindberg shows quite clearly the extent to which any standard of the objective importance and social significance of people and their destinies has gone by the board in the era of decadence.

The general decay of all literary forms in this period is not an immanent artistic process, not a struggle against 'traditions', as the decadent writers and artists imagine, it is rather the socially necessary, objective and unavoidable result of these writers' lack of criticism (as writers) of the surface appearances of capitalism, their uncritical capitulation to this superficiality, and their uncritical identification of illusion (distorted semblance) and actual existence.

We repeat once again that the writer's possession of such a standard is the foundation for any literary composition. Any plot is an actual validation or repudiation of concrete, socially determined persons in concrete and socially determined situations. Any literary construction is a heightened and concentrated reflection of the social relationships and the human-moral relationships between individuals. Only the objective correctness and subjective sureness of this standard can open up for the writer a path to the fullness of life.

The internal richness of a literary character arises from the fullness of its internal and external relationships, from the dialectic of superficial life and the more profoundly operating objective and spiritual forces. The more genuine this standard in the writer, i.e. the more it corresponds to reality, then the deeper he is able to dig, the richer the determinations and the more dynamic the life he will arouse and bring to light. For the more genuine this standard, then the more it reveals the great internal contradictions of social development, and the more organically the writer will uncover major social conflicts in the individual destinies that he depicts. Relativism by itself impoverishes the human being, both the writer and his characters. The dialectically recognized unity of the absolute and the relative, raised to a higher level – i.e. relativity correctly understood as a moment of the process – enriches these. Here we find the basis in world outlook that explains why the literature of the decadent era has not managed to create even a single genuinely enduring and typical character.

The fertility of the conflicts portrayed likewise arises from this objective truth and from the subjective certainty of standard. Only if the writer knows and experiences accurately and surely what is essential and what is secondary, will he manage to understand, even as a writer, how to give expression to the essential, how to portray the typical fate of a class, a generation, or an entire epoch, in terms of the private destiny of a single individual. With the loss of this literary standard, the living interrelation between the private and the social, the individual and the typical, gets lost. The abstractly conceived social can in no way find embodiment in a living human being, it remains poor, dry, abstract and un-literary. On the other hand, in the literature of decadence the most un-interesting trivialities of the philistine world, which are abnormally private from the word go, are inflated into 'universal destinies'. At both extremes, the same poverty and literary breathlessness reigns supreme. But if the literary standard is present, then in the hands of a major writer an apparently petty event can develop into an infinite wealth of human and social determinations. Here again, the truth is demonstrated that relativism impoverishes, living dialectics enriches.

Great realism, therefore, perishes in the era of decay. And besides the overtly apologetic anti-realism and pseudo-realism of the literature promoted by the reactionary bourgeoisie, we have a long chain of tendencies that try in a very 'radical' and 'avant-garde' fashion to liqui-date the very foundations of realism. Whatever may be the intention behind the representatives of these tendencies, objectively they only help the bourgeoisie in its struggle against genuine realism. This objec-tive social function is shared by the entire literature of the decadent epoch, from naturalism through to surrealism.

It is impossible to repeat often and strongly enough that the tendency of literary decay is not a predestined fate of the individual writer, but rather a question of the normal social situation. Naturally, the further this general ideological decay progresses, the greater are the intellectual and moral demands placed on the writer if he is to avoid falling into decadence and seeks to tread the path of genuine realism. This path is dangerously narrow, and surrounded by tragic abysses. We should therefore treasure all the more highly those writers who have still managed to struggle through to realism despite this unpropitious time.

A Correspondence with Anna Seghers [1938/9]*[1]

28 June 1938

Dear Georg Lukács,

As I recall, we had our last evening's discussion at a table in a Friedrichstrasse bar. The present table is immeasurably longer, and you are sitting far indeed from me. Nevertheless, I would like to proceed in this letter in more or less the same fashion as in those discussion evenings. I don't intend to make a contribution, simply to raise a few questions on points where I still find your arguments unclear. In the last few years you have worked on various different themes of extreme importance for writers, probably even the most important themes. You have led my own thoughts forward – and those of others – to aspects that we should not have come to by ourselves. You have brought us clarity on many questions. And where we disagree, this disagreement is pithy and direct, and hence also useful and enlightening for our work.

Your most recent work on method, on realism, has also explained a great deal.[2] And here, too, I have read your essays, including the most recent concluding one, with the full involvement that this subject must arouse in a writer. Yet although much is again explained here, and on the important points I have no *fundamental* disagreement with you (the objections that I do have will emerge in the course of this letter), I was still not completely satisfied when I finally closed the journal in which the discussion on realism is concluded. I spent a whole week wondering what lay at the root of this dissatisfaction, for as I said, my specific objections are not such as to account for a certain empty feeling that this long and complex discussion has left in me. I believe therefore that it is not *what* was said that is to blame, but rather what was not said, and what you have perhaps not yet said at all.

I should like to cite an episode from German literary history in which we may be able to see many things that your discussion leaves out of account. It is well known how Goethe, especially in one particular

*First published in *Internationale Literatur*, no. 5, 1939.

period of his life, spoke disparagingly about certain characteristics of the younger generation of writers. His sharpest antithesis, that 'classical equals healthy, romantic equals sick', you are well familiar with, also his little work on 'exaggerated talents', etc. He took a dim view of Kleist and many others. On the other hand, however, he treated Zacharias Werner, whom no one remembers today, with extraordinary warmth, and gave him whatever help he could – though Werner was simply an average philistine who happened to agree with Goethe on questions of method. It is by no means uncommon, however, for men of genius, who represent a certain important concept, to be unable to think except in terms of this concept, and to better understand mediocre work of a similar kind to their own than work that is altogether different. In the case of Goethe and Kleist, the question is one of two different generations of writers. And just look at what happened to Kleist's generation: he himself died by suicide in 1811, Lenz died a lunatic in 1792, Hölderlin lived till 1843, but had also been mad since 1804, Bürger died mentally ill in 1794, Günderode also by suicide, and so on. Goethe, on the other hand, lived to a very ripe old age, he finished a body of work that has been admired ever since, a work that has had a mighty influence on the German people, and is almost inexplicable in its depth and breadth, its compactness and its totality – a work that shows humankind in all its human potentialities. Subjectively, however, the price of this work was its author's firm adherence to the society of his time, while a rejection of this society might well have endangered it. Goethe had a great dislike for any kind of dissolution – the disharmony of the generation of writers whose sickness he saw as only logical (see Gorky's essay 'On the Social Significance of Madness', and the analysis of death made by Goethe's friend Schiller, etc.). I have omitted to add that in 1830 Goethe's son August died. His father had refused him permission to take part in the war of liberation, as he wanted to see his 'earthly existence continued on earth'. We could also add here the letter of a candidate for a clerical incumbency who travelled through Saxony-Weimar in Goethe's time and maintained that in no region where the German language was spoken had he met with so much filth, ignorance and superstition, which was astonishing for a small principality whose capital was the meeting place for the most celebrated and enlightened minds of the German people. If I dwell on these things here, it is not to embark on the question of 'heritage', but for a quite different purpose, which I shall make clear later on.

To take first the question of Kleist and Zacharias Werner. From

Goethe's point of view, what was specifically artistic in Kleist (and many others) remained in the background if it did not seem to lead to any genuine synthesis. In this case, to the benefit of a man who was at least to make a certain progress in the field of literary method. It would not be hard to give a dozen other examples. We must now ask what this 'specifically artistic' actually means. I do not have in mind here such questions as talent, gift, genius, etc., whatever these may be, but rather the specifically artistic process as depicted most finely perhaps by Tolstoy, though it has also probably been described by all those who have observed it correctly. In his diary, Tolstoy maintains that this process of creation has two stages, as it were. At the first stage, the artist receives the reality apparently unconsciously and immediately, as something completely new that no one had seen before, so that what has long been known becomes unknown; at the second stage, however, the question is to make this unknown known again, and so on.

All these arguments, which you are also familiar with, are by and large in general agreement with your own, and this is readily understandable. Now the major part of the debate on realism, because it is a debate over method, pertains to this second stage of artistic creation, i.e. what has to happen to this unconscious reception of reality if it is to become a genuine, social work of art, one that points towards the future. The question arises as to whether so great a concern with method might not to some extent get divorced from the first stage of the artistic process. I hope you don't misunderstand me here. I know, as you do too, that method is just as much something 'specifically artistic' as is the first stage. And yet even if it is tremendously important to get beyond this first stage of primary reaction to reality, it is no less important that it not be forgotten, for this primary reaction is the very precondition and premiss for any artistic creation, and without it it is no more possible to reach a synthesis than without method. Perhaps you see all this as something that can be taken for granted, and this is why you do not explicitly refer to it. Unfortunately, however, nothing can ever be taken for granted. In the last five years I have frequently had dealings with comrades, talented, partly talented and untalented alike, who had full command of the realist method and at least saw themselves as genuine portrayers, not just describers. The story of the sorcerer's apprentice was an idyll compared with the performance of these friends. They managed completely to *dis*enchant the whole world. In their case the primary reaction (of which Tolstoy says that the whole of reality must first of all act on a person quite freshly and unconsciously, if he is subsequently to portray it in full awareness) was either completely smothered, or else it was simply not present at all. They depicted a world which they had not actually experienced, which remained closed to the reader, too. They therefore tried to force great moments in the life of the working class which they had perhaps experienced, into the straitjacket of some artificial plot. At this point in their maturity they were unable to invent any genuine plot, and yet they believed they had solved in this way the division between 'portrayal and description'. There were some talented people among them, and with these, it was only necessary to refer them to their own basic experience. The more consciously a person lives, in fact, and the clearer his understanding of the social interconnection, the harder it generally is for him to 'make things once again unconscious', as Tolstoy puts it. When he does manage this, however, the result is all the more successful. Now you may well say that you are in no way to blame for misunderstandings, let alone for unsuccessful novels. I mention all this, therefore, only because very frequently the question of method is brought in when the mistake actually has its origin at a much earlier point in the artistic process.

Back again, now, to Kleist. Of course, it is impossible to compare his generation with our own. If we do have something in common, it is perhaps a certain sticking to the 'first stage'. The reality of their time and their society did not exert a gradual and persistent influence on them, but rather a kind of shock effect. The reason why an artist does not rise above this first immediate influence, either being unable to do so and tormenting himself with this, or else not wanting to do so and getting stuck, can vary a lot depending on subjective reasons, although of course these always go back to his social position. Both yesterday and today, the hesitation of an artist in orienting himself towards reality can have all kinds of causes. Pure incompetence (for example, the kind that inflates itself into an 'ism') or, among other things, the so-called 'fear of deviation'. This has an effect that is very adverse to realism. The artist then forgets that boldness and responsibility are as indispensable for him as for any other person in his actions. But before we come on to method once again, and discuss the overcoming of immediacy, we must deal first of all with the first procedure, the immediate stage. And so as not to be misunderstood, I do not of course have in mind some kind of magical inspiration, but rather that what matters is *what* it is in the reality that makes an impression on *whom*.

This double task, therefore, which you yourself describe, necessarily becomes harder, the stronger is this immediacy (for the harder it is then to overcome it, and correspondingly greater i.e. the achievement in so doing), and the more savagely and powerfully the reality acts on the artist. The present reality, with its crises, wars, etc., must thus first be endured, it must be looked in the face, and secondly it must be portrayed. Countless so-called artists, however, do not see it at all, or they only appear to look it in the face. These times of crisis have always been marked in the history of art by wild breaks in style, experiments, peculiar mixed forms, and in retrospect the historian can see which road proved truly navigable. I believe, therefore, that failure and emptiness are not necessarily absolute. And I doubt whether many of these attempts were really quite so empty. During the collapse of classical antiquity, in the centuries when Western Christian culture was first developing, there were any number of attempts to deal with the reality. So, too, at a less remote time, the end of the middle ages, when we had the beginnings of bourgeois art: the burgher as patron was depicted on altarpieces, monuments, etc. Eventually, we had the first proper individual portraits, which however inadequate, were still the forerunners of Rembrandt. Seen from the standpoint of classical antiquity, or from the high tide of medieval art, the eventual outcome was purest accident – even in the best of cases absurd or experimental. And yet it was for all that the beginning of something new. You can reply to this, in the title words of your last contribution, that in all these cases it was a question of realism. And here I would like to interpose a few simple requests. Please again define exactly what you understand by realism. This request is not superfluous. In your discussions, you use terminology in various different ways, and often without precision. It is ambiguous, for example, whether you mean the realism of *today*, or realism *in general*, i.e. an orientation to the highest possible reality attainable at a particular time. Many religious ideas, for example, which have no reality for us today, were undoubtedly a step towards reality in their own time. If there are some artists today who still work from some invalid standpoint such as this, or who have gone back to doing so, is the method to blame for the result, or does the mistake lie rather at an earlier point in the creative process? And 'mistakes' of this kind are certainly very frequent today, as I see myself from many manuscripts coming out of Germany, because in some respects Hitlerite fascism has regressed to a barbaric level of culture, so that by comparison, stages of human history that had long been superseded again appear to have reality and are reoccupied. I very much hope you understand me here. If we take the concepts that you used in the discussion, then even Gothic art, for example, had something of a naturalistic tendency. Undoubtedly there have been completely non-realist periods in art, if you use the concept of realism as it generally, though not always, was used in the discussion. In the centuries-long course of the art of classical antiquity, with its various stylistic periods, artists applied all kinds of possible methods. If sculpture and vase-painting are taken together, then we can see the variety that was possible in classical antiquity. Before Myron's Discobolos, antique art was in some respects different in nature to how it subsequently became. Every new generation, as you well know, favours a different antiquity. The antiquity beloved of Goethe and Winckelmann was different from the period of antiquity that my generation best appreciates, as different as Roman art is from Gothic. And within each period, many methods competed with one another. (It would also be good to write about the relationship between method and style.) Although I am only indicating here, and have formulated my ideas hurriedly and rather vaguely, you will certainly understand the general direction of my questions, and the point at which I believe there is a gap missing in the discussion on realism.

There is also another aspect, and once again I believe it can be most clearly shown in connection with visual art. Like many others have done, there were certain artists whom I did not take to be realists until I had the opportunity to familiarize myself more closely with their social existence. What idealist and insipid descendants Italian painting has had in Germany! Only in Italy was it possible to discover that these Italian painters were in fact genuine realists, and in no way idealist; the colours of their country, and the totality of their lives, were as they painted. And vice versa. El Greco exerts a great influence on painters of our time. But only last summer, when I travelled to Spain for the first time in my life, did I realize the extent to which he was a realist, despite the anti-realist influence he has had on many people today. His colours were not visionary, but the colours of his country. His proportions really do approximate to the proportions of his people, it is simply that he dared to see these as they were. A further phenomenon that belongs here is that frequently painters who were seen in their youth as revolutionary, fantastic, etc., suddenly seem, when seen again many years later, as more softened and moderate, as far more realist than before. In the exhibition of a thousand years of French art at the Paris World Exhibition, it was not just my own subjective impression how the great French impressionists had become classics in a very short time, who had set down the reality of French society in their age, for future generations and other societies, just as much as Rembrandt or Titian did for their own societies. Only later, in other words, did the juxtaposition of apparently accidental elements prove to be the elaboration of the typical, the essential moments in the characteristic face of the class. It was only that the viewer was previously accustomed to perceive in a face qualities that were not essential. For nowadays it is very often the case that people bring the reality into accord with the image, instead of the other way round. 'A sunrise like a painting', 'a face like a Rembrandt'.

You yourself allowed an exception in the cases of poster, montage and humour. Durus[3] concedes a further exception, that illustrated by Marc, who characteristically stresses the fairy-tale aspect in his painting of the blue horses, and is not fairy-tale a kind of antithesis to jokes? You start off by asking whether there is a single authentic expressionist. I should like to ask in return whether there is any authentic work of art which does not contain a substance of realism, i.e. a tendency towards bringing reality into our consciousness. There is, however, a great danger here – not in this letter, and not in a conversation between ourselves, but rather for the artist and for what is specifically artistic. Only the really great artist can bring completely to consciousness a new piece of reality; others only see this piece of reality in isolation, and only succeed in bringing it partly to consciousness, or only with great difficulties. But even with the really great artist, this process of making conscious does not always succeed for his own point in time and the society in which he is working. After *The Night Watch* Rembrandt was laughed at and ruined. And all great syntheses have been preceded by preliminary surveys of the new reality, experiments, etc., both in the case of the individual artist and for the whole generation to which he belongs. Even the realist artist has as it were his 'abstract periods', and these are absolutely necessary.

All important points developed in connection with the *critique of methods*, if they are correct, also have their relevance for the *method of criticism*, for the instruction of anti-fascist writers. All these aspects, such as totality, the overcoming of immediacy, the profound knowledge of social connections, certainly maintain their validity. The object of the critic, or the teacher, is the artist and his work, a unique and specific social linking of the objective and subjective factor, a switching from the object to the subject and back again to the object. If all these aspects are to be applied to the method of criticism, we must demand that this penetrates into the totality of the artistic process in a different way than before, that it sets individual works in the context of the overall work of the writer in question, and that it is able to react immediately to art, but at the same time to rise above a spontaneous judgement, so that it genuinely mediates a work of art and does not apply slogans, giving not the 'montage' of a critique, but a genuine criticism. Only then will it be possible in our critical work to avoid such errors of judgement as are in part attributable to a complete distortion of any immediate artistic feeling, and in part to the inability to rise above an immediate impression. If this is successful, then, to take a random example, we shall no longer praise a novel such as that of Gläser as a model epic of the popular front, no longer maintain that Brentano was inspired by Gläser, but examine more seriously his serious book *Chindler*. We shall then see that Marchwitza, in his *Kumiaks*, has attempted something new, and will help him with it. Even before Hitlerite fascism, Vicki Baum wrote some very respectable things.[4] There is a very good piece of realism, for example, in her Hollywood novel of almost ten years ago; I must confess this as an honest reader over many years of the *Berliner Illustrierte Zeitung*. But if we review Döblin extremely cursorily in one or two columns, and Baum in great detail in very many columns, it seems to me that something is badly wrong with someone's sense of proportion, that very same sense of proportion that is one of the most important aspects of realism.

I hope you will permit me now, dear Lukács, to turn directly to yourself. In the last few years I have learned a great deal from you. Now of course you write not only for me and for our close friends, nor do you write only as a literary historian. In the last analysis, you write as a teacher, and you address yourself to all anti-fascist writers. When you pass judgement on certain groups of writers, your judgement itself may well be correct, if you see their work as nothing more than a stimulating experiment, and reproach them for having made German literature into a playground for toying with form. But even assuming that this judgement is just, it is still necessary to ask whether it is correct in this form, and really does serve as a help and instruction.

To bring in again poor Dos Passos as a typical example, should we not admit that he has enriched the literature of our time with great new material? With shreds of material? That may well be, but in any case such threads as the story of the unemployed lovers who, expelled from the docks, and given notice by their landlady, cannot find any place in New York to lie down. Or the burial of the unknown soldier, which is surely a poem in itself.

Romain Rolland and Thomas Mann, whom you counterpose to the 'Don Passoses', are certainly great writers, and certainly in the vanguard. But quite apart from the fact that they grew up in a different epoch to that of most writers whom you criticize, even if Shakespeare, Homer and Cervantes were to rise from the dead, they could still not give the new writers the immediacy of basic experience. They could only show them, at most, the methods by which their own experiences were made into eternal works of art. Precisely through the method of realism, you will reply, precisely by solving this double task.

But what is demanded of the anti-fascist writers is not just this double task that you have yourself presented, it is rather a triple task: all-round physical and intellectual application, or as we might say, the reconversion of their work into reality. If the anti-fascist writer succeeds in such a powerful synthesis, then our goal is fully attained. Writers who find themselves in this key position need the most impassioned and far-reaching instruction, and the most careful and differentiated criticism. Besides, writers are perceptive and sensitive people, these qualities being indeed part of their profession.

In the creation of a work of art, as with any other human action, what is decisive is the orientation to reality, and as you yourself say, this can never stop still. But what you see as decay, I see rather as a preliminary survey; what you see as experiment in form, I see as a forceful attempt at a new content, an attempt that is unavoidable.

Finally, dear Lukács, this is only a letter. It simply contains a few impressions that I gained from reading your work, impressions that are thus spontaneous and unformed. Many of these are perhaps mistaken, and many again may be unimportant. I think, however, you will be glad I have written. And if you have the desire to answer, you must bear in mind that you can discuss and debate among yourselves, while here I have only the printed result of your debating.

Greetings,
Yours
Anna Seghers.

29 July 1938

Dear Anna Seghers,

In coming to reply to your objections and questions, I too remember the old Berlin discussions, which we are unfortunately no longer able to continue personally and directly. But you will understand, and certainly not expect anything else, if, just as in these Berlin times, I leave aside here everything that does not pertain to our specific and fairly narrow theme.

First of all, you should not forget that my article was a reply to a specific discussion. (And this discussion, in passing, was not on the question of realism. It was simply that I sought to direct attention to realism.) In my arguments and examples, therefore, I had to confine myself to the preceding articles in the discussion. I brought in Joyce and Dos Passos, for instance, for the sole reason that Bloch held them up as the towering figures of modern, avant-garde literature.

I must also leave aside here everything that you say about criticism in general. I shall only defend my own position. The proportionate space given to individual writers in our journals, for example, is something on which I have virtually no influence whatsoever. I shall similarly leave aside what other critics say, even if they happen to refer to my writing. It is not only literature that is presently in a difficult state of transition, but criticism is as well. There is no other possibility, then, but to march separately and strike together. In other words, whatever one or other of us does correctly becomes an advantage to all. Each of us, however, has to bear reponsibility for his own mistakes. And I for my part shall stand up only for what I have personally maintained.

One final small preliminary: you speak of comrades who had 'full command of the realist method, portrayers, and not just describers', but who, as you certainly rightly see it in most cases, have produced artistically terrible works. Believe me, dear Anna Seghers, that I have not even lent these apprentices an *un*enchanted broom. Remember the winter of 1931–2 in Berlin. As far as I recall, I was the first critic in our literature who pointed out weaknesses in portrayal of precisely this kind. You will also remember how bitterly I was reproached for this at the time, and charged with overrating bourgeois literature to the detriment of proletarian. But you will remember again that I stressed at that time how these writers replaced portrayal with journalistic reportage. Air and paper are tolerant elements. Anyone can appeal, both in speech and in writing, to what suits him best. But there are none the less objective connections, and these permit me to say that an appeal of this kind to my essays is quite without material foundation. To come now to the really important questions. You are completely right to emphasize so forcibly the two steps or moments of the creative process. I would go along with you to a considerable degree, except that you have misunderstood me on one important point. I should now like to make this a little more precise, without being at all polemical about it. In my essay I frequently spoke of writers remaining stuck at the level of immediacy. At first sight, this concept of immediacy might appear to coincide with the immediacy that you speak of as the first stage in the creative process. But this is not in fact the case. In my essay, immediacy does not mean a psychological attitude whose antithesis or development would be the growth of consciousness; what I mean by immediacy is rather a definite *level* of the reception in content of the external world, quite irrespective of whether this reception is effected with more consciousness or with less. I would remind you of the economic examples that I adduced, the reason for this being that these are clearer and more precise than those drawn from literature. If for example someone sees the essence of capitalism as lying in monetary circulation, this indicates that the level of their outlook is an immediate one – even if they write a learned book of two thousand pages on the subject, after ten years' hard work. If on the other hand, however, a worker grasps the concept of surplus-value instinctively, then he has already risen above this level of economic immediacy, even if the words in which he presents his insight, both to himself and to others, are spontaneous, emotional, and 'immediate'. What I demanded of our writers is that they should overcome this kind of immediacy.

Viewed abstractly, the two kinds of immediacy are independent of one another. So I would agree with you when you say that the classical figures of literature 'could not give the new writers the immediacy of basic experience'. This is completely correct. Without such immediate basic experience there can be no literary talent, and it is impossible to produce any work worth a single word of criticism. And if any comrade or colleague should say to you that I am against this kind of immediacy, then please tell him he is being ridiculously stupid and should first learn to read before expressing himself on theoretical questions. This immediacy of basic experience, which you define quite correctly, is thus a common premiss from which we shall now attempt to elucidate some questions more clearly than was possible in my essay.

You will certainly agree with me if, while recognizing the necessity of the immediacy that you emphasize, I maintain that this is not some isolated thing-in-itself, not something that exists in mystical separation from the life-process of the writer (and hence that of society as well). You yourself rejected this idea in a completely justified fashion. For my part, this rejection was not even necessary, as it did not occur to me to ascribe to you any such decadent and mystical fetishism.

The immediacy of basic experience, therefore, is a moment in the writer's life-process. And as such a moment, it is connected with his whole past, and is indeed a summary, an explosive expression of this past. On the other hand, as you correctly say, it points towards the later process of creation – and not only to this, but also to the entire later life of the writer.

Let us now look somewhat more closely at this connection with the writer's past. It is clear that this does not consist simply and solely of such moments of immediacy. The entire conscious and unconscious life of the writer, his intellectual and moral work, is what decides the content of such experience. If we are dealing with a genuine writer, then even the most energetic and conscious intellectual and moral work that has gone before will in itself subtract nothing whatsoever from his spontaneity, from the genuinely experiential character of his work. On the contrary. We can see precisely from the lives of the greatest writers and artists how such intensive work deepened and enriched the spontaneity of their basic experience. On the other hand, however, any half-digested knowledge (even if this purports to be Marxist), and any ambiguity in the moral sphere (self-deception, etc.), has an unfavourable effect on the breadth, depth, productivity, fruitfulness and genuine spontaneity of this experience.

If we thus consider the spontaneity of the creative reception of the world as part of the writer's life-process as a whole, if we see that the conscious work of the writer already has very profound effects on this experience (even if these are often very complex and mediated), we can then proceed, without being distracted by misunderstandings, to investigate the connection between this immediacy and the immediacy which I spoke of in my essay.

In themselves, the two things are quite independent. It is possible, in other words, immediately to experience the essential relationships of the world, which are objectively not immediate, in the artistic sense (and this is the experience of all really great writers), but it is also possible to remain at the immediate surface of capitalist relations despite exhausting conscious effort – for instance my earlier example of money.

This independence, however, exists in so pure a state only in abstraction. In reality, there are highly complex interactions. And you will not quarrel with me, indeed from your own experience you can illustrate this with countless examples, if I say that there is a certain affinity, sometimes a very effective one, between the objective immediate content of the surface appearance of a social condition and the cult of a mystic and isolated immediacy of the process of artistic creation.

Artists, in other words, who do not strive vigorously to develop themselves intellectually and morally as human beings, generally also remain in their experience at the level of this objective immediacy of the social surface.

Once again here, I would like to point out the very great complexity and mediation of these interactions. In the case of the writer's intellectual work, what is of first importance is not the kind of intellectual, scientifically formulable results at which he aims. It is rather the extent to which this work carries him beyond the immediate surface objective, in the very spontaneity of a basic experience. In my discussions, I have pointed to the case of Thomas Mann, since with him this inherent literary fruitfulness of intellectual and moral work is so clearly visible. What he portrays is incomparably more profound and closer to objective truth than is what he states to be the intellectual result of his investigations.

I am in full agreement with you, therefore, when you write that the question is '*what* it is in the reality that makes an impression on *whom*'. The question now is to specify more concretely what we mean by this 'what' and 'whom'. And as long as we do not artificially isolate the spontaneity of artistic basic experience, and hence mystify it, but rather consider it in connection with the life-process as a whole, then the matter becomes quite self-evident.

If you have read my writings of the last few years, you will not reproach me for seeking in any way to underestimate the pureness and spontaneity of the artists' reception of the world. I would remind you here of the third section of my essay on Maxim Gorky (*Internationale Literatur*, *Deutsche Blätter*, 1937, 6). I would ask you to read through this section once again, and you will see more clearly than I can express it in a letter what my view of this question is. I quoted there a saying of Gorky's, that:

> The writer is no longer a mirror of the world, but only a small splinter of it, from which the social backing has worn off, and having lain about in the mire of the city streets, it is no longer able to reflect with its facets the great life of the world; all it mirrors is fragments of street life, little scraps of broken souls [quoted from Lukács's article 'Gorky's Human Comedy', translated in *Studies in European Realism*, London, 1950, p. 223].

You see, then, how a great writer, a great realist, also believes that the question is *what* in reality makes an impression on *whom*.

And yet the second step in the creative process should not be artificially isolated from the first. The artistic reception of the world already contains most of the formal problems of conscious portrayal – at least in intention and tendency. At one point in your letter you speak of the inability of certain writers to invent a genuine plot. One might well believe that this is truly an artistic problem of the purest and most immanent water. But the real situation is quite the opposite. Whether a writer is able to create a plot out of his reception of the world, whether his characters are able to figure in the various steps of such a plot with growing lifelikeness and conviction, depends precisely on whether the spirit of the writer has really become a mirror of the world or only gives a distorted reflection of disconnected fragments of this, as a little splinter of this mirror. For a genuine plot drives what is fundamental, the essential and very complex connections between an individual and his world, into the broad light of day. Simple observation by a single person, however artistically refined, is never sufficient for this. Any plot forces the writer to bring his characters into situations that he could not possibly have observed himself. And if the writer invents such situations, he must also develop his characters further than his own immediate observations allow. Whether he manages to do this depends on how broad, how wide, and how deep has been his artistic basic experience. And we are already agreed, I hope, that this basic experience is again dependent to the greatest extent on the energy and depth of the artist's intellectual and moral work.

There is thus a very complicated dialectical interaction between the first and the second step in the creative process. This second step can take very different directions. To simplify things, I am confining myself here to genuine and honest writers. But even with these, the question still arises as to whether the writer draws this objectively essential component from his own experiential material, whether he strengthens and completes his character as a mirror of the world in a deliberate creative process, or whether he seeks 'artistic' means to join disconnected splinters into an artificial semblance of unity. Subjectively, this latter procedure is quite compatible with the greatest talent, and with the greatest and most dedicated honesty; objectively, however, the result is simply a shambles of interesting cases.

We thus come on to my central problem, the question of decadence. Allow me here a small detour into literary history, as an answer to your argument about Goethe's relationship to the younger generation that followed him. Please do not take offence, dear Anna, but the incidents you quoted belong to romantic legend, and have not been examined at close hand. If you look more closely at the judgements made by Goethe in his later years, you will find he took a passionate interest in Byron, in Walter Scott, in the young Carlyle, in Manzoni, Victor Hugo, Mérimée, etc. Indeed, it is impossible to consider the freshness and lack of prejudice of the old Goethe without being touched with admiration, how at eighty years of age, and busy with the second part of *Faust*, he read Balzac's first major novel *Peau de chagrin* and Stendhal's *Le rouge et le noir* with great interest, understanding, and even enthusiasm. I would ask you therefore, if Goethe in 1830 was neither too old nor too classicist to read Balzac and Stendhal correctly, why should we introduce 'age' and 'classicism' to explain his negative judgements on Kleist some twenty years before?

You know my own opinion on Kleist from my essay in *Internationale Literatur*. The conflict between Goethe and Kleist is of course impossible to go into in a letter, however lengthy. I would, however, like to draw your attention to one point, i.e. the position that the two men took towards France and Napoleon. Whatever else Napoleon may have done, for parts of Germany he acted to destroy the residues of feudalism. And in this capacity he was honoured by the greatest Germans of the age, Goethe and Hegel. Heine later wrote quite correctly that without the French Revolution and Napoleon, classical German literature and philosophy would have been completely trampled down by the petty absolutism that otherwise prevailed in Germany. Kleist, at this time, represented a mixture of reaction and decadence. *This* was why Goethe rejected him. (I have discussed Kleist's artistic stature at length in my essay.)

It goes without saying that German development in this period was very full of contradictions. The war of liberation against Napoleon contained both democratic and reactionary elements. But precisely in Kleist's case it should not be forgotten that he was linked with the expressly reactionary wing of the resistance to Napoleon. So if Goethe was in some respects unjust to Kleist, which I do not doubt, from the standpoint of world history there were very justifiable reasons for this injustice.

If I have gone into this question in some detail, dear Anna, it is not in order to correct an error in literary history. My point is rather that we have experienced in our own time, and are still experiencing, much that is analogous to this, and that it is therefore not unimportant today to get down to the basic question, the underlying behaviour, and contrast the real Goethe with the real Kleist, so as to learn something from the contrast that is still relevant today.

Since we last saw one another we have had the experience of fascism.

I do not intend to repeat here things that you know just as well as I do. On political questions, I take our common standpoint for granted. I want simply to speak of those questions of world outlook that are most intimately bound up with artistic creation. And if we gather together the experiences of the last few years from this standpoint, we can then emphasize two important perspectives.

First of all, it has become evident that the influence of decadence, of various different reactionary ideologies and prejudices, is far wider and deeper than we believed in our earlier self-satisfied complacency. It is widespread not only in the so-called petty-bourgeois masses, but even among ourselves, in the actual vanguard of the anti-fascist struggle. Out of this appreciation, I have made in my essay an unflinching self-criticism of the objectively reactionary character of my earlier writings. I used my own writings so as to give an example that none of my opponents would contradict. But do you really believe, dear Anna, that I am the only anti-fascist writer whose past shows such objectively reactionary works. Without any self-complacency, I believe that I do not stand alone in this. The difference is simply that I have recognized and expressed this, whereas very many people, even today, cherish the most tender regard for their reactionary prejudices, and sometimes even perpetuate them in the name of Marxism.

Secondly, we have learned that there are far greater, stronger and more healthy forces around us that are opposed to fascism than we believed in our former complacent era. We must therefore subject our judgements as to the progressiveness, popular character and genuine humanism of many writers to a fundamental revision, and not remain stuck in the narrow schematism of a clique-like 'avant-gardism', which has served in our midst only as the antithesis to the narrow pseudo-Marxism that shows contempt for everything artistic, and in sectarian fashion only values what is immediately of service for agitation.

These lessons for our present situation are most intimately connected with what in our narrow former standpoint has now to be abandoned. Here again, the seeming polar opposites simply complement one another: the pseudo-Marxist narrowness that would strike out of German history everything that is not immediately proletarian and revolutionary stands on the same footing as the narrowness of that 'avant-gardism' which puts Negro sculpture and the drawings of the insane on the same level as Phidias and Rembrandt, even preferring them where possible.

It is impossible for me to go into my conception of decadence in any further detail here. Some of this you know already from my articles, particularly from the last essay in the discussion. The seventh number of *Internationale Literatur* contains a major essay on this subject;[5] and when it is published, we can then discuss it in more detail. For the moment, since my letter has already become very long, I want simply to deal with one further question. You say of the discussion: 'It is ambiguous, for example, whether you mean the realism of today, or realism in general, i.e. an orientation to the highest possible reality attainable at a particular time.' I believe that it is impossible to separate the two questions. If, as a critic, one does not set out to investigate the conditions and laws of realism *in general*, then the result will be an eclectic position towards the realism of *today*. We shall then not demand what you yourself quite correctly emphasize, the highest reality today possible. Correct criticism must show time and again, by means of artistic, historical and social analysis, what is *objectively* possible today as far as realism goes, and this it can only do if it has a standard – realism in general. Otherwise, we will rest content with what is accepted today as realism (even if its basic tendency is anti-realist), and will *canonize* the weaknesses, errors and defects of our time, the decadent tendencies that are still alive in it, as 'contemporary realism'. Of course, certain elements of realism can be found all over the place (realistic details, etc.), even in anti-realist works. A completely consistent anti-realism is almost as impossible in the field of art as a completely consistent solipsism in the field of philosophy, something that I also spoke of in our discussion. But this does not in any way affect the basic question (in both cases). Criticism of this kind, in my view, would be objectively reactionary, quite irrespective of what the critic might himself intend.

In your letter you bring up a number of examples designed to show me how easily a critic can go astray in assessing new artistic phenomena. Here you are completely correct. I will not challenge certain of your examples which are problematic, as I could myself extend the number of both possible and actual errors. The point, however, is not this, but whether the critic, in the struggle against decadence that is absolutely necessary today, should exhibit a fearsome caution, or should rather immerse himself in the struggle quite untroubled about his reputation, his 'unerring judgement', etc., so long as he achieves something useful in the struggle against harmful tendencies and for the necessary clarification.

This then is my position, dear Anna. You have known me a long time, and you know how for all the decisiveness of my views, I am very far from personal complacency. So if I now introduce a great historical example in order to shed light on the situation of criticism today, and on my own position as well, you will understand that I would not think for one moment of comparing myself with any great historical personality. The man I have in mind here is Lessing, and his battle against *tragédie classique*. Was his assessment of Corneille aesthetically correct in this respect? Not at all. For my own part, there is very much in Corneille that I am fond of, and I do not lose any sleep worrying whether I should let my enjoyment of his or Racine's works be affected by Lessing's criticism. Did Lessing make a 'mistake', then, in attacking Corneille so passionately and, as we see, so 'unjustly'? Not at all. Without this 'mistaken' and 'unjust' criticism, the entire flowering of classical realism in Germany would have been impossible. The Augean stables of courtly decadence had to be cleaned out, to make way for the great realist and humanist art that was then just arising in Germany.

Historical examples must always be used with caution. In this case, and its application to the present, I would myself see something as not equivalent: Corneille and Racine were in no way decadent. In Germany, this courtly decadence arose only in imitation of French absolutism, and a century later both socio-politically and artistically. The decadence of the bourgeois class, however, and particularly in the imperialist era, has an altogether different character. The only common feature is that on the one hand, tendencies that are dangerous for further developmemt must be combatted, while on the other hand, mistakes cannot be ruled out in the heat of the struggle. Lenin once said very wisely to Gorky, who was complaining at the rigours of war communism, that in hand-to-hand fighting it is impossible to say precisely which blows are necessary and which superfluous. I believe, however, that our present situation is that we have failed for a long time to strike sufficient blows, and sufficiently pertinent blows, against decadence.

This is one point, then, on which I cannot agree with you. You advise me to caution. This advice certainly contains a justified aspect, and believe me, dear Anna, I never pass judgement on a writer before I have studied him very thoroughly. But the principle of caution, out of fear of possible error and the possible verdict of history, is something I do not accept. If I have made mistakes in too many individual cases – and between ourselves, I do not think I have done – then let future literary historians declare me stupid. (Many of my present opponents have long been doing so. This is an unavoidable side-effect of ideological conflicts, when these become more or less conscious of the decisive questions.

One should not get too worked up about them, however.) Even if I really have often been mistaken, then future historians will put matters right, and my ashes will not protest against their judgement. But if we are to wage the struggle against decadence that is needed today, then we must not be afraid of such things. I am deeply and firmly convinced that this struggle is necessary and correct, precisely at this present time.

In old friendship,
Yours
Georg Lukács

February 1939

Dear Georg Lukács,

On receiving your letter of last July I could not immediately answer. I found the second letter more difficult than the first. Then all kinds of things were happening. The discussion on realism was abandoned, and we forgot about it. Our windows had already been painted blue against air attacks, and sand brought into the houses against fire-bombs. Then the war was again postponed, the protective paint stripped off, and Hanns Eisler replied with unabated ardour in the *Neue Weltbühne* to the charge of the previous summer that he was simply plagiarizing the German classics.

If anything has turned out to be tough and immobile, it is the discussion on realism. This shows there are really important questions at stake, even if what is most important has not yet emerged, and we have so far only been skating round on side issues.

I want now to try and answer your letter. I find this hard, firstly because this is again a month – like every month this year – in which letter-writing is especially difficult, secondly because your letter was only in part a proper reply to me. Certainly, you went into a number of questions, but taking up and varying the original theme rather than actually answering. This is not important, however, and I shall now stick page by page to your letter.

You would like to leave aside everything to do with criticism. You must understand, however, that this is already difficult for me. For this very passage on criticism in my first letter was particularly important for me. The question, in other words, as to whether the art of criticism must not be subjected to precisely the same methods and laws that you yourself demand of works of art. But you say that you have no influence on criticism, and so: march separately, strike together. I do not know whether such striking-together has always gone off so well. Over the years, many writers have had both blows and caresses showered on them simultaneously – though even this would not be damaging, if the dosage was correct. Many have never received any blows – not that you are to blame here. Nor can you be blamed for misunderstandings. I realize very well that you never intended to provide an enchanted broom. The sorcerer's oversight, in any case, did not lie in the broom, but simply in leaving it standing around. Perhaps the oversight in our case lies in the way that we have made method into a standard. The fiction could thus arise that method in itself can produce something. I did not mean to replace this illusion by the other illusion that everything can be done by immediacy alone.

The part of your letter that deals with immediacy is something that I go along with completely, and find very good indeed. I would only quibble at the term 'moral and intellectual work', not out of disagreement, but rather for fear of a certain misunderstanding. For we know enough people who work desperately on themselves, true 'wrestlers', both intellectually and morally, and yet completely fail in penetration, in depth of genuine immediacy, whereas there are on the other hand many François Villons, Verlaines, etc . . . Immediacy goes astray because this work on themselves, this wrestling, is an illusory way of solving things, only 'in-itself' and unrelated to anything else. This is not intended as a new hymn to immediacy. You are right, and nothing could be better said about the two immediacies than what you have said in your letter.

You then introduce, as evidence as to how the artist should receive the world in an all-round way, a quotation from Gorky. Lukács, dear Lukács, don't be cross, but isn't there always something of the magic broom in the application of a quotation, however splendid this might be? In other words, once again the possible illusion that because a wise and understanding person finally found a particular door, all similar doors can be unlocked in the same way?

What kind of 'mirrors' did we have during the war and after, when we were growing up? These reflected either a past world of basic experience that was foreign to us, and to which we could not do justice under the weight of our own experience, or else they gave a distorted reflection of society, as trick mirrors. (I accept the terminology here, even though art certainly does not just 'mirror' reality.) We had no German Barbusse, no German Romain Rolland. Today we can more or less explain the reason for this. But at least we preferred those splinters who honestly reflected a fragment of our world to any of the distorting mirrors. Again I accept the term 'splinter', even though it expresses something broken, which is in no way the case. What happened was not that something new got broken, but rather that something was beginning that is still not completed: the portrayal of the new basic experience, the art of our own epoch. For clarity's sake, I would like to take an example from art history. In late antiquity, the 'backing' had indeed often worn off, but the 'splinters' that were left were the first forms of expression of early Christian art, i.e. no longer simply 'splinters' of the great art of antiquity, but different in nature. In general, when dealing with the art of an age of transition such as our own, it is always good to consider parallel eras in history, 'transitional eras' from the past, not so as to tie artists to such beginnings, but rather because it gives us a different feeling for the passage of time and for the initial difficulties faced by anything new. The work of art contains the relation of the artist to his material. Criticism here has to find out where the striving for reality begins, and come to grips with the writer on this basis.

Now comes the most important part of your letter. You refer to Lessing. Lessing saw his main enemy in feudalism. And as Lessing battled against feudalism, and against its expression in art, so – you say – we must do battle against decadence.

Our main enemy is fascism. We combat it with all the physical and intellectual powers at our command. It is our enemy, in the way that feudalism was Lessing's enemy. And as Lessing combatted the courtly and feudal art of his time, so we combat the expression of fascism in art. But can this struggle be equated with the struggle against decadence?

You say 'we have failed for a long time to strike sufficient blows, and sufficiently pertinent blows, against decadence'. Who is it that deserves these blows? The fascist writers, the poets of war, the blabberers of blood and soil. The Marinettis and D'Annunzios. Their staunch German colleagues. For these, there cannot be too many blows. We have indeed not even struck the first real blows against them. But the hand-to-hand fighting you refer to takes place on a different terrain. Here it is a question simply of survivals, infections and pieces of the past that have not been overcome. It is certainly true that many of our writers are trapped to a greater or lesser extent by these infections and survivals. But does this make them decadents? If you are helping them to rise out of this, then this is not a struggle against decadence, not a 'hand-to-hand fight' at all. In this case, it is not even a question of blows. Great caution is needed, not on account of one's reputation or fear of misjudgement, but rather so that nothing living and new is damaged as well.

To stick to the case of Lessing, his fearless battle against feudalism in art did not prevent him from condemning *Götz von Berlichingen* completely and absolutely. He called this play an empty and inflated entrail, and failed to recognize in it the work of a great contemporary. Goethe was indeed Goethe, but a writer should not gain recognition *despite* his critics. Lessing linked the question of struggle against feudalism in art with certain methodological ideas and questions. Later, Goethe was just as unsuccessful in his way – and if you do not like the example of Kleist, you can take Hölderlin or one of the others in question. Moreover, if Goethe cut the *Broken Jug* in two parts and interposed a pantomime, this was certainly not because he saw Kleist as a reactionary.

Your starting-point, and it is a correct one, is that the struggle against fascism in literature can only be waged effectively if our own minds are quite free from poison and infection. You go on, however, to link this struggle very closely with particular methodological questions.

My fear is that this leads to a restriction precisely where you have yourself succeeded in gaining space, but in a different aspect: in the fullness and diversity of our literature. I am afraid we are being faced with an alternative where it is in no way a question of either-or, but in this case rather of combining the two, of a strong and diverse anti-fascist art, in which everyone who qualifies as an anti-fascist and writer can take part.

If we want to help people find their way towards reality, then we must give them suitable support. I am not sure whether this discussion on realism always held the same course towards reality that is demanded from the writers themselves.

In a letter such as this, queries and objections only take so passionate a form because we leave aside, as taken for granted, agreement on the most important questions.

Now something amusing. Many of our colleagues and friends read and listen to discussions of this kind, so I notice, with the most remarkable feelings. They wait tensely and eagerly to see who is going to defeat whom. One side alone, they believe, must be left on the field, otherwise the game is worthless. But in a discussion on an equal basis, where the point of departure and the goal are held in common, only one thing is left on the field, and that is whatever is still unresolved. I have tried once more in this letter to present a few things that are still unclear to me. I know that they cannot simply be answered on a few pages, and that they need a good deal of work. I have seldom been so sorry in a correspondence that I have to write instead of speaking.

With warm greeting, dear Lukács,
Yours
Anna Seghers

2 March 1939

Dear Anna Seghers,

Your reply gave me great pleasure. It is always gladdening to feel that an exchange of views has brought greater closeness on the main points. If you are in basic agreement with my views on immediacy, then we have already achieved the most important thing. I am well aware, of course, how slippery and unstable such 'agreement on main questions' can be. And it is precisely in this connection that I also find it painful that we cannot discuss this problem through to a conclusion verbally, by question, counter-question, immediate answer, etc., as only then would we be in a position to dispatch all the minor misunderstandings that still remain.

I am also in agreement, for my part, with your assessment of the kind of discussion that we writers necessarily have among ourselves. Your formulation that it is only what is still unresolved that is left on the field is a very good one. I would simply add that what is false is left as well. For differences of opinion do not arise only from unclear views that are not thought through, but also from false views. I know, of course, that these false views, too, have their social and personal reasons, and also that very many people feel greatly attached to them. This is the difficulty of a sharp but pertinent discussion. But you know me well enough to know that I always struggle against views and tendencies, never against people as such. To come then to one major question, I struggle against decadence, against outlooks and sentiments that derive from a decadent basis, but not against those writers who express such outlooks and sentiments. A great many of these I have a high regard for, both as writers and as human beings, and it is no contradiction, but precisely on this account, that I am upset to find survivals of these outlooks and sentiments still present in their work.

A small misunderstanding seems to have crept between us in connection with what I wrote on the subject of criticism. I intended to say that *our* discussion should be confined to the theoretical and critical ideas I have expressed, so that we might come to as close an agreement as possible on these questions. If I spoke, therefore, so as to clear the ground for our specific discussion, of how we critics should today march separately and strike together, this was naturally meant as a specific recommendation, not that such striking together would always or even frequently work out. If you were present here, and could take part in our internal discussions, you would see from your own immediate experience how little content we are with the present level of our criticism, and how much I myself am one of the least content. I hope we shall succeed here in improving at least something, and avoiding in the future crass mistakes of the kind there have undoubtedly been in the past. But I did not intend to deal with this whole wide field, which would only divert our discussion from the major questions.

There is here, however, a question of principle, and also the semblance of a possible misunderstanding, which we will I hope also succeed in dispatching. You ask in your letter 'whether the art of criticism must not be subjected to precisely the same methods and laws that you yourself demand of works of art'. If all you mean to say here is that in criticism, too, the same reality is reflected in thought as it is in the work of art, then I am in complete agreement. In this case, the word 'art' means nothing more than genuine command of the material. But if you are using the word in its full sense, and do not see criticism as a branch of science and propaganda, then our views on this point are divergent. In this case, we would have to begin a completely new discussion, since I view the claims of modern critics to actually create works of art as a comfortable self-deception, which flatters their inflated subjectivity and permits them to remain superficial and immediate (in the sense we have already explained) on all fundamental questions of aesthetic theory.

As I said, though, this would provide the subject for an entire new discussion, and I shall confine myself for the moment simply to indicating this possible conflict, and present the following arguments on the assumption that criticism is not art, but rather science and propaganda. In this connection, we must deal first of all with the question of so-called method. It is only natural that writers, for whom the poetic mode and their own creative activity forms the central pivot of their interest, initially miss this 'specificity' in any criticism that focusses on principles and method. I believe, however, that the fruitfulness of correct and good criticism for literary creation only becomes effective if this feeling is overcome. Quite recently, I found in the correspondence between Gottfried Keller and the critic and literary historian Hermann Hettner that even Keller shared the feeling you express *vis-à-vis* arguments of principle. But in the course of his development he corrected this feeling: 'I have accordingly bade a final farewell to this private fancy for the so-called specifically poetic, inasmuch as I find that this feeling must be taken purely as pertaining to the producing individual, and does not belong in a principled discussion.'

This quotation also expresses something else that I believe should be said for once quite openly and bluntly among us: a writer needs talent. It would lead us far afield if we were to start debating here the reasons why we have often made mistakes in this respect. And you are as familiar with these reasons as I am. But I don't want even the slightest misunderstanding to persist between us on this question. And so, once again taking my own case as an example, assuming that I still had fifty years ahead of me in which to immerse myself in the principles of literature and study as fundamentally as possible all questions of method, do you believe, dear Anna, that after fifty years spent in this way, I would imagine myself able to write even an artistically successful short story? I am quite well aware that this is impossible, the reason being that I lack the talent for artistic production. But I do not believe I am the only person in our literature who lacks such a gift. And what is the inevitable result when lack of talent appeals to misunderstood and vulgarized 'methods'?

I have a slight suspicion, dear Anna, that you would want to make me responsible for vulgarizations of this kind. This seems to be suggested by the simile of the broom which the sorcerer left lying around. I believe, however, that I have no more left my broom lying around than did my immortal predecessor. At least not in the sense I infer from your letter. In a very general sense, of course, anything written down is left 'lying around'. And particularly so, in that criticism is simply a part of science. No work of criticism, in other words, can be complete and entire in itself; only a complete system of aesthetic theory would be at least relatively complete, and this would also contain a complete history of artistic development. Any individual critical work is inevitably divorced from this overall connection, more or less forcibly so, no matter how multifarious and comprehensive the overall outlook on which it is based. It is never enclosed in itself in the way that a work of art is. How difficult this is is something I know from my own work experience. My friends often make fun of my habit of saying that 'this is not the place to discuss' a certain question. But you will understand how this precisely expresses a feeling for the all-round linkage of each problem with all others, the feeling that any statement can lead to misunderstandings if this overall connection, and thus the tendency to one-sidedness, is not at least indicated. And as I am already making these personal confessions, I shall add another one: other friends reproach me for not writing in a sufficiently 'quotable' and epigrammatic way. I do this deliberately, out of the very same feeling. For in any particular utterance I am concerned to at least indicate the overall connection, the systematic and historical development.

It goes without saying that any particular statement, even if objective, has something fragmentary about it. And the reader will necessarily fragment it still further. The extent to which this invariably happens, and readers *make* sorcerer's brooms out of such fragments, can be shown from a passage in your letter. I asked you to read a section from my essay on Gorky, so that you would have my conception of artistic receptivity more firmly in mind. In that section I quoted a few words of Gorky's as a way of indicating his basic sentiment. You then went and attacked this isolated quotation. But what is sauce for the goose is also sauce for the gander. Others will do the same. And I am as little responsible for the one thing as for the other, as in no case can I prevent what I write being read in such a way.

Even in your own case, your attack on this isolated quotation involves a misunderstanding of my views. You counterpose to Gorky's splinters a so-called distorting mirror, and take a stand in favour of the splinters – understandably, given the false premiss. For such a dilemma is not involved here at all. The 'distorting mirror' cannot be counterposed to the splinters, as it is in fact rather a parallel phenomenon, a consequence of the same social forces. I indicated this question in the introductory lines of my article on realism; and in an earlier essay, which also formed part of this discussion ('The Ideal of Harmonious Man in Bourgeois Aesthetics'),[6] this entire complex is presented in detail. So you can only understand my position, and only really attack me – if you are not in agreement – if you are aware that I am as much against the 'distorting mirror' as I am against the splinters. (The same applies to the question of talent. The contention that artistic talent is indispensable does not mean sharing the modern conception of talent, which sees this, as Tolstoy well put it, virtually as a biological quality of man that is isolated from all human and moral qualities.) Only if you understand the direction of this double battle will you see why I ascribe such central importance to the writer's intellectual and moral work. Of course this cannot make an artist out of someone devoid of talent, but it is still the only way in which talent can achieve something that is of genuine artistic significance.

Why do I criticize these splinters time and again? Because it is precisely here that we see the weakness of the talented representatives of our literature. I hold the optimistic belief that untalented writers sooner or later fade into oblivion, though of course the psychology of many talented writers is just as splintered as is that of many untalented ones. Perhaps the most important point, however, is that the great age in which we are living, and the experiences of the anti-fascist struggle, work *spontaneously* in the direction of overcoming this splintering. There is scarcely a talented writer in our midst who has not made decisive progress in this very direction in the course of the last five or six years. I see this as a sign of the times, and believe that it is the task of criticism to consciously accelerate this spontaneous process.

You speak in the same connection of how we Germans had neither a Romain Rolland nor a Barbusse during the war period. This is completely correct, and bears precisely on the central point of our discussion. For where did Rolland and Barbusse draw the force for their unsplintered portrayal, for their realistic syntheses? Here I must refer back to the quotation from Gorky: because in their case the 'social backing' was more strongly present than it was with the best German left-wing writers of the same period. And what this 'social backing' means here – as I have already explained in detail in my article on realism – is the unity of democratic tradition in social life and realist tradition in art; the consequence of this unity being a constant striving to give art a popular character, and an inseparable connection with the great problems of national life. All this was lacking with the German writers of the war period. I believe you will not misunderstand me if I go on to say that both the shameful capitulation of so many German writers to the ideology of the imperialist war, and also the specific kind of opposition of a small minority, an opposition which was so disposed, both in content and artistic form, that it was unable to arouse the people against the war, derived from the undemocratic development of Germany, from the 'German wretchedness'. And if we are today summing up the experiences of the Weimar period, we must bear in mind that the left intelligentsia – both Communist and non-Communist – did not really overcome this weakness of German development, not in fundamentals; indeed for the greater part they did not even attempt the task.

You should not say that the blame for this falls on the objective historical situation. I am well aware of this. But the question is that none of us made the attempt to link up with the living democratic and popular forces that did exist in the German present and past as intensely as was objectively possible and necessary. In this way, we, the German left intelligentsia, became splinters, and in the interest of the anti-fascist struggle we must now overcome this splintering, this lack of the social and national backing.

We lack democratic traditions, and for this reason our realism is not decisive enough, not comprehensive and deep enough. I know that Germany's democratic traditions are weaker and less glorious than those of France or England. But for this very reason we should cultivate them more intensely, strengthen and develop ourselves with them, and carry them back to the German people. (I would remind you that fascist demagogy calls democracy a 'Western import'.) Even today, we are doing this far too little, and with far too little resolution and awareness. And you must understand that if I speak time and again of the German past, I do so in this connection, as speaking for the democratic future of Germany.

In criticism, too, we lack democratic traditions. In our critical judgements, therefore, we proceed from a formal-artistic standpoint, which is too narrow. You unfortunately do the same thing in the example of Lessing and Goethe. It is an unquestionable fact that Lessing took a very sceptical position towards *Götz von Berlichingen* (and also towards Goethe's *Werther*, which you fail to mention). But it should be added, firstly, that he was in complete agreement with the young Goethe's 'Prometheus' poem. Secondly, you should read what Goethe said of Lessing throughout his life, as you will find nothing but gratitude and the yearning for a contemporary critic who had the same social and human qualities as Lessing. (For there were contemporaries of Goethe who were in no way inferior to Lessing in artistic sensitivity.) Thirdly, Goethe's development completely justifies Lessing's criticism. For Goethe never took a further step along the path indicated by *Götz von Berlichingen*, neither in social content nor in dramatic form. Goethe's naïve and primitive opposition to the 'German wretchedness' led on this one occasion to a glorification of a completely reactionary figure. In *Egmont*, however, the dramatic subject of a more mature Goethe already points in a completely opposite direction. And the development of Goethe's dramatic form takes a similar course. Lessing cleared the way for an understanding of Shakespearean drama. The fluid, epic form of *Götz* is a step backward by comparison with Lessing's theory and dramatic practice. And Goethe was very quick to grasp this. His *Clavigo* already breaks quite radically with this epic form, and *Egmont* shows how profoundly Goethe had already understood the dramatic form of Shakespeare and how originally he had developed this. (Despite all this, I would not impugn either the aesthetic or the historical importance of *Götz von Berlichingen*. But 'this is not the place to discuss that question'. I have done so several times, however, for example in my book on the historical novel.)

This is of course only a very sketchy outline of the relation between Lessing and Goethe; a lengthy essay would be needed to even indicate the actual connections in full. In a letter such as this, I must confine myself simply to stating the facts. I only broached this question, however, because I wanted to point out at least some of the perspectives that are decisive for presenting this relationship both historically and aesthetically. I can immediately see how hopeless it is to do this in a letter. For to make the connection really comprehensible, it would be necessary to indicate at least the affinity and difference between French and German developments in the late eighteenth century. Only then could one show how on the one hand both the strength and the limitation of Lessing was connected with his rejection of the Rousseau line of the French Enlightenment, and how on the other hand the German classicism of Goethe and Schiller meant a step backwards from Lessing in relation to democracy, even though it was the only concretely possible path, given the social situation, which German culture could take at that time. You will understand that I cannot even attempt here to sketch these connections, since this would require an analysis of the contradictions within the plebeian class in the bourgeois revolutions of that time, an analysis of the difference for literature and culture between the actual revolution in France and its ideological effects in Germany, etc. (When my book on the history of realism is published, you will find some indications of this relationship.)

It is not obstinacy or the hair-splitting of a literary historian, dear Anna, if I take issue so stubbornly with your anecdotes from literary history. You have an unusual sensitivity for the phenomena of our own time. So it makes me a little sad that you are content to treat the greatest figures of the German past with such abstractions as failure to understand new things, difference of generations, etc., and do not attempt to think through in the same sensitive manner the real underlying reasons for the apparently paradoxical and at first appearance surprising statements of these great German writers. For if even you are satisfied with such anecdotes, how do these figures appear to the average representatives of our literature?

All this I see as a question of pressing relevance today. I do not want to repeat everything I have written you in my previous letter about the present political importance of the literary battle against decadence. You yourself admit I am right that fascism can only be combatted 'by minds quite free from poison and infection'. Once again, I am extremely glad we agree so closely on this decisive point. The only thing on which I do not agree with you is that this struggle has to be confined to combatting the most pronounced reactionary figures of decadence, the Marinettis and D'Annunzios. Of course, the decadence of fascist barbarism is the thing to combat above all. But there are also problems of development internal to the anti-fascists. And here I would ask you, on whom do the Marinettis and D'Annunzios still exert a real influence? On the other hand there are innumerable and very important decadent tendencies (such as irrationalism, etc.), that still have an extremely strong influence within our own ranks, on the best minds, the most important writers, and the most convinced anti-fascists. If these minds are really to be free from poison, as you desire, then we must combat the survivals of decadence that persist and exert an influence in our own ranks. I know this is a very unpopular task, and that even so good and faithful a friend as you has sometimes got angry with me and will most probably also have occasion to blame me in the future. And yet no compromise is possible, once one is convinced of the necessity of this struggle. Here I can only echo the sentiment that Plutarch's Themistocles expressed at the council of war before the Battle of Salamis: 'Strike me, but hear me out'.

In as much as I can judge recent events in Germany, I am further strengthened in this conception. Time and again, new opposition movements rise up against fascism. Social strata and individuals who previously tolerated every form of imperialist capitalism without contradiction, and even promoted this themselves, now reject ever more decisively this total barbarism. The manner of their opposition, however, and their ideology, are of course deeply permeated with fascist influences. Only very slowly, instinctively and spontaneously do they attain clarity. In this connection, these people are far more deeply bound up with German national life than is generally assumed. Naturally, they often share highly reactionary conceptions of Germanness. What can we give them, to ease and accelerate their struggle for clarity? Certainly not disconnected tatters of a decadent ideology only half overcome, or a variant of decadence that lacks the national backing and must therefore always remain foreign to these people? I believe that only by demonstrating the real strength of the German past, showing the connection between the great German past (which is certainly very different in form from how most of them imagine it) and the future greatness of a genuinely democratic Germany, can we aid a democratic culture in Germany. Just as I am deeply convinced of the connection between realism, the popular character of literature, and anti-fascism, so too I am certain that our discovery of the democratic past of German culture is not a path leading back, but rather a path into the future, an ideological aid to the liberation of Germany.

This letter has again become a long one, and yet I have not said a tenth of what I would have liked to say. The stronger the elements of agreement appear in our dialogue, the more painful I too feel the lack of actual conversation. For in letters, petty differences and nuances always turn out sharper than in the direct exchange of ideas. I rely however on your literary sensitivity, as you have already been able to empathize with knottier figures than I am.

In old friendship,
Yours
Georg Lukács

Tribune or Bureaucrat? [1940]*

Literature deteriorates only to the extent that people deteriorate. [Goethe]

1. THE GENERAL SIGNIFICANCE OF LENIN'S ANTITHESIS

Lenin's *What is To Be Done?* was designed to expose the opportunist philosophy of 'economism' that was influential at the time of its publication (1902). The 'economists' objected to the theoretical and organizational unity of the Russian revolutionary movement; all that was important, in their view, was the struggle of the workers for their immediate economic interests, their spontaneous action against the reprisals of the factory-owners. They saw the role of the conscious revolutionary as restricted to giving aid and succour to local and immediate working-class struggles. The idea of recognizing these particular class conflicts as parts of the general historical task of the proletariat, of illuminating these individual moments of struggle by political propaganda based on socialist doctrine, and combining these resistance movements in a revolutionary political movement designed to overthrow capitalism and bring the victory of socialism, was in the eyes of the economists a 'violation' of the working masses, harbouring the risk of isolating the revolutionary intelligentsia from the masses. The 'economists' confidently held that the spontaneous movement would always produce consciousness through a simple process of growth.

Lenin demolished this opportunist 'theory', and showed that 'economism' actually leads the proletariat away from the political struggle, making the workers abandon the overthrow of capitalism and content themselves with temporarily improving the condition of particular sections of their class. But in Russia at that time, Lenin held that the primary task of the revolution was to overthrow the autocracy, which provided the capitalists with their most reliable protection. As Lenin saw it, the 'economists' struggle against organizational unity in the name of spontaneity made them the bringers of bourgeois influence into the working class.

* First published in *Internationale Literatur*, nos 1–3, 1940.

In the course of elaborating the ideological foundations of the Marxist party and exposing the bourgeois nature of this reformist 'theory', Lenin counterposed two different types of ideologists: the revolutionary tribune and the bureaucrat. He maintained that both in the capitalist West of the time and in backward Russia, the predominant type was that of the trade-union secretary, the bureaucrat. The 'theory' of opportunism — both international and Russian alike — sought eargerly to perpetuate this backwardness and distortion. Lenin's book was directed against this dual tendency, which had a combined influence under the conditions of tsarist Russia. For the spontaneous development of a new workers' movement, in a country where capitalism was relatively backward, immediately encountered the phenomena of decay characteristic of the imperialist epoch: the 'theory' of Bernstein, the practice of Millerand, and the entire international gathering of opportunism. Lenin's militant work, which theoretically annihilated all these tendencies at their very root, thus not only marked a turning-point for the Russian workers' movement, it was also a milestone for the entire history of revolutionary thought: the first principled rejection of opportunism at an international level.

Lenin's counterposing of people's tribune and trade-union bureaucrat as characteristic types, produced by the two contending tendencies in the workers' movement, revolutionary Marxism and opportunism, has a significance that goes far beyond the specific conditions of time and place that were its original occasion. In Lenin's own words:

> It cannot be too strongly maintained . . . that the Social-Democrat's ideal should not be the trade-union secretary, but *the tribune of the people*, who is able to react to every manifestation of tyranny and oppression, no matter where it appears, no matter what stratum or class of the people it affects; who is able to generalize all these manifestations and produce a single picture of police violence and capitalist exploitation; who is able to take advantage of every event, however small, in order to set forth *before all* his socialist convictions and his democratic demands, in order to clarify for *all* and everyone the world-historic significance of the struggle for the emancipation of the proletariat [*Collected Works*, Vol. 5, p. 423].

The concrete colours of this picture are taken from the Russian conditions of the time. The portrait of the type, however, has such a pertinent universality that it is still completely valid for us today.

It goes without saying, given the objective nature of this subject, that Lenin's investigations necessarily went beyond the working class and its organizations. The vulgarizing flattening of Marxism that found political expression in opportunism, whether of the right or the 'left', always presented the life of the proletariat in isolation from the overall movement of society. And this flattening, moreover, demagogically proclaimed itself to be 'genuinely proletarian', keeping the workers' movement away from alien influences. Lenin's argument, on the other hand, reveals the true state of affairs, the many-sided and indissoluble connection between the fate of the working class and the society as a whole. On the one hand, the proletariat cannot liberate itself without demolishing all oppression and exploitation, whatever classes and social strata are affected. On the other hand, the life and development of the working class reflects all the social and economic strivings that are of real importance for the further development of society, as well as the negative tendencies that inhibit such development, and in the imperialist era even the parasitic tendencies. In his critique of imperialism, Lenin repeatedly pointed out how the parasitic character of this period should not be viewed in a narrow and superficial manner, but had rather to be grasped as a universal social tendency, and as such it was also expressed in the workers' movement itself. As a result of the ever more strongly reactionary character of capitalism, together with the corruption of the 'labour aristocracy', the general demoralization of political life and the restriction of democracy, a tendency towards bureaucracy, separation from the masses and divorce from real life arose also in the reformist organizations of the working class.

As far as capitalism itself is concerned, bureaucracy is a necessary phenomenon, an inevitable product of the class struggle. Bureaucracy was one of the first weapons of the bourgeoisie in its struggle against the feudal system, and it becomes ever more indispensable, the more the bourgeoisie has to start wielding its power against the proletariat and the more its interests come into open contradiction with those of the working masses. Bureaucracy is consequently one of the fundamental phenomena of capitalist society.

What is of particular importance for our consideration here is the cultural aspect of this question. We have already seen the general features of the two antithetical types in the workers' movement, one of which Lenin indicated as an ideal to be striven for – on the basis of a profound analysis of capitalist society and of the conditions for the liberation of the proletariat – the other as a negative example to be overcome. We shall now go on to investigate in brief the basic features of this negative example, so as to grasp it as something necessary and socially universal under capitalism.

Lenin's analysis links bureaucracy in a profound sense with spontaneity. Spontaneity, here, means that the object of interest and activity is immediate and only immediate. An immediate relationship to the object, of course, is the obvious starting-point of all human activity. What is peculiar to the phenomenon we are investigating here is simply that the 'theory' of spontaneity — the ideological glorification of bureaucracy – demands a confinement to this immediate object, tabooing as inauthentic and false anything that goes beyond this, though in fact this is precisely the expression of genuine theory (theory without quotation marks). 'Economism', the tendency to a bureaucratization of the workers' movement that was characteristic of that period, dressed up this confinement to immediacy, this glorification of spontaneity, as something 'purely proletarian', restricting the fighting activity of the workers to a defence against their immediate economic exploitation in the factory, the immediate clash of interests between factory-owner and labour force. In this way, however, this 'purely proletarian' standpoint handed over all the major battlefields of democratic social transformation to the liberal bourgeoisie, and abandoned – in fact, if not in words – any struggle for socialist transformation.

Restriction to a subjective spontaneity in behaviour is the necessary counterpart to this objective immediacy of the object. Everything that goes beyond this, depending on a knowledge of the objective connections and laws of motion pertaining to society as a whole, is rejected 'on principle' as 'not proletarian', as an 'alien element'. The primitive spontaneous reaction to immediate stimuli is counterposed to theoretical understanding of the totality as a higher form of subjectivity, as a more adequate relationship to reality.

It was only the full development of imperialism that revealed the true depths of the Leninist critique of the theory of spontaneity. From this perspective, it is possible for the first time really to grasp the actual social and theoretical foundations of international opportunism. Whereas upholders of 'orthodoxy' such as Kautsky sought to present their differences with Bernstein as questions of tactical detail, Lenin was already quite clearly aware at the time that the Bernstein phenomenon involved a decisive abandonment of the struggle for socialism, indeed even for the realization of all revolutionary-democratic demands, and was an adaptation of the revolutionary workers' movement to the limits acceptable to the liberal bourgeoisie.

This liquidation of Marxism ran its course in the imperialist milieu. Since the bourgeoisie has ceased to be the bearer of social progress, its ideology exhibits to an increasing degree such phenomena as disbelief in the knowability of objective reality, mistrust of all theory, and contempt for understanding and reason. The appeal to spontaneity and the glorification of simple immediacy as the final court of appeal for command of reality is accordingly a primary cultural and ideological tendency of the imperialist period. The bourgeois kind of spontaneity, sticking fast to immediacy, grows necessarily out of the capitalist division of labour. Its ideological product completely corresponds, therefore, to the narrow and egoistic class interests of the bourgeoisie. The undisturbed operation of bourgeois domination is made easier by the fragmentation of the popular masses, craft ideology, contentment with the specialized tasks allotted by the capitalist division of social labour, and by the deliberate acceptance of the forms and possibilities of thinking, the modes of perception, that spontaneously arise from this division of labour.

The more reactionary the bourgeoisie becomes, the more energetically does this aspect of its ideology come to the fore. As long as the revolutionary-democratic tendencies still have strong support in the bourgeoisie and petty-bourgeois strata, and in the bourgeois intelligentsia, this objective spontaneity of the specific ideology of the capitalist division of labour and its promotion by the narrow class interests of the bourgeoisie is time and again broken through. The reactionary parasitism of the imperialist period, however, makes this into the dominant tendency in bourgeois society, reaching right through into the political movement and ideology of the proletariat.

It is easy to see why the bourgeoisie has an interest in views of this kind. Spontaneity means the mental obliteration of those all-round connections of social development that are objectively present and effective in every phenomenon of social life. It therefore means a renunciation of knowledge of the laws of motion of capitalist society, the laws that clearly indicate the irresolvable contradictions of this society and the necessity for a revolutionary transcending of it. The more firmly people's mental and emotional strivings remain locked in the pitiful abstract prison of spontaneity, the greater is the ruling class's security. This is naturally true most of all for the working class, but it holds for all areas of cultural life as well.

It is certainly true that many spontaneous reactions to capitalism are rebellious in kind, and they frequently maintain their subjective oppositional or insurgent intent even when they do not rise above the spontaneous level. Objectively, however, expressions such as these, by remaining spontaneous, generally flow into the stream of tendencies that maintain the prevailing regime. Rebellion must rise to a certain consciousness of objective connections if it is to turn against the system of oppression and exploitation in deed, and not only in intent.

Lenin's tribune of the people is the herald of this revolutionary consciousness. If the type he represents is to be properly understood, then it is not enough to see only the outward features of the tribune. For what makes the tribune is not verbal brilliance and rhetorical eloquence; the genuine tribunes of the French revolution were neither the dazzling orators Mirabeau and Vergniaud, nor even Danton, but rather the simple Marat and the dry Robespierre.

A consciousness familiar with the objective properties of the social totality in its movement, according to the stage of historical development of the time, and the decision with which the deepest needs of the liberation of the working people are championed, are what raise someone into a tribune. And it was as tribune of the revolution himself that Lenin took up the battle against spontaneity. If Lenin managed to transcend immediacy and gain a clear consciousness of the movement of the social totality, he did so – borne up by a deep and embracing love for the oppressed people, such as fills all knowledge with the emotion of outrage and the call to liberation – on the basis of the adequate understanding that has only been made possible by the materialist dialectic, by Marxism. On no previous occasion has the superiority of reason striving for all-round knowledge over mere immediacy been so sharply proclaimed.

But this sharpness contains transcended in itself all the dialectical transitions of reality. The metaphysical separation of spontaneity and consciousness is a general ideological weakness of the era of bourgeois decline. It is expressed not only in those who capitulate before spontaneity, but also in most of the latter-day descendants of the Enlightenment, who while struggling for consciousness, have still failed to overcome the rigid separation between spontaneity and consciousness that is characteristic of the decadent era, so that they only reiterate the doctrine of decadence with its signs changed. Here, too, Lenin saw the dialectical unity of life. He objected to spontaneity as an ideal, as a barrier, but he recognized it as an expression of life, as one part of the overall movement, and a correctly understood moment of this. In drawing the lessons of the Russian strike movements, Lenin stressed this relativity of spontaneity and consciousness, and the continuous turning of each into the other. 'This shows that the "spontaneous element", in essence, represents nothing more nor less than consciousness in an *embryonic form*' [ibid., p. 374].

This was the first time in the history of social thought that the real interaction of these two categories was defined. And it is only if the combination of the two is recognized, for all their most sharp separation, that the Leninist conception of the relationship of consciousness and spontaneity can be seen in its true light. Spontaneity as the 'embryonic form' of consciousness expresses the priority of being over consciousness, the necessary rise of an adequate reflection of reality out of the movement of reality itself. But this movement is not an automatic one. The development of consciousness into a true grasp of the world, and the human task of transforming it, cannot be accomplished without conscious work, without becoming conscious of the external world and oneself. For this, the break with spontaneity is indispensable. For it is only through this break that the totality of socially effective forces, their directions, laws, and the possibilities of influencing them, can be recognized, subsequently becoming an intellectual possession of those fighting for a better reality.

These two sides of the connection between spontaneity and consciousness must be clearly borne in mind if we are correctly to evaluate Lenin's formulation that revolutionary consciousness is brought into the proletariat 'from without'. The correct meaning of this blunt 'formulation', as Lenin himself called it, is, however, as simple as it is profound and significant:

> Class political consciousness can be brought to the workers *only from without*, that is, only from outside the economic struggle, from outside the sphere of relations between workers and employers. The sphere from which alone it is possible to obtain this knowledge is the sphere of relationships of *all* classes and strata to the state and the government, the sphere of the inter-relations between *all* classes [ibid., p. 422].

The embryo of spontaneity only develops into a genuine adult through the work of such a consciousness, the class-in-itself thereby developing into a class-for-itself. The tribune awakens this consciousness. His all-round knowledge quickens the growth of the bud into a flower; he goes ahead of the development, promoting and pursuing it. Those who glorify spontaneity, on the other hand, who thoughtlessly share in it and perpetuate it, must confine themselves simply to recording accomplished facts, finding themselves, as Lenin put it, 'at the tail of the real movement'. No matter how enthusiastically 'revolutionary' or 'proletarian' a tone they may sound, their activity remains barren and unfertile, a bureaucratic recording of others. It is bureaucratic even in the most general and worst sense of the term, as a drag on the living development. For it channels the spontaneity that is in no position to bring about any results of itself into false and stunted directions, through the way that it so falsely fixes it in consciousness and raises it into the sole principle, inevitably leading to distortions. The spontaneous movement of the proletariat has a bourgeois content, and to fix this in theory is not unpolitical, but reactionary.

2. BUREAUCRACY AS A BASIC FORM OF DEVELOPMENT OF CAPITALIST CULTURE

But what has all this got to do with literature and its destiny? It is evident right away that Lenin's analysis and his contrasting of types have an extraordinary scope, their significance reaching beyond the occasion that induced them, and indeed beyond the field of the workers' movement altogether. This means, however, that this contrast extends even to the deepest problems of literature. The objection may be raised here that while the contrast between tribune and bureaucrat certainly grows out of the social division of labour and the class struggles of capitalism, and the subjection of all spheres of ideology to the dominion of commodity exchange and the debasement of all ideological products to the level of commodities has been a generally known fact ever since the *Communist Manifesto*, it does not necessarily follow that the contrast of types made by Lenin is immediately applicable to the most recent and fundamental problems of literature in our own day.

The possibility of such an expanded application, however, is contained evidently enough in the Leninist counterposition. Lenin's analyses always get down to the basic questions of social culture, and always grasp the most universal and decisive tendencies at work. Lenin's historical genius in grasping the next link in the chain was never practicistic or relativist. For example, it was neither confined simply to the specificity of the moment of time under investigation, nor did it remain tied to the particular character of the class to which Lenin's interest was expressly directed. He always saw the unity of society as a dialectical and contradictory historical development.

But even for Hegel, and far more for Marx and Lenin, this dialectical unity is the unity of unity and difference. In an expanded application of Lenin's idea, therefore, this moment of difference must be emphasized right from the start. What this concretely means is that the problem of consciousness is qualitatively different for the working class than for all other classes of capitalist society, or all earlier revolutionary classes in history. The connection between the spontaneity of proletarian class consciousness, even proletarian class instinct, and socialism, is something specific, and cannot be applied to other classes or historical periods.

Yet it in no way follows from this that the antithesis between spontaneity and consciousness, and the corresponding antithesis between bureaucrat and tribune – *mutatis mutandis* – is not a general phenomenon in the history of society. It must simply be always borne in mind that this consciousness always contains a greater or lesser measure of what Engels depicted as the specific features of 'false consciousness'. In investigating art, where, as Engels also showed, an adequate grasp of reality in its totality and movement was achieved by the great realists despite a false consciousness (the triumph of realism), it is particularly possible to apply Lenin's contention in this way, even if the difference already indicated must naturally be always borne in mind. This qualification, however, does not mean that we should draw back in fear at the – socially necessary – appearance of a difference between particular social phenomena.

In appearance, there is certainly a strict and exclusive antithesis between the bureaucrat criticized by Lenin and any genuine literary phenomenon. There is indeed an industrialized literature that is produced with bureaucratic routine and has become simply a commodity on the market, but we scarcely need waste any words on this here, since the position is too simple and self-evident. Literature proper, and the human, social and artistic type of the genuine writer, seems, however, to constitute the purest opposite to the bureaucrat. On the one hand soulless objectivism, the demise of human subjectivity, the simple rule of the most empty and formal material relations, on the other hand an ever stronger cult of the ego, of a subjective experience that is ever more purely insisted upon, of the object of experience grasped in subjective immediacy and serenity, no matter how conscious the purely artistic work of achieving such spontaneity.

The attentive reader of *What Is To Be Done?*, however, will call a halt at this point. He will recall the excellent passage in which Lenin shows how the terrorists of his time stood in the same relationship of bowing to the spontaneity of their intellectual origin as did the trade-union bureaucrat. And is Oscar Wilde, for example, more distant as a type from Tolstoy's Karenin than Ivan Kaliayev, the romantically enthusiastic bomb-thrower, 'the poet', as his comrades called him, from an ossified if cunning bureaucrat such as Leipart?[1] If a polar combination of types that are at first sight sharply antithetical is possible in the one case, then why not in the other? Let us study this antithesis somewhat more closely.

It would be wrong to vulgarize and simplify either the capitalist division of labour itself or its subjective reflections in the ideas, emotions, etc., of human beings. Plekhanov's view, that a 'psychology' arises on the economic base, forming in turn the basis for ideological patterns, has a rectilinear character about it that jeopardizes concrete research. For the objective social meaning of immediate reactions (such as are also conceptually fixed at the level of immediacy) can ultimately be the same, even though these reactions themselves appear polar opposites in their psychological immediacy.

Lenin fundamentally expanded and deepened the Marxist line of a battle on two fronts. And the elaboration of this doctrine – which already reached a highly developed form in *What Is To Be Done?*, with the counterposing and combination of economists and terrorists – is precisely based on the fact that both right and 'left' deviation from Marxism similarly amounts politically to opportunism, the influence of the bourgeois environment similarly winning influence on the workers' movement in each case.

Lenin never neglects the difference within this unity. Not only can the psychology of the two extreme but correlated poles be extremely different, but the specific strata within bourgeois society which according to concrete circumstances form the specific social base of such a tendency, need in no way always be the same at each pole. Yet the elucidation of their specificity does not abolish the unity, it simply underlines the decisive social and historical moments of the concrete historical situation in which this unity makes its appearance.

Thus Lenin characterized economism as the 'spontaneity' of the 'pure workers' movement' – to come back to our original example – while terrorism was the result of 'the spontaneity of the passionate indignation of intellectuals, who lack the ability or opportunity to connect the revolutionary struggle and the working-class movement into an integral whole' [ibid., p. 418]. The result is necessarily a completely different and even opposite psychology, yet in no way does this abolish the similarly spontaneous character of the two so sharply contrasting types, the similarity of social origins and of the effects of this spontaneity.

It is important to avoid simplification, too, in analysing bureaucracy as a general cultural phenomenon under capitalism. The antithesis between anarchy and mechanization that characterizes the capitalist economy finds expression in a manifold and intricate fashion. The basic contradiction between social production and private appropriation is sufficiently well known. This contradiction defines the specific character of the capitalist division of labour, as well as the antithesis between the division of labour within the individual factory and in the society as a whole. The same economic forces that in the one case produce a situation of anarchy, create in the other case the strictest planning and authority, which is why Marx formulated it as a law that an inverse relationship obtains between the two divisions of labour.

As a result of this contradiction, the spontaneous effect of capitalist industry on human beings is very complicated and diverse. In spontaneity, therefore, in the simple and immediate relationship to the immediate object, we find both the anarchy of the totality (which remains unrecognized as such), and the strict, self-enclosed, authoritarian and mechanized immanence of the individual factory (whose objective connections with the totality remain similarly unrecognized). The mixture of the two components is always different, but in almost all cases both can be made out.

If we now consider the capitalist bureaucrat in the narrower sense, the first thing we perceive about him is the mechanistic and automatized aspect, as his fundamental attribute. Even the higher level bureaucrat — not to speak of the petty employee (post office clerk, cashier, etc.) — is to a large extent mechanized. Max Weber once said that capitalism conceives justice as an automatic machine, with 'cases' being fed in at one end and 'decisions' popping out at the other. It is evident in this connection that a 'decision' of this kind has to be something that can be rationally calculated in advance. Thus we have in appearance the greatest antithesis to spontaneity.

Yet precisely here, such spontaneity can only be denied by a vapid and short-sighted romanticism. Max Weber, in his attempt to characterize the bureaucrat, describes his highest ambition in something like the following words: If he has a measure to put through that goes against his convictions, then he is concerned to achieve his task in the best possible way, *lege artis*, with all the finesse of his handling of files. These files, which as far as he is concerned appear intrinsically disconnected from the overall social context, obtain a still more isolated existence that seems to function by itself. Bureaucratic execution becomes a formal and 'artistic' task.

In this way the capitalist bureaucracy obtains an 'immanence' which, while objectively determined by the totality of society, economy and class struggle, has its true character obliterated in its spontaneous effects on the individual participants. It is precisely the unreserved surrender to the spontaneity of such an 'immanence', i.e. the complete immediacy in the subject's behaviour towards the objects of his activity and hence the maintenance of the isolation and self-seclusion of the individual office in its 'immanence' from the movements of the totality, that secures correct functioning in the capitalist sense, and constitutes the ideal bureaucrat of capitalist society.

There can of course be very differing sub-types within this framework. These range from those officials who have surrendered themselves quite unconsciously to the spontaneous operation of the bureaucratic mechanism, with body and soul (i.e. completely soullessly), and who function as true cogs in the great machine, through to the 'artists' and 'moralists' of bureaucracy.

To speak of 'artistry' here is a paradox only in form. We could refer to Tolstoy's ingenious diplomat Bilibin, whose mode of operation is described as follows in *War and Peace*:

> He put in equally good work whatever the nature of the matter in hand. It was the question 'How?' that interested him, not the question 'What for?' He did not care what the diplomatic business was about, but found the greatest satisfaction in preparing a circular, memorandum or report skilfully, pointedly and elegantly [trans. R. Edmonds, Harmondsworth, 1978, pp. 175–6].

Alongside this 'artistry', which already touches on the theories and modes of behaviour of art for art's sake, we find the other sub-type of bureaucracy with a moral pathos. Here again, we have to restrict ourselves to a single characteristic example. No less a writer than Kant gives us the following version of the motto '*fiat justitia, pereat mundus*', already in itself a bureaucratic one, a version that is both grotesque and scurrilous: 'Even if civil society were to dissolve itself with the consent of all its members . . . the last murderer in prison would first have to be executed, in order that each should receive his deserts' [*Kant's Political Writings*, ed. H. Reiss, Cambridge, 1970, p. 156].

Yet this bureaucratic narrowness of Kant's view did not remain unchallenged even in bourgeois literature. Under the ideological influence of the French revolution, Hegel subjected the formalism of Kantian ethics and legal philosophy to a devastating criticism. The details of this criticism are not important in the present connection, and we want rather to indicate its historical preconditions. The French revolution (and in part even the Napoleonic period) had so forcefully brought to the fore the general interest of nation and people that at certain points of time and place the bureaucratic relationship of people to their activity was superseded even in the state apparatus.

It is not superfluous to remember this here, for it shows that even in bourgeois society bureaucracy is a far more comprehensive concept than officialdom, while on the other hand not every official need necessarily exhibit a bureaucratic behaviour in his activity. Balzac, as the great chronicler of French society, gives us some striking examples of the spirited operation of Napoleonic officials, an operation that came to grips with the concrete content, with the totality. His Brideau may have died young, but he dies on the battlefield of his work.[2] His Rabourdin may have experienced a tragicomic debacle in the Restoration period, with this attempt to organize the work of a ministry according to the fundamental public interests, and not according to the spontaneity of the bureaucratic operation. But it is precisely only in its great periods of transformation that bourgeois society goes beyond this 'normal' spontaneity, and then only in exceptional cases, even if these are not isolated, but rather symptomatic.

But it is precisely exceptional cases of this kind that show us the insuperable character of bureaucracy in capitalist society. The objective economic forces of the capitalist division of labour produce and reproduce it continuously, both on a mass scale and as the crowning achievement of the most varied practices. The specific class interests of the bourgeoisie promote this development with all possible means.

At the same time, this coincidence of bourgeois class interests and bureaucratic spirit should not be conceived in a vulgar, simple and rectilinear way. When Engels described the rise of the legal profession in the capitalist division of labour, he especially stressed that a sphere was now opened up 'which, for all its general dependence on production and trade, has also a special capacity for reacting upon these spheres' [letter to C. Schmidt, 27 October 1890]. This 'special capacity for reacting', the 'immanent' spontaneity of the legal sphere (and also of others that have arisen for similar reasons), can in individual cases even lead to sharp conflicts; the subjectively honest bureaucrat, who gives the spontaneity of his particular sphere and his spontaneous behaviour towards it a 'philosophical' deepening, investing it with moral emotion to make it the content of his own life, can very easily come into conflict with the class interests of the bourgeoisie in an individual case. But whatever the upshot of these conflicts: tragic, comic, tragicomic or simply fizzling out, their necessary (if necessarily sporadic) appearance in no way alters the basic fact that the bureaucracy that arises on the basis of the capitalist division of labour, with the 'immanent' spontaneity of its particular individual spheres, provides the securest protection for the overall interests of the bourgeoisie. The conflict in the individual case simply serves as a backdrop for the general convergence.

The elaboration of spontaneity into bureaucracy is only a sharpened consequence of its general society-preserving and socially stabilizing effect, i.e. of habit. Lenin viewed this as so important a social factor that he ascribed it an important role also in the rise of socialism – naturally in a very different direction, and with quite opposite content. Under capitalism, the normal functioning of society requires everyone to be accustomed to the positions allotted them by the spontaneous division of labour; a habituation to duties that spontaneously grows out of these positions assumed in the social division of labour; habituation to the overall course of social development proceeding on its way independent of their will and desires, so that they can only view this development as spectators, any decision as to its direction being removed from their hands. Marx, Engels and Lenin repeatedly showed how the illusion of popular self-decision in the capitalist democracies is precisely just an illusion, forming part of the system of this habituation to the normal functioning of capitalism. The only exception is given by periods of genuine democratic people's revolutions. Remember, for example, how sharply Engels distinguished between the periods before and after 1798 (in his *Critique of the Erfurt Programme*), and called the Third Republic an empire without emperor.

Under capitalism, therefore, habit means a general stupefaction. Through the fact that people view capitalist spontaneity as natural and normal, learning to react to its expressions as to such natural events as a thunderstorm or heatwave – possibly unpleasant, even upsetting, but which can only be accepted as they are – they become habituated to capitalist inhumanity. This habit is of tremendous importance for the ideological aspect of capitalist stability, for it prevents both the rise of any persistent rebellion, such as can develop into a rebellion of principle, against injustice and inhumanity, as well as any enthusiasm for great human uprisings that goes beyond mere spectation and sensation, uprisings which always contain, whether consciously or not, a tendency towards revolt against the capitalist system.

This habituation creates in the people of capitalist society a spontaneous and mechanistic relationship to living events, a relationship of bureaucratic recording. Neither good nor evil decisively interrupts the peaceful 'operation' of this way of life. All really great writers incessantly rage against this stupefaction. Dickens, for example, gives a very pertinent description of the situation in *Dombey and Son*. The civil servant Morlin has failed to notice anything of the radical change in the character of a man whom he sits with each day in the same office. Ashamed of this fact, he lets slip the following true and bitter confession:

> If we were not such creatures of habit as we are, we shouldn't have reason to be astonished half so often. . . . It's this same habit that confirms some of us, who are capable of better things, in Lucifer's own pride and stubbornness – that confirms and deepens others of us in villany – more of us in indifference – that hardens us from day to day, according to the temper of our clay, like images, and leaves us as susceptible as images to new impressions and convictions. . . . [I] was quite content to be as little troubled as I might be, out of my own strip of duty, and to let everything about me go on, day by day, unquestioned, like a great machine – that was its habit and mine – and to take it all for granted, and consider it all right [Chapter 53].

Dickens's justified resentment, however, only paints here a gloomy grey on grey. And this is the ultimate truth of capitalist habit. Its everyday practice, though, in no way rules out sensation, empty excitement, fruitless intoxication. Indeed, just as working people desperate with their lives drug themselves on spirits, or the idle, bored rich on champagne, as a continuous response to this grey-on-grey meaninglessness of capitalist life, so the intoxications and sensations of politics, of public and private life, literature and art, follow a similar course.

Goethe vividly described this situation for a stage of development when the petty-bourgeois element was still predominant in German society. In *Faust* he has one of the burghers say:

> When Sunday comes, or times of holiday,
> Let's talk of fights: there's nothing I like more
> Than news of Turkey: or lands far away,
> Where malcontents have loosed the dogs of war.
> You stand at windows with your drop of drink . . .

> [*Faust*, Part One, translated by Philip Wayne,
> Harmondsworth, 1949, p. 59].

Both style and technique of sensation have since radically changed with capitalist development. But its social function in the process of habit remains the same: the petty-bourgeois philistines, men who had become ossified bureaucrats even in their own personal lives, accepted for years as something 'natural' the hecatomb of the first imperialist world war, including the death of their own sons and brothers; the sensational stories of the daily news only shored up this habit.

This situation can be most clearly illustrated by a counter-example. When first of all an intellectual vanguard, but later followed by broad masses, no longer came to accept the fate of an individual man, the unjustly condemned Captain Dreyfus, as normal and natural, refusing to 'accustom' themselves to it, then a state crisis developed in France. Sensationalism and genuine arousal are in fact mutually exclusive, even if their external appearances are at times very similar. Genuine arousal, however, is turned against the bureaucratic habituation of capitalist spontaneity, and calls for an effort to gain consciousness of the overall process, whereas sensationalism leads back after its barren intoxication to everyday habit, buttressing and reinforcing capitalist spontaneity through the relief it provides.

3. TRAGEDY AND TRAGICOMEDY OF THE ARTIST UNDER CAPITALISM

What the class interests of the bourgeoisie demand of literature and art are habit decked out with sensationalism, stupefaction made tasty by intoxication. The writer as specialist in tension, in 'gripping' stories, intoxication and pacification, is a product of the capitalist division of labour. The class interests of the bourgeoisie accelerate and strengthen this development.

Yet this is a development that in no way proceeds without resistance, no matter how strong the effect of the decisive objective socio-economic factors. Engels showed how the greatness of the men of the Renaissance, the Leonardos and Michelangelos, was based precisely on the fact that they were not yet subject to the capitalist division of labour. This advantage of operating in a still undeveloped capitalism is increasingly lost for the ideologists of the recent period. But the significant people of the post-Renaissance period have felt that the preservation of their universal personal development, their link through many threads to the life of the people, their participation in the most diverse fields of social life, in brief, their non-capitulation to the demands of the capitalist division of labour, is a vital interest of culture. Just as genuine people's revolutions, above all that of 1793–4, fought for the goals of bourgeois democracy against the will of the bourgeoisie, so in the last few centuries ideological progress has taken place in an incessant struggle with the objective conditions and subjective requirements of the rule of the bourgeoisie.

Swift and Voltaire, Diderot and Rousseau, Lessing and Goethe, all wrestled to create glorious islands of human culture against the pressing flood of bourgeois barbarism. But social progress cannot be stayed. Even these brilliant heroic efforts and individual successes necessarily remain individual cases. Capitalism and its economic victory overwhelms ever more the resistance of the genuine bearers of culture. To the degree that the commodity economy becomes universal, all cultural goods also become commodities, and their producers specialists in the capitalist division of labour. At first sight, the development of commoditification – despite the common features that have already been emphasized – seems to form a strict opposite to the path to bureaucratization as sketched above. For in this latter case we observe a growing abstraction from experience, an ever stronger dessication into formal routine (despite or even because of spontaneity), whereas in the former case we have an ever more highly stressed exclusiveness of experience, an ever more stressed rejection of everything that goes beyond experience. The writer becomes a specialist in experience, a virtuoso of immediacy, a recorder of the soul.

There are certainly attempts in the development of modern art to mollify this sharp polarity. From naturalism on, tendencies have time and again emerged that seek to make literature into a 'science' and exclude poetic subjectivity. It is very typical how the founders of German naturalism criticized Zola for his subjectivity, seeking to improve on him precisely by eliminating this. The 'new objectivism', and the literature of 'montage' and 'fact', also displays profound contempt for the experiential subjectivism of the earlier naturalists and objectively goes still further in the direction of the mere recording of naked empirical facts and a dry commentary on them. The worst qualities of the 'specialized sciences' of the era of ideological decline are thus glorified as features of the modern writer: a creeping empiricism, a bureaucratic specialization, and a complete estrangement and divorce from the living connections of the totality.

But this is simply a secondary tendency. It is instructive, for it shows the polar correlation of the cult of experience and bureaucratized 'science' within literature itself. Yet we do not need this assistance to understand the fetishized effects of debasing literature into a commodity even in the case of an emphasized and over-emphasized subjectivity. Experience, the 'personal note', has become the use-value that is needed for marketability, being indispensable if a literary work is to have an exchange-value.

In the self-critical literature of the era of decline – and we shall see later on that a certain self-critical tone is a characteristic feature of this decadence – the comparison with prostitution emerges time and again. Without going into the barren (because practically ineffective) emotional basis of the breast-beating tone that is expressed here, and thus without underlining the value judgement involved in such comparison, we can say that it is correct from an economic standpoint, in that both involve debasing the final remaining human subjectivity into a commodity.

This comparison emerges in Arthur Schnitzler's witty one-act play *Literatur*, being very vividly and convincingly presented. The plot revolves around a man and a woman writer, who have had a love affair together. Naturally, each of them makes their own experience into a novel, and both use the 'experiential' and 'authentic' documents of their love. Both novels, therefore, contain the same complete exchange of love letters, to the mutual surprise and shock of both parties. The man is beside himself with moral outrage because the woman had rewritten each letter before sending it and kept the original drafts for later use. The woman, for her part, is just as violently indignant that her partner had copied his out, and similarly kept them for literary purposes.

This is of course a grotesque extreme case of the prostitution of experience. But the grotesque is always only an imaginary exaggeration of something that really exists already in fact. And the internal contradictions of the experiential basis in the decadent writer become visible here in a manner that is true to life.

In this connection, the common features shared by aesthete and bureaucrat come extraordinarily sharply to the fore. We can remind ourselves again of Tolstoy's *Anna Karenina*. The bureaucrat Karenin has learned of the blossoming love of his wife for Vronski. He prepares himself to reproach Anna and prescribe her rules of behaviour. This is how Tolstoy depicts his train of thought:

> And everything that he would say tonight to his wife took clear shape in Alexey Alexandrovitch's head. Thinking over what he would say, he somewhat regretted that he should have to use his time and mental powers for domestic consumption, with so little to show for it, but, in spite of that, the form and contents of the speech before him shaped itself as clearly and distinctly in his head as a ministerial report [translated by Constance Garnett, London, 1977, p. 145].

In both cases, the stunting of human beings has the same social foundations: divorce from the overall social process, the fetishized acquisition of autonomy by particular partial spheres of activity, the surrender to spontaneity ossified into a 'world outlook' which an autonomizing of this kind necessarily produces. Here we again find the automatic machine depicted by Max Weber, simply that this time it is not judgements or decisions, but rather experiences, that drop out when a coin is thrown into the slot. Here the dance of the dead involved in the rationality of the commodity market is yet a further shade more sinister. A warehouse of pure and immediate experiences is established, a bazaar of 'ultimate things', a bargain sale of human personality at greatly reduced prices.

This is the grotesquely comic final act. But the satire of the kind that we indicated in the case of Schnitzler was preceded by a whole cycle of genuine tragedies. We have already discussed the resistance that the really great representatives of literature opposed to the culture-destroying effects of the capitalist division of labour. The general social lack of prospects of this resistance, however, does not lie only in the fact that the subsumption of the entire society to the capitalist division of labour brought with it for a long while a previously unsuspected unleashing of the productive forces, and thus could not but be irresistible, on account of its economically progressive character, no matter how damaging its effects in culture. The increasing rarity and declining force of this resistance would have necessarily followed from this fact alone. But a further factor also entered in, that of a qualitative change in content.

The decisive new theme is the change in the relationship of the significant artist to the culture of his age, and to the social foundations and developmental tendency of this culture. In other words, the position of such an artist towards the bourgeois class has become problematic. And with the greater shakiness of this basis, the struggle against the cultural consequences of the capitalist division of labour takes on a new and tragically desperate character. For the change in the artist's relationship to his own class now receives the form of appearance of a change in the relationship of art to life. What does it mean, if we recognize in the great writer the type of the tribune in contrast to that of the bureaucrat? In no way necessarily always an immediate political position taken on the concrete questions of the day, or at least not adhesion to one of the parties in struggle, the literary proclamation of their slogans, which is precisely what we do not find with so many great writers. Their character as tribunes, their 'party' character in the

Leninist sense, is often expressed precisely in a rejection of parties altogether. For example, if this rejection is based on the fact that a writer such as Lessing in Germany, or Shelley in England, could see none of the parties, tendencies or groups in existence as suited to represent that great cause of the people, the nation and freedom to which he devoted his life's artistic work. The question is one of this devotion, its intellectual and artistic depths, the intimacy of its roots in the genuine wishes and hopes, the genuine joys and sorrows, of the working people.

The contradiction between the narrow class interests of the bourgeoisie and the culture that arises on the economic and social basis of the development of the productive forces by capitalism is already familiar. The further this development proceeds, the sharper grows the gulf between the bourgeois class interests and the vital demands of culture, even a bourgeois culture. Its social foundations were always pregnant with conflict, and it now ends up in a state of tragic division.

The Archimedean point from which the great writers turn the world upside down, the perspective from which their comprehensive and faithful, deep and generously realistic reflections of the truth of bourgeois society arise as mirrors of human development, has always had something utopian about it. The tragic wisdom which enabled Shakespeare to criticize both the declining feudalism and the birthpangs of capitalism with equal justice, indicating both the tragic splendour of the one, and the demonic forces of blood and dirt invoked by the other, had deep roots in the popular life of his time. From the social standpoint, it was determined by the contradictions that lead the process of humanity on difficult and contorted paths, through unending pain for the people, through the destruction of entire civilizations and the annihilation of flourishing and powerful social strata. But the point from which Shakespeare correctly saw and assessed these human tragedies still had a utopian character; he was chained by the unreality of the unachievable, even if this was true as a popular yearning, and authentic as an impassioned plea for humanity and civilization.

From the social and political point of view, the Archimedean point may well be illusory, yet it subsequently wins reality through its all-round and complete portrayal of life, and through its more genuinely popular character. To express it better, it is indispensable for the portrayal, and seen from the standpoint of the achieved portrayal, it functions for us almost as an ancillary construction, almost as a foreign body when set against the portrayal's realism. This dialectic of the true and the false, the realistic and the utopian, arising from the contradictions of social development itself, the detour via (historically unavoidable) illusion to the firm grasp of historical authenticity and moral eternity, arises from the contradictions of social development itself, and forms the basis of what Engels called the 'triumph of realism'.

In the course of history, however, it becomes ever more difficult to obtain Archimedean points of this kind. Goethe, Walter Scott, Balzac and Tolstoy owe their immortality to a similar dialectic of contradictions (the concrete, historical and social forms and contents of these being of course completely different in each case), but we can already observe with them how this foundation becomes ever more problematic, and the contradictions ever more difficult to resolve.

This development, indeed, turns into something qualitatively opposite. The Archimedean point ceases to provide a comprehensive survey of the whole of human social life, so that emptiness and alienation from life gain the upper hand within it; the contradictions between the utopian starting-point and the comprehensive reproduction of reality give rise ever less frequently to a 'triumph of realism', and a utopianism that often displays its reactionary secondary features plays an ever stronger and more disturbing role in their portrayal itself.

The secret of such Archimedean points is that with writers who have raised themselves to this level, an unbroken love for the people, for life, together with faith in human progress and linkage with the problems of the present, are not cancelled by their unfearing and unreserved utterance of everything that exists, by the most devastating criticism of the inhumanity of social life. To see everything and to love life is a paradox in any class society, a dialectical contradiction, but one that could for a long time have a fertile and creative effect. Only when it is deepened into an alternative devoid of prospects does the writer's tragic dilemma arise, the period of tragedy for art.

It is only the productive interaction of these two contradictory factors of acceptance and negation that prevents artistic work, and the elaboration of specifically aesthetic means of expression, from being distorted into the classic culmination of 'specialization'. Only the love of life gives the artist his unreserved truthfulness towards everything that he perceives and reproduces, his breadth, scope and depth of vision. If a social condition arises in which the artist is forced to hate life, to have contempt for it, and he even begins to develop an attitude of indifference, then the truth of even his best observations is constricted. The surface and the essence of human life grow apart, the former becoming empty and vacuous, requiring invigoration by trimmings that are foreign to the material itself, while the latter becomes alien to life, trivial, or full of simply subjective and false profundities. (So as to avoid any misunderstanding, I should stress again that the contemptuous hate which Shchedrin or Swift poured on the social regime of their time was quite different in kind. Both these men were able to love mankind and life even through this hate, indeed precisely by means of it – certainly in very different ways, according to their differing historical positions.)

The other side of the coin is that when this dissolution arises, when society stamps out the love of life, then art becomes counterposed to life in a deleterious way, art and life growing apart from one another and even mutually hostile. Autonomy is certainly the indispensable atmosphere for the existence of art. But there is autonomy and 'autonomy'. The one is a moment of life itself, the elevation of its richness and contradictory unity; the other is a rigidification, a barren self-seclusion, a self-imposed banishment from the dynamic overall connection.

It is precisely here that we can rightly judge the depth of the Leninist characterization of the relationship between spontaneity and consciousness, with spontaneity as the embryonic form of consciousness. Without a genuine and immediate grasp of life, its surface as well as its depth, without the spontaneous passion of forming the material, there can be no art. For art always involves certain concrete questions: in relation to the writer's own immediate experience of life, the question as to what this is the embryo of, and in relation to the poetic (also spontaneous) passion for beauty and perfection of form, the question as to what the form expresses, what beauty it perfects.

The relationship between lived experience and the vision of form is concealed in a mystic and irrational obscurity, as far as modern discussion on art is concerned. But the objection to its elucidation, i.e. that the theory and history of art are in no position to disclose, for example, the reasons why Leonardo da Vinci was inspired by the model of the Mona Lisa, is no more reasonable or convincing than the stupid demand that the rightly forgotten Professor Krug raised to Hegel, i.e. that if he claimed to have established a system of dialectic, he should be able to 'dialectically derive' his, Professor Krug's, quill pen.

The moment of accident in every detail and specificity can never be abolished, being a moment of the process itself. The task of theory can only be to disclose the general law-like properties of the dialectic of accident and necessity, and to concretely analyse its concrete modes of appearance in the individual cases. The question is therefore one of the general relationship of spontaneity (in both lived experience as in the vision of form) to conscious artistic work (including the artist's work at his world outlook). For in both these spontaneities, as also in the conscious further development and elaboration of the embryos contained in them – objectively, and independent of how the artist sees himself – the reflection of reality lies concealed, so that it depends on the tendencies in social life whether these tendencies converge or diverge in the particular artist.

What is the meaning of the artistic creation for the artist who is still able to love life, whose connection with his fellow men has not yet been broken? Tolstoy's depiction of the work of the painter Mikhailov in *Anna Karenina* sheds a clear light on this whole complex. Mikhailov is making a purely artistic, 'purely formal' change and improvement to his painting.

> But in making these corrections he was not altering the figure but simply getting rid of what concealed the figure. He was, as it were, stripping off the wrappings which hindered it from being distinctly seen. Each new feature only brought out the whole figure in all its force and vigour . . . In all he had painted and repainted he saw faults that hurt his eyes, coming from want of care in taking off the wrappings.

And Tolstoy counterposes to this relationship of artistic work to life the prevailing modern conception in which talent is 'an inborn, almost physical aptitude apart from brain and heart' [loc. cit., pp. 458, 463, 465].

The fact that Tolstoy, who introduces similar oppositions into his aesthetic writings as well, often reaches false conclusions as to the intellectual and social foundation of this antithesis, in no way affects the underlying truth of the contrast itself. And just as little does a similar (or sometimes still greater) lack of consciousness as to the social foundations of this phenomenon reduce the testimony of other modern artists who unreservedly love the truth as to this state of affairs.

On the contrary. The more immediately such writers feel the hostile antithesis between art and life, the more vividly they are able to depict something that is generally valid in modern society, though naturally only if they do not themselves submit without resistance to the immediacy of this experience, but are able rather to gain a human and artistic consciousness of the contradiction contained in it. We can take a very simple example here. In his interesting novel *Le lys rouge*, Anatole France depicts the love between an artist and an aristocratic lady. Only one small episode of this concerns us here. The woman asks her lover on one occasion why he does not want to make a sculpture of her. 'Why,' he replies, 'just because I am a moderately good sculptor. . . . In order to create a figure that is really alive, one has to treat the model as dead matter, tearing from it the beauty that one presses and violates, in order to extract the essence.' In the woman he loves, everything is essential, so that as artist he would stick slavishly to details and never create a total composition.

Were we to try as a thought experiment to apply this view to a Raphael or Titian, we should immediately see that it would be impossible to find a common language between the artists of the Renaissance and those of our own day. The relative autonomy of the process of artistic creation, governed by its own specific laws, had not yet cut adrift from the overall context of life for these earlier artists, indeed the specific laws of the artistic process meant for them the highest subjective increase in their feeling for life, their love of life. This precisely corresponds to the objective situation that the work of art is a concentrated and intensified reflection of life. Even Goethe, who himself vividly experienced the impending approach of the tragedy of the artist in the world of capitalism, and deeply portrayed this, left us an imperishable monument to this earlier unity of art and life, for example in his *Roman Elegies*.

The relationship that the significant artist has to his model is only a special and immediately palpable case of the changed relationship between art and life in general. In Flaubert and Baudelaire, this entire complex stands at the very centre of their aesthetic of desperation, of a philosophy of art that arose from a hatred and contempt for developed bourgeois society. The same is true of Henrik Ibsen: at the end of a long life, and one full of struggle against baseness and the debasing effect of this society, a struggle that developed with his rising despair as to the lack of any escape into a self-criticism of his existence as a writer, this man once again depicted his self-accusation in terms of the tragedy of artist and model.[3] What with Anatole France was only a passing episode (even if important and significant), here becomes the centrepiece of tragedy; i.e. if the artist wants to be honest and true to himself as an artist, and to pursue his path as an artist to its end, then he has necessarily to kill all life in and around himself. The awakening of penitent humanity is delayed with tragic necessity. For being human would have meant renouncing art and the living-out of existence as an artist. Flaubert already proclaimed that '*L'homme n'est rien, l'oeuvre est tout*' ('man is nothing, the work is everything').

This 'dramatic epilogue' of Ibsen's was the tragic summary of a conflict that matured in the nineteenth century and became ever more insoluble. Diderot and Goethe already experienced its approach. In *Rameau's Nephew*, the young Rameau tells the Diderot of the dialogue the story of how a Jewish renegade 'artfully' abducted a fellow believer and delivered him to the Inquisition's torture chamber. Rameau admires the 'art' involved, and arranges his story so that the naked relationship of deceit emerges as the superiority of stronger energy and intelligence over weaker. What is he relating here, if not a modern novel constructed according to the rules of art for art's sake! (Compare Oscar Wilde's *Pen, Pencil and Poison*, and the Karenins, Bilibins and their ilk.) In his dialogue, Diderot still objects with righteous indignation: 'I do not know which I should be more enraged about, the wickedness of the renegade or the tone in which you have spoken of it!' But is this really Diderot's complete meaning? He did after all write the dialogue and create the character of Rameau, and Hegel was right to see in Rameau's 'divided consciousness' the real spirit and authentic dialectic of reality, in contrast to the 'unformed thoughtlessness' represented in the dialogue by the 'honourable consciousness' (the Diderot character).

Yet Rameau is still presented as a depraved outcast. Goethe, however, already saw very clearly, and portrayed this in his *Tasso* in a tragic sense, that authentic artistry has the tendency to drive its bearer out of any human community. A great part of his life's work, in fact, consisted in a struggle against this tendency. Tasso himself is an intensified Werther, and throughout *Wilhelm Meister*, even in *Faust*, there is the attempt to overcome the fate of Tasso in such a way that art and the authentically artistic relationship to work and life is still saved. With Diderot, therefore, we have the perfected type of the estrangement of art from life, yet only as a morally disreputable and witty exception. With Goethe, we have the tragic progress of this estrangement and the unceasing striving to overcome it. Goethe's greatest works revolve around the reestablishment of an already direly threatened universalism, the active reconciliation of the all-round developed personality with bourgeois society. It is important and characteristic in this connection that in *Wilhelm Meister* the artistic life becomes the superseded moment (as similarly does the scholarly life in *Faust*). Goethe investigates broadly and deeply the social foundations of the Tasso tragedy, and he finds (in this breadth and depth, for this breadth and depth, and hence also for Goethe's own life's work) a solution of reconciliation that is of course full of resignation. The tragedy of the fate of Tasso, however, is not cancelled out by this solution; it is rather confirmed and underlined.

It must still be insisted on here that in Goethe's case this conflict is viewed with a far more profound vision than that with which Baudelaire, Flaubert or Ibsen viewed its tragic victims later in the nineteenth century. These writers experienced the modern tragedy of the artist and expressed it as a confession of faith. The real modern tragedy, however, the tragedy of art itself, remained for the most part something unknown to them; only here and there do outlines of it begin to dawn. Their interest in the problem of the hostile alienation of art from life was centred on the human destiny of the isolated creator. They scarcely saw that art itself was falling to pieces.

It was precisely this side of the question, however, that Goethe saw so clearly. Precisely because he could maintain the integrity of his many-sided personal development better than the later tragic figures, he could view the individual victim of the newly approaching conflict in cold blood; his hopes and fears hinged around the fate of art itself. He saw the objective advance of estrangement. He knew very well that man only has access to the macrocosm of the world from the microcosm of his own life, and that the degree of perfection, the fidelity and lifelikeness of artistic and scientific reflections of the macrocosm are dependent on how the microcosmic experiences are directly arranged, and how they are brought to artistic and scientific consciousness. He therefore approached the question 'from without', which in this case meant that he chose a standpoint outside that of the immediate relationship of the artist to the living material with which he was faced. This profound insight led him to prophetic predictions about later artistic development. Thus he said among other things: 'Each thing that exists is an analogy of everything that exists, so that existence always appears to us as at the same time separated and combined. If this analogy is followed too far, then everything coincides as simply identical; if it is shunned, then everything is scattered into infinity. In both cases, reflection stagnates, in the one case being hyperactive, in the other case being killed off.'

This prediction was completely fulfilled at the turn of the twentieth century. Those major writers who immersed themselves deeply in the problematic of their time already had to view the Flaubert-Ibsen problem in a (tragically deepened) Goethean fashion, i.e. to extend the tragedy of the artist into the tragedy of art itself. In this way – either behind the immediate occasions (e.g. the 'model' tragedy), or against abstract backgrounds à la Flaubert – the social and human kernel of the question, the relationship to bourgeois society and its culture, became more clearly apparent than with their predecessors.

The great revolt that fills Romain Rolland's cycle of novels *Jean Christophe* does not complain against 'life', but rather against the bourgeois society of the imperialist age. Rolland, like Goethe, approaches the question of art 'from without'; he takes up the accusation that Balzac made against the reduction of art, and (with it) of artistic experience, to a commodity in his *Lost Illusions*; he depicts the loneliness of the artist, in connection with this universality of the market, as a necessary regression and an equally necessary banishment. The life that has become hostile to art ceases to appear something abstract, and to the same degree the artist's struggle for his external and internal self-preservation becomes a courageously desperate and undaunted attempt to save art itself from drowning in the waves of the capitalist commodity market.

Thomas Mann's well-known short story *Tonio Kröger*, when viewed superficially, seems narrower and less militant. In essence, though, it wages the same struggle. The hostile antithesis between art and life is here, too, already an accomplished fact. But the tragic hero of this important story, Tonio Kröger, already knows that no art is possible without the love of life, while his – very problematic – bourgeois status and his love for life are one and the same thing. Both are similarly and tragically devoid of prospect in the social conditions of imperialist Germany. To Tonio Kröger – and here the story overtly attacks the stylized cult of the demonic of decadence – life appears in the forms of simple girls and boys devoid of problems. The writer, excluded from their homely community, develops against his yearning for life and the impossibility of satisfying this yearning. And he knows (Mann himself of course knowing still better) that this unsatisfied and hence ever renewed yearning, this wound consciously kept open, is a new and specific form of connection with life, with the life of the people, despite all the obstacles and barriers that capitalism in its imperialist stage opposes to such connection; that the renewal and preservation of life is only possible if the artist does not allow 'the social spontaneity of his enforced isolation, the social spontaneity of the hostile antithesis between art and life, to operate unhindered in himself and in his work.

All these stories of Thomas Mann's are of interest for us in a further respect, too, i.e. through their contrasting characters. These brilliantly drawn types of the modern artist find themselves in the same position as Tonio Kröger, simply without his genuine yearning for community with people, for life, and without his pain at the impossible satisfaction of this yearning. They veil themselves proudly in their isolation, establishing

themselves in this hostility to life as in a naturally necessary environment, and then allow all the perceptions and ideas to arise in them that
grow spontaneously out of this condition and are immediately adequate
to it. What is original in them, however, is that in this way they become
comic figures. Of course, others have also depicted the comic aspect in
modern literary life, and we have already recalled Schnitzler's example.
But in Schnitzler's case, his satire precisely bears only on the completely
lifeless, completely commercial and bureaucratic representative of this
type, who is exaggerated in caricature. The really typical modern
aesthete, however, Schnitzler can still see as tragic and noble. In
Thomas Mann's stories, however, the comedy bears on the pure type
itself, his 'nobility' and 'tragedy'.

This is the justified triumph of even the most ordinary and simple life
over a puffed-up barrenness. Here the criticism does not embellish the
victorious side; its hollowness and lifelessness, its inhumanity and lack
of civilization, are pitilessly and sharply illuminated. But the triumph of
even this life, in the tragicomic satire of modern art, opens a perspective
and access to the life which rightly triumphs, with genuine force, over
the conflicts of the era of decay and the types that this produces.

This distinction must be maintained because critical self-laceration is
one of the basic characteristics of the stage of development of our
problem that is now to be discussed. The estrangement of art from life
has already developed here to such an extent that no writer who is at all
serious can possibly remain completely silent about it. All the less so,
when in this era it is the great tragic figures of transition who enjoy the
greatest honour, and are even glorified as models, so that at some points
it is simply seen as a sign of good breeding to proceed via isolation and
estrangement from life into despair. Self-laceration, therefore, can be
easily combined here with self-satisfaction.

But even in those cases that deserve more serious consideration, the
value of such self-criticism is problematic. It remains barren, trapped
within the spontaneity of imperialism and even reinforcing this, in as
much as it lends the writer the aura of sham consciousness and sham
criticism. Hugo von Hofmannsthal has given us the exemplary model of
such a false self-criticism in essay form. This purports to be a letter
written by Lord Chandos to Bacon of Verulam, discussing the singular
conditions of his soul (the decadent soul of the early twentieth century).
He relates how he misses more and more the connection of things, how
he can no longer bear any comprehensive abstraction, how he cuts
himself off inwardly from the human community and lapses into a state

of apathetic indifference. Only purely accidental and empty stimuli –
poisoned rats, a watering-can under a nut tree, and the like – tear him in-
toxicatedly from this spiritual death. He then feels a supernatural dread
beyond any words or concepts, before collapsing again into his twilight
state until the next intoxication.

Hofmannsthal depicts his Lord Chandos as a man in decline, who is
moreover aware of his decline. But this awareness is not honest, for it
remains open whether these states of intoxication are not supposed to
represent something infinitely superior to the normal mode of experience and perception of 'ordinary life'. And indeed, if we peruse Hofmannsthal's critical writings, we do find Chandos-like ecstasies
described as the highest impressions that art can evoke, modern art in
particular (Wassermann's short stories, the paintings of Van Gogh). By
a 'criticism' of this kind, therefore, the decadent type is erected into the
crowning figure of profound refinement.

Hyperactive or deadened, that was how Goethe characterized the
modern distortion of art. We should certainly not go against the intention of Goethe's criticism were we to add that these polar opposites are
found side by side in the art of the decadent period, and constantly
collapse into one another. Hofmannsthal's Lord Chandos and his ilk
can hardly be any better characterized than in these words of Goethe's.

We have now returned, however, to our earlier definition, to intoxication and stupefaction as general spiritual characteristics of habituation
to the most fearful inhumanity of declining capitalism, to what the class
interests of the bourgeoisie require of art. This sterile intoxication is not
only an ancillary phenomenon to the dullness of habit, it actually
strengthens the worst aspects of this. The more noble and select it
makes itself out to be, the more critically it behaves, then the more this
tendency is apparent. And in this way the art of decadence flows into
the stream whose waters are designed to protect the threatened citadels
of imperialism from the revolt of the working people – quite irrespective
of what the individual artist may have intended. In the spontaneous
embryos from which this kind of art grows, an oppositional intent may
well be expressed from time to time. But the confinement to spontaneity,
and its theoretical and critical glorification, make no other development
possible save that of a monotonous and barren alternation between intoxication and stupefaction.

Talent and acumen are of little use here. Few writers have exposed
the 'counterfeit' character of modern decadent ideologists more acutely
than André Gide. But this did not prevent Gide himself from ending up
among the counterfeiters.

4. THE ACTUALITY OF LENIN'S ANTITHESIS

The victory of socialism ends the period of tragedy for art as well. The hostile separation of art and life comes to an end once the exploitation and oppression of the working people are abolished, and the people organize their social life in accordance with their own economic and cultural interests, i.e. according to the interests of everyone except a tiny handful of exploiters.

The victory of socialism produces a fertile interaction between artist and life, at a level that has previously never been attained. The abnormal disunity in the relationship between the writer and his public is ended, so that the writer once again comes to share the people's deepest feelings, struggling with them in their most important battles. By striving for the genuine specific goals of art, the artist fulfils at the same time certain important social tasks. And because human progress is expressed in his works, life, art and thought are combined into a deep organic unity. Because he proclaims the actually solvable character of all former conflicts in social life, he does not force on the artistic material, the literary form, any demands that are foreign to it, but simply draws realistic conclusions from what is happening every day in reality itself.

The relationship of the artist to life, and hence also to art itself, thus also takes a radical new turn.

But does this mean that the experiences of the history of art in the last century, and the lessons that we have tried to win from this history with the aid of Lenin's brilliant insights, have lost all actuality? Are they already doomed for the realm of oblivion, having at most a purely historic interest for us today?

We believe this is not the case. Above all, we must not forget that any social transformation means, for the ideology that arises on its basis, at first only a possibility, a change in the direction and kind of effect, in the intensity of the space in which social forces contend. The transformation of this possibility into reality is never an automatic result of the social moments, but rather of the conscious activity of human beings on the basis of such a change.

Bolshevik self-criticism, as a basic feature of the Lenin-Stalin period, rests on comparing what has been realized with what is objectively possible on the basis of the social situation. The acuteness and unreserved character of this self-criticism is therefore a token of sureness and strength. It discloses defects that are necessary products of former development, but which, as survivals of a social world that has partly perished already, and is partly condemned to perish, not only should be overcome, but also can be overcome. The possibility of the new that is inherent in the social conditions and forces is not only the measure of what has been achieved, but at the same time also the motor of achievement. The sharper this self-criticism appears, the greater is this justly impatient conviction.

This dialectic of possibility and reality thus determines our assessment of Soviet literature from the standpoint of our present problem. We must consequently direct our attention to the social phenomenon of bureaucracy in Soviet life. And as long as we cannot yet say that bureaucracy has vanished from the social reality without trace, then we are still obliged to investigate very carefully its ideological influences in all areas, including those of literature and art, and to combat these unreservedly. Naturally, bureaucracy in socialist society has a different significance from bureaucracy under capitalism, so that the corresponding literary phenomena are also different in kind. And because interactions in the spheres of ideology are extraordinarily complex, we must be prepared right from the start for very great distinctions. But as long as the social phenomenon of bureaucracy is still present, its ideological effects and influences can also not cease to be relevant. Bureaucracy also exists in our socialist society. Lenin already began the struggle against it in 1918, and anyone who would say that this battle is completely at an end with the rout of the enemy would fail to see the full complexity of the real situation. It is sufficient to recall the criticism of bureaucracy that Stalin and Kaganovitch made at the Seventeenth Congress of the CPSU(B). Both Lenin and Stalin viewed the perpetuation of bureaucracy as a damaging inheritance of capitalism, as well as an inheritance of the particular economic and cultural backwardness of prerevolutionary Russia. The abolition of bureaucracy thus forms part of the Stalinist programme for liquidating the economic and ideological survivals of capitalist society.

This struggle and programme already clearly show the fundamental distinction, i.e. while under capitalism bureaucracy is an important and indispensable social component, under socialism it is a foreign body to be dispensed with. In capitalist society, ideological resistance to the 'spirit' of bureaucracy is an aspect of the general fact that everything that is culturally progressive and valuable can only prevail against the tide of specifically bureaucratic spontaneity. The contradictions that emerge in this connection form a characteristic feature of capitalist society, and are inseparably bound up with it.

The situation under socialism is quite different. It is true that the survivals of capitalism also have their pernicious spontaneity in socialist society. And the danger of this is yet further increased by the influence of the capitalist encirclement of the Soviet Union and the planned activity of the enemies of socialism. This danger must not be conceived in too narrow a sense. It does not just involve certain dubious or vacillating elements being corrupted, seduced and recruited by the enemy. The mere existence of bureaucracy in a Soviet institution, even if the individual bureaucrats are subjectively honest, objectively amounts to assistance to the hostile powers. On the one hand, because bureaucracy objectively establishes a protective wall behind which the enemies can comfortably conceal themselves and readily manoeuvre. On the other hand, because the bureaucratic treatment of any single question – even when there is no deliberate evil intent – inhibits the economic and cultural development of socialism.

L. M. Kaganovitch, in his articles against the '*funktionalka*', indicated how the organization of the national economy as a unitary whole is foreign to capitalism.

This organization is one of the central questions for the construction of socialism. For the bureaucrat, though, it is characteristic, as we have seen, that his activity does not stand in any connection with the dynamic unity of the totality. (This is of course a question of deeds and not words. In words, the Soviet bureaucrat always declares himself an enthusiastic supporter of overall economic planning.) Even in the case of subjective honesty, he commits actions that cannot possibly serve this unitary organization of the economic whole, but necessarily produce disorder, disorganization, and estrangement from the interests of the people.

Bureaucracy is a foreign body under socialism. This means first of all that it can only have a damaging effect, whereas under capitalism it is something useful (even if in a contradictory and relative way), or at the very least something indispensable. Under capitalism, accordingly, the spontaneity of the economy not only reproduces bureaucracy at an ever higher level, but the ruling capitalist class, its state and its ideological apparatus, deliberately foster the extension and development of bureaucracy. Under socialism, on the other hand, the development of the economy itself, the awakening of the masses to cultural life and the ever stronger unfolding of democracy all bring into play a counter-movement against bureaucracy, and the state, the Communist Party and the social organizations all wage a conscious struggle for its liquidation.

The question of the spontaneous and immediate reaction of the masses to the social reality must also be tackled from a new perspective under the conditions of victorious socialism. There can be no doubt that the life built on socialist principles necessarily exercises a spontaneous effect on the masses, a broad and strong effect. And here we come up against Lenin's question of social habit once again.

In Lenin's depiction of the economic conditions for the withering away of the state in socialist society, he stresses how:

> freed from capitalist slavery, from the untold horrors, savagery, absurdities and infamies of capitalist exploitation, people will gradually *become accustomed* to observing the elementary rules of social intercourse that have been known for centuries and repeated for thousands of years in all copybook maxims. They will become accustomed to observing them without force, without coercion, without subordination, *without the special apparatus* for coercion called the state [*The State and Revolution, Collected Works*, Vol. 25, p. 462].

Lenin stresses that the expression used by Marx and Engels, that 'the state withers away', precisely indicates 'both the gradual and the spontaneous nature of the process'. 'Only habit can, and undoubtedly will, have such an effect', once social life is so constituted that 'there is nothing that arouses indignation, evokes protest and revolt, and creates the need for *suppression*' (Lenin's emphasis).

This elementary educational effect of socialist society can be scarcely too highly assesed. But the continuously harmful (opportunist) influences of an undialectical understanding of this question precisely show what new relevance falls to Lenin's old doctrine of the relationship of consciousness and conscious activity to spontaneity under the conditions of socialism. In a concretization and further development of this doctrine that is as original as it is profound, Stalin applies it to the problem of the withering away of the state, in his speech to the Seventeenth Congress of the CPSU(B). Here he showed clearly and convincingly how the conception of this development as a 'spontaneous process' leads to carelessness, passivity and disarmament in the face of the enemy. The proponents of this new and supposedly 'socialist' theory of spontaneity believed 'that soon there would be no classes, and therefore no class struggle, and therefore no cares and worries, and therefore [that] it is possible to lay down one's arms and go to bed – to sleep in expectation of the advent of a classless society'. Stalin showed, on the contrary, that 'a classless society cannot come of its own accord, as it were. It has to be achieved and built by the efforts of all the working people, by strengthening the organs of the dictatorship of the proletariat, by intensifying the class struggle, by abolishing classes, by eliminating the remnants of the capitalist classes, and in battles with enemies, both internal and external' [*Works*, Vol. 13, pp. 358 and 357]. We see, therefore, that the dialectical relationship between spontaneity and consciousness as depicted by Lenin is still valid under the fundamentally different circumstances of socialist society. Here, too, spontaneity is simply the embryonic form of consciousness. Here, too, socialist consciousness, the activity of socialism aware of its goal, must intervene so that this embryo develops into a flower. 'Of its own accord', through spontaneity alone, distortion, confusion and error can arise from the same possibilities that are inherently contained in the spontaneity of socialist life.

And yet the environment in which this struggle is waged has now radically changed. The disposition towards socialism is no longer spontaneously alive only in the working class. The economy rather develops in all strata of the working people a readiness for socialism, a willingness to be reeducated in a socialist direction, to be transformed as human beings, a 'habituation' to the conditions of a truly human life. Here again, however, the transformation of these possibilities into reality has to follow the road of socialist consciousness.

All this clearly shows the general relevance of Lenin's antithesis today. And it is similarly illuminating that under the conditions thus depicted the realms of ideology in the narrower sense are also not free from capitalist survivals, no more than they can be from bureaucracy. It is sufficient here to refer to the judgement of the situation made in the last decision of the Central Committee of the CPSU(B) on the condition of party propaganda. This decision recognized a serious backwardness among a section of theoretical workers 'in their fear to boldly raise topical theoretical questions, in the widespread presence of hairsplitting and over-nice distinctions, in the vulgarizing and trivializing of certain principles of Marxism-Leninism, in a backwardness of theoretical ideas, and in the insufficient theoretical generalization of the powerful practical experiences that the party has collected in all areas of socialist construction'. What does this criticism mean, if not that a section of these workers on the theoretical front are not tribunes of the people, but bureaucrats – precisely in the sense of Lenin's *What Is To Be Done?*.

Are these considerations also applicable to literature? It would be ridiculous to try and find 'bureaucratic' tendencies in the work of the broad stratum of eminent Soviet writers. Socialist literature, when taken as a whole, is one of the strongest champions of genuine socialist culture and the struggle against the survivals of capitalism. And even among those writers who may be justly criticized in the spirit of the above quotation, such criticism should not be mechanically transferred from the other ideological fields to which it was originally directed, without the specific problems of literature being borne in mind. Of course there are capitalist survivals also in literature, an excess of them; but their forms are specific and complex, their characteristics rarely appearing as immediate and direct in their appearance.

Under the conditions of socialism, we must find our starting-point among the survivals of capitalism. We can refer to the 1936 discussion on formalism and naturalism. There is no question but that both literary tendencies are survivals of capitalism, and indeed, if we are not to trivialize and do violence to literary history in a vulgarly sociological fashion, we must say that they are survivals of its ideological decline. If they were therefore relatively widespread for a time in Soviet literature, this means that their social roots were akin to what Lenin and Stalin have pointed out about bureaucracy.

These literary styles arose on the basis of capitalist decadence out of an ideology that has lost the will and ability to grasp the social totality in its movement and reproduce it in a true-to-life fashion. All the forms of expression that subsequently arise are surrogates which essentially remain simply on the surface of things.

Socialism, however, is the actual overcoming of all economic and social foundations of this decadence. So if the ideological encirclement of capitalism has the effect that forms of expression of bourgeois decadence are taken over into the literature of socialism, the proximate causes of this lie in the survivals of the former general cultural backwardness of Russia that was the legacy of tsarism. Just as half-educated provincials like to blindly imitate even the most crackpot 'fashions' of the metropolis, so one section of our writers have taken over the literary 'achievements' of the imperialist West. Both the form of this appropriation and the certain effect it has had indicate that the backwardness of literary mass culture is still not completely overcome, just as the bureaucratization of our state apparatuses (as Lenin wrote in the early 1920s) indicated the lack of education of the popular masses in regard to democracy, their inability at that time to really govern and actually administer their own affairs.

But the affinity with bureaucracy is still more striking when we consider the question from the aesthetic point of view. We have already seen how indifference towards content and context is a characteristic of the bureaucratic relationship to life. The bureaucrat lives within a world of forms with apparent laws of its own, being the bearer of its spontaneity.

I have already shown, both here and elsewhere, how questionable are the means of expression peculiar to bourgeois decadence. Yet they are in a certain sense adequate to the very restricted, narrow, crippled and often mendacious perceptions which they arose to give expression to. Only a writer, however, who has a deeply bureaucratized, inwardly indifferent relationship to both forms and contents of the new life, a relationship that is only concerned with external form, could try and portray the rise of the new socialist society and the birth of the new socialist man in terms of the decadent means of expression.

When formalism and naturalism arose in Soviet literature, therefore, they were necessarily even more abysmal than their bourgeois prototypes. For every concrete artistic form is the form of a specific content. Its character depends on the one hand on the breadth and depth with which objective reality is reflected at a particular period, and on the other hand on the feelings, ideas and experiences which it arose to give expression to. The modern prejudices as to a supposed independence of forms of expression from these foundations of experience and world outlook (which are at bottom of course social foundations) are no more than prejudices, whether they are proclaimed with pseudo-scientific objectivity, or whether they serve to declare certain literary means of literary expression, such as those of naturalism, impressionism and expressionism, to be 'eternal forms' of human subjectivity in general.

This self-deception on the part of modern writers has nothing to do with the real objectivity of artistic forms, which precisely involves the necessity of historical changes in concrete forms of expression. From this standpoint, any particular form appears to stand in the closest dialectical connection with changes in those social and historical contents to which it gives temporary expression. The authentic objectivity of artistic forms rests on an agreement with the content, on a profound, comprehensive and correct reflection of the general features of the objective reality itself, those that recur in a law-like manner.

The reason why modern decadence is so dubious is precisely because it does not possess either the will or ability for this deep and comprehensive reflection of reality. Wherever something humanly touching and gripping does occur, despite everything, within the general framework of this problematic, something like a genuine artistic value, then this has its origin in the agreement between the form of expression and the experiential foundation. Hence there is at times something moving in the trembling despair in the face of the uncomprehended inhumanity of later capitalism that certain naturalist works exhibit, when they touchingly embody this very despair in the trivial everyday disunity of their language, the banal plotlessness of their construction and the stupefied and crippled humanity of their characters. Even the blind and goalless explosion of rage over certain especially blatant acts of inhumanity can in certain circumstances contain a kind of pathos that enables the naked fact, the unelaborated, artistically unworked 'document', not linked up with totality, movement or law, but abstractly containing simply a human destiny, to appear sufficient to expose the absurdity of capitalism. Even montages, produced out of a deep despair over the disunity and disconnection of existence, the heap of heterogenous splinters which is how the writer experiences life under capitalism, can movingly produce a feeling of this kind.

But the claim that these tendencies produce on such foundations any genuine picture of the world, i.e. genuine works of art, must be sharply rebuffed. Where they do have the above described effect, they do so – without knowing or intending – as documents of the destruction of all humanity by capitalism, which in its death-throes spreads the plague of decay. But precisely this extremely just verdict on the products of literary decadence requires the most decisive rejection of its influence on the literature of socialism. These decadent forms cannot be used to portray the rise of a new world and its new human beings. The sparse, thin and problematic poetry of despair, which only manages to create a subjective authenticity out of the depths, cannot find tones for celebrating the rebirth of humanity and humankind. If this is attempted, one is immediately struck by the barbarically backward lack of culture that is expressed in this crude incongruence between form and content. If this impression is given a concept, however, then what we have is simply a dubious artistic and human bureaucratism. The naturalists and formalists of Soviet literature take over these forms from Western literature – uncritically following the spontaneity of a literary existence that has become abnormal under socialism – without paying the slightest attention to their experiential foundations. They form the conception of a 'professionalism' and 'mastery of technique' independent of reality, content and world outlook, as an 'almost physical aptitude apart from brain and heart' – as Tolstoy put it. The more cleverly this is developed, the more bureaucratic is the relationship that such writers assume to the literary forms. They develop into literary Bilibins.

With this bureaucratic relationship to the content, we are dealing with a phenomenon that stretches beyond the supporters of naturalism and formalism. The worshippers of Western decadence are now on the retreat. There was a period when they were almost completely concerned with transferring psychological 'problems' of bourgeois decadence into Soviet actuality. The development of socialism has led to the disappearance of this kind of 'literature'. (Certain individual regressions are not important.) But those artists who have not completely overcome the survivals of decadence within themselves, went on to find new forms of anti-realism. One such form is the formal, empty, bureaucratic 'optimism' expressed in certain works that appear at first sight to be socialist, but are in actual fact dead, devoid of ideas, and useless and ineffectual both from the standpoint of aesthetics and from that of propaganda.

An optimism without quotation marks, such as fills the work of the great teachers and tribunes of socialism, grows out of a comprehensive understanding of the dialectic of overall human development. Even amid the horrors of the capitalist world, they proclaimed the irresistible final victory of liberated humanity, and this prediction based on profound knowledge illuminated the dismal descriptions of capitalist hell that Marx and Engels gave of England, and Lenin and Stalin of Russia. This optimism without quotation marks let the light of hope for a successful outcome shine in the speeches and writings of Lenin and Stalin, even in the most difficult times for the direly threatened Soviet republic. But the same optimism led Lenin and Stalin to see in socialism the weapon, object and goal of a serious battle, an arduous process of the birth of the new that was hemmed in with danger. The optimism of the tribunes of the socialist revolution consists in fearless contemplation of the external and internal threats, in the fearless exposure of obstacles and barriers, and the full understanding of the dialectical contradictions that lead by various routes to the final liberation of humanity.

And this is also the creative road pursued by the socialist revolution's greatest literary tribune, Maxim Gorky, as well as by his talented and worthy successors in Soviet literature. Bureaucratic 'optimism', on the other hand, makes the process with its contradictions and difficulties simply vanish. For this school, the only events that exist are victories won without struggle or effort: the resistance of the external enemy, and the internal resistance within men themselves, hindering the birth of socialist man and in individual cases frustrating this, does not exist for them. It is only brought in as a bogy, and the clown of bureaucratic 'optimism' easily despatches it with a well-aimed blow of his stick.

The bureaucrat, likewise, faces no real resistance in his world of files, where everything is settled smoothly and without friction along the well-travelled rails of precedent and classification that are always to hand.

The struggle against those tendencies to a bureaucratization of art that still obtain can only be successfully waged 'from without', i.e. from outside the immediate relationship of the artist to his material. For its roots lie in the social existence of the individual artist, in the survivals of the capitalist division of labour, which, as we have seen, produced the separation of the artist from the life of society, and the false 'specialization of the artist'. This division of labour has been destroyed by the victory of socialism, as far as its foundations are concerned. Yet this still does not mean that its survivals, in both being and consciousness, have been everywhere liquidated without a remainder.

The construction of socialism in one country requires tremendous efforts. The all-round appropriation of culture, the conquest of all of its areas, is not an easy or rectilinear process. It must necessarily involve the detour of specialization. The task, however, is to bring every real conquest of a partial area into a living connection with the development of the society as a whole. For wherever this connection is broken or ossified, the bureaucratic distortion of specialism necessarily arises. This is what Marx says of the position of the artist under communism:

> The exclusive concentration of artistic talent in particular individuals, and its suppression in the broad mass which is bound up with this, is a consequence of division of labour . . . with a communist organization of society, there disappears the subordination of the individual to some definite art, making him exclusively a painter, sculptor, etc. . . . In a communist society there are no painters but only people who engage in painting among other activities [*The German Ideology, Collected Works*, Vol. 5, p. 394].

Our socialist development has not yet reached this stage. But the clear perspective of this development is an important signpost even for today. Communist human universality, the shaking off the yoke of the division of labour, does not in any way mean dilettantism, but on the contrary the highest development of all abilities, the specialized ones naturally included. The question today is to bring these two still contradictory and opposed poles into a fruitful harmony: the complete mastery of individual fields that is indicated today, and the living and many-sided connection with the development of the society as a whole that must fertilize the individual work.

The classical inheritance, the model of Leonardo and Michelangelo, Diderot and Goethe, provides us here with an indispensable guide. What the primitive level of division of labour made possible in class society must be fully attainable for the first time in the period of its socialist transformation.

But the most relevant and effective reminder is the Leninist ideal of the tribune. This most clearly expresses the concrete connection with the demands of the day. Maxim Gorky took this road that Lenin had pointed to. His writings most strikingly show how little a great writer need be 'only a writer', how in such an individual the political is transformed into the human and the human into the political, so that a unitary and high level of literature arises from the interaction of the two. They show how fruitful it is, precisely in the aesthetic sense, to approach the problems of literature 'from without'. The great artists have always striven to work in this way. It is precisely the really great artists, who loved life and studied it, who became conscious of the real significance of the immediate phenomena that they grasped with their senses and created new artistic means for correctly reflecting newly developing aspects of life in their art.

These final considerations seek above all to demonstrate the living relevance of the antithesis of tribune and bureaucrat. But the foundation of this argument still remains capitalist society, whose survival and encirclement still exerts a certain temporary influence upon Soviet literature.

No detailed explanations are required to see that the struggle of progressive writers in the capitalist countries against reactionary and decadent barbarism is waged under far more difficult conditions, and that there the spontaneity of the capitalist economy continuously produces and reproduces bureaucracy, the reactionary bourgeoisie also fostering with all means in literature the development of the bureaucratic spirit in its most diverse manifestations.

The revolt of progressive writers against the barbarism of imperialism and in defence of culture is a struggle for the deepest vital interests of literature, when it seeks to tear this from its bureaucratic and aesthete-like isolation and turn the writer back into a tribune. It is only in this form, as a tribune of the people, that progressive literature can win the people back for literature, and literature for the people, by way of this victory driving the capitalist enemy of culture ideologically from the field and so helping to prepare his political defeat.

Notes

Introduction

1 The following are the English-language editions of Lukács's works referred to in this introduction (all are published by Merlin Press except where otherwise stated): *History and Class Consciousness (H & CC)*, introduced and translated by Rodney Livingstone, 1968; *Political Writings, 1919–1929*, introduced by Rodney Livingstone, translated by Michael McColgan (New Left Books, 1972); *Studies in European Realism*, introduced by Roy Pascal, translated by Edith Bone (Hillway Publishing Co., 1950; reprinted, without the introduction, Merlin Press, 1978); *The Young Hegel*, introduced and translated by Rodney Livingstone, 1975; *The Historical Novel*, translated by Hannah and Stanley Mitchell, 1962; *Soul and Form*, translated by Anna Bostock, 1974; *The Theory of the Novel*, translated by Anna Bostock, 1971; *Goethe and His Age*, translated by Robert Anchor, 1968; *Writer and Critic*, translated by Arthur Kahn, 1970.

2 Ferenc Feher, 'Lukács in Weimar', in *Telos*, 39, Spring 1979, p. 132 (hereafter Feher).

3 Michael Löwy, *From Romanticism to Bolshevism*, New Left Books, 1979 (hereafter Löwy).

4 Review of Löwy in *New Society*, 24 January 1980, p. 125.

5 'Der Nachruhm Balzacs', in *Die Rote Fahne*, no. 193, 26 April 1922.

6 *Mimesis*, Princeton University Press, 1968, pp. 433–4.

7 A good general account can be found in Fredric Jameson, *Marxism and Form*, Princeton University Press, 1971, Chapter 3.

8 *Die Rote Fahne*, 17 October 1920 (quoted in Helga Gallas, *Marxistische Literaturtheorie*, Luchterhand, Neuwied/Berlin, 1971, p. 26).

9 See Fritz Raddatz, *Lukács*, Rowohlt, Reinbek, 1972, p. 70.

10 *Lef* (i.e. Left Front in Art) was a periodical published by Mayakovsky from 1923 to 1925. Its contributors were members of the literary avant-garde, such as Viktor Khlebnikov and Viktor Shklovsky, and it defended modernist views based on Futurism and Constructivism. Its successor, *Novi Lef* (1927–8), called for a literature of facts.

11 See 'Brecht on Lukács', in Ernst Bloch et al., *Aesthetics and Politics*, New Left Books, 1977, pp. 70–1.

12 In 'Georg Lukács and Critical Realism', in *Marxism in Our Time*, Oxford University Press, 1972, p. 285.

The Novels of Willi Bredel

1 Willi Bredel (1901–1964) joined the Socialist Youth Movement while an apprentice lathe-operator; he was a member of the Spartacus League in 1918. He spent two years in prison for taking part in the Hamburg Uprising of October 1923. In 1929 he was sentenced to a further two years' gaol for criticizing the Berlin chief of police for his handling of a riot. While in gaol he wrote *Maschinenfabrik N & K* which made use of his experiences working for Nagel & Kaemp. After a period in the Soviet Union he was put in a concentration camp for thirteen months. He escaped via Czechoslovakia to the Soviet Union in 1934. He was co-editor, with Bertolt Brecht and Lion Feuchtwanger of *Das Wort*, a German-language literary journal produced in Moscow (1936–9). He served as a political commissar in the Spanish Civil War, spent the Second World War in the Soviet Union, and returned to East Germany where he became president of the Academy of Arts in 1962.

2 Ernst Thälmann (1886–1944) was general-secretary of the German Communist Party, and Heinz Neumann (1902–1939?) one of its leading members.

3 Emil Ludwig (1881–1948) was the author of best-selling biographies in Germany in the twenties, for instance of Goethe and Napoleon.

4 For Gotsche's reply to Lukács, see Introduction, pp. 14–15.

5 Leopold Averbach (1903–1938) was head of the Russian Association of Proletarian Writers from 1930 to 1932.

6 H.R. was one of the workers quoted by Gotsche in his reply (see Introduction, p. 15).

7 Stalin attacked the historian Slutsky, accusing him of 'smuggling' Trotskyism into the Bolshevik movement, in 'Some Questions Concerning the History of Bolshevism' in 1931 (Stalin, *Collected Works*, Vol. 13, Moscow, 1955).

'Tendency' or Partisanship?

1 Georg Herwegh (1817–1875) and Ferdinand Freiligrath (1810–1876), both associates of Marx, were leading poets of the German revolutionary movement in the nineteenth century.

2 Franz Mehring (1846–1919), biographer of Marx and a leading Social Democrat historian, also wrote influential essays on literature and philosophy.

3 *Philosophy of Mind* (Part 3 of the *Encyclopedia*), translated by Miller and Findlay, Oxford, 1971, para. 389, p. 30. [G.L.'s note.]

4 This tendentious adjustment of reality, designed to introduce in an artistically organic manner a 'tendency' that does not arise organically out of the material of reality itself, is not only to be found in the bad literature of the declining bourgeoisie. To give but a few examples, we find it in the

second half of Goethe's *Elective Affinities*, in the dramas of Hebbel after 1848, and in Dostoyevsky, of whom Gorky justly says that he slanders his own characters. [G.L.'s note.]

Reportage or Portrayal?

1 Ernst Ottwalt (pseudonym of Ernst Nicolas, 1901–1943). Ottwalt made his way from the extreme right (he belonged to a *Freikorps* after the German defeat in 1918) to the Communist Party and the League of Proletarian Revolutionary Writers. He wrote a number of anti-fascist novels and stories as well as collaborating with Brecht on the script of the film *Kuhle Wampe*. After emigrating in 1933 he went to Denmark, Prague and Moscow where he was arrested in 1936 and all trace of him was lost. His wife, who had survived after the Soviets had handed her over to the Gestapo, tried to discover his whereabouts when the Soviet prosecutor at Nuremberg included a lengthy quotation from Ottwalt's *Deutschland Erwache!* ('Germany Awake!') in his opening speech. Her plea went unanswered but it was later learnt that Ottwalt had died in a labour camp in Archangel in 1943.

2 Ernst Ottwalt, *Denn sie wissen, was sie tun. Ein deutscher Justiz-Roman*, Berlin, Malik Verlag, 1931. [G.L.'s note.]

3 Jens Peter Jacobsen (1847–1885) was a Danish novelist influenced by Flaubert, best known in Germany for his novel *Niels Lyhne* (1880). He was also the author of the late romantic poetry set to music by Schoenberg as the *Gurrelieder*.

4 Engels on the legal profession in his letter to C. Schmidt of 27 October 1890, Marx–Engels *Selected Correspondence*, Moscow, 1965, p. 422. Engels goes on to state that this principle, if in modified form, applies also for 'the realms of ideology which soar still higher in the air' (ibid., p. 423). [G.L.'s note.]

5 The 'no longer' here pertains to the creative methods of the bourgeois class, when this was still revolutionary, the 'not yet' to those of the proletariat. Nothing is to be gained by harking back to the revolutionary literary traditions of one's own class, if this class has no further revolutionary future ahead of it. Achievement of the revolutionary proletarian creative method requires that the writer should make a complete break with his own class, and that includes the ideology of this class. Membership of the proletarian political party is in no way sufficient by itself, let alone mere sympathy with this party. On the other hand, a necessary objective factor is that the development of the revolutionary workers' movement has reached the level at which these questions can be posed. [G.L.'s note.]

6 The same applies to the great realist writers of the revolutionary period of the bourgeoisie, with the provision that in their case this recognition is constricted by their class position, so that their method can only be based on a naïve materialism and instinctive dialectics. [G.L.'s note.]

7 A reference to H. R. Knickerbocker's *Deutschland, So oder So* (Berlin, 1932).

8 Superseded in the dual Hegelian sense – i.e. on the one hand the abolition of the moment's autonomy, its reduction to a mere moment, the demonstration that it is a mere appearance, and on the other hand the insistence that it does have an objective existence as an appearance, a moment, as a part of the overall process – even in its relative autonomy. [G.L.'s note.]

9 At the Leipzig Cheka trial in 1925 German communists were accused of planning to set up a party secret police, or Cheka, in connection with alleged assassination attempts prior to the abortive communist uprising of October 1923.

10 Tolstoy's limitations are not at issue here. On these I would refer yet again to Lenin's essays. [G.L.'s note.]

11 Lenin, 'Leo Tolstoy as the Mirror of the Russian Revolution', in *Collected Works*, Vol. 15, p. 206. [G.L.'s note.]

12 Hegel, *Logic*, trans. Wallace, Oxford, 1975, section 133; p. 189. It goes without saying that Hegel, as an idealist, does not emphasize the content as the overriding moment. [G.L.'s note.]

13 Sergei Tretyakov (1892–1939), avant-garde Soviet writer, leading protagonist of 'the literature of facts', and translator into Russian of Brecht (see Introduction, pp. 15–16).

14 *Den-Schi-Chua*, Berlin, 1932 (English translation, *A Chinese Testament*, New York, 1934). [G.L.'s note.]

15 It is impossible here to depict the social foundations for the turn towards reportage as a creative method in the case of worker writers. Behind certain similarities of method there undoubtedly lie similarities of social existence: the narrowness of class basis. But in the case of worker writers this usually derives from sectarian tendencies, for example the consideration and description of reality exclusively from the standpoint of a party functionary, generally leading to ultra-left errors (underestimation of the difficulties facing the developing revolution), etc., whereas, in the case of the petty-bourgeois writers who are coming round to a proletarian position, the narrowness of the class basis which we have analysed tends for the most part to give rise to rightest errors. [G.L.'s note.]

16 Ottwalt's reply to Lukács had appeared in the *Linkskurve* in October 1932 (see Introduction, p. 15 above).

17 I feel all the more obliged to take a strong stand against this error in that it plays a certain role in my own book *History and Class Consciousness* (1923), naturally on different philosophical premises. My wrong view at that time had the same social basis as Ottwalt's present error: an inadequate integration with the revolutionary workers' movement and hence a rigidity of method: the slide from materialist dialectics into idealism or mechanism (or both). [G.L.'s note.]

18 A few words are necessary here on what Comrade Ottwalt says about the

role of science. The great representatives of literary portrayal took it for granted that they should make use of and depict in their writing the highest results of the science of their age (cf. Fielding, Goethe, Balzac, etc.). It is around Zola's time, however, and in his own writing too, that science begins to become an inorganic component of literature itself. Ottwalt's example of Ibsen's *Ghosts* shows this very clearly, for here the theory of genetic inheritance is used in a way that is more than questionable, as far as its content is concerned, being also mythologized in form so as to express a mechanical fatalism that does not exist in the real world. [G.L.'s note.]

19 New Objectivism (*Neue Sachlichkeit*), which flourished in Germany in the late nineteen twenties, represented a non-political recoil from the emotional effusions of expressionism. Typical exponents included the left independent Erich Kästner and the right wing Ernst Jünger. The accent on cool detachment also left its mark on Brecht, even though he satirized its conformist ideology.

20 Jacob Wassermann (1873–1934). A highly successful popular novelist, friendly with Hugo von Hofmannsthal, Arthur Schnitzler and Thomas Mann. He was the bourgeois novelist *par excellence*; his works are now forgotten.

21 Fyodor Panferov (1896–1960) attracted attention with his two-part novel *Brusski* (1930) which portrayed the conflict between old and new in a Russian village.

22 I refer to Gorky and Panferov here simply as two major examples (without wanting to compare them in any other way), as they both apply a similar creative method. I assumed that these examples were familiar to everyone. I was not prepared for such an outrageous judgement as that Panferov 'prettifies the gigantic reality and transforms it into romantic heroics'. I quote this without any further comment. [G.L.'s note.]

Expressionism: its Significance and Decline

1 Ludwig Rubiner (1881–1920), an expressionist poet and theoretician committed to a humanist brand of socialism.

2 The USPD was the Independent Socialist Party of Germany. At the party's special conference in Halle in October 1920 a majority voted to join the Third International, and joined the Communist Party a few weeks later.

3 Johannes R. Becher (1891–1958) began as an expressionist poet who in turn joined the USPD, Spartacus and the Communist Party. A co-founder and chairman of the League of Proletarian Revolutionary Writers, he was forced into exile in 1933 and was from 1935 to 1945 in the Soviet Union. He returned to East Germany where he was prominent in the literary bureaucracy, serving as Minister of Culture from 1954 until his death.

4 We shall confine our discussion here to Germany, even though we are well aware that expressionism has been an international movement. But even

though its roots are to be sought in the imperialist system as a whole, the fact of uneven development between different countries necessarily produced different forms of appearance. Only after studying expressionism in the concrete forms it assumes in various countries is any summary possible, if we are not to remain on a purely abstract level. [G.L.'s note.]

5 Ernst Bassermann was the leader of the National Liberal Party when it agreed to form the Bülow bloc with the Conservatives against the Catholic Centre Party in 1906–7.

6 Kurt Hiller (1885–1972) founded a group of revolutionary pacifists. In the journals he published during the First World War he tirelessly advocated a utopian activism which sought to establish the hegemony of an intellectual aristocracy. He emigrated from Germany in 1934 after internment in a concentration camp, and was active in the anti-fascist emigration in London where he lived until 1946 when he returned to West Germany. Ludwig Ganghofer (1855–1920) and Joseph von Lauff (1855–1933) were popular regional writers.

7 Rudolph Leonhard (1889–1953) took part in the revolutionary upheavals after the First World War before establishing himself as a poet in Berlin and later in Paris. He was active in the anti-fascist organizations in France where he lived illegally throughout the German occupation, narrowly escaping capture by the Gestapo.

8 Hans Blüher (1888–1955) was active in the Youth Movement and is mainly known for his writings on that subject.

9 Franz Werfel (1890–1945) was one of the leading expressionist poets. His best-known work outside Germany, *The Song of Bernadette*, was written in gratitude for the refuge he found in Lourdes when escaping from the Nazis.

10 Hanns Johst (b. 1890) was a minor expressionist whose early play *Der Einsame* ('The Lonely One') provided Brecht with a target which he parodied in *Baal*. In later years Johst dedicated his work personally to Hitler.

11 Alfred Lichtenstein (1899–1914), Ernst Blass (1890–1939) and Jakob van Hoddis (1887–1942) were expressionist poets whose work was cut short: Lichtenstein died at the front during the First World War; Blass who had been almost blind since 1930 was banned by the Nazis in 1933 and died of tuberculosis; van Hoddis was mentally ill from 1912 and died in transit when the Nazis deported all the inmates of the Jewish mental home in which he had been living.

12 It is not accidental that anarchist ideologies, or such as stand close to anarchism, play a major role in this connection. On questions of imperialist war, anarchism reaches at best a USPD position. [G.L.'s note.]

13 Max Picard (1882–1965) was a doctor who turned to writing. He started as an art critic but soon went on to write cultural-philosophical works in which he maintained that modern man could only find salvation if he were able to reverse the flight from God.

14 Walter Hasenclever (1890–1940) wrote one of the representative expressionist plays – *The Son* (1916) – in which the conflict between the generations, but also between the idealist radicalism of the young and the old patriarchal society, was fought out. A radical and pacifist, he lived in France after the First World War. Interned by the French at the outbreak of war, he took his own life when the Germans invaded France.

15 Ernst Toller (1893–1939) was one of the leading expressionist dramatists. He took part in the abortive soviet uprising in Munich in 1919 and served five years in gaol after it was put down. A leading anti-fascist writer in exile in England, France and the USA, he committed suicide in New York.

16 Georg Kaiser (1878–1938) was, with Toller, the leading expressionist dramatist. The Nazis banned his works in 1933 and he emigrated to Switzerland in 1938. Carl Sternheim (1878–1942) wrote grotesque satires on Wilhelmine Germany which, long forgotten, are now being revived.

17 Alfred Ehrenstein (1886–1950) was an expressionist poet and writer of prose associated with *Der Sturm*, a periodical in the vanguard of expressionist painting and literature.

18 Franz Pfempfert (1879–1954) was the editor of the literary and political magazine *Die Aktion*, one of the main expressionist journals. Highly radicalized, Pfempfert was an early supporter of the Spartacus League. After the First World War the journal was openly communist in its sympathies. Pfempfert emigrated in 1933 to Prague, moving to France in 1936 and Mexico in 1940.

19 Herwarth Walden (1878–1941) was the editor of *Der Sturm*, the best-known expressionist journal. In the twenties he became a communist; in 1931 he emigrated to the Soviet Union where he taught modern languages until 1941 when he was arrested and disappeared.

20 Otto Flake (1880–1963) was a cultural philosopher who worked to foster the spirit of international humanism; he also wrote expressionist novels.

21 'Simultaneism' was a theory developed by Robert Delaunay who, with Wassily Kandinsky, was a pioneer of abstraction in art. In his series of 'Window' paintings starting in 1912, Delaunay fused the colours of Cézanne's later period with the forms of analytical Cubism, and claimed that the result, a simultaneous impact of two or more colours, gave the picture a dynamic force.

22 Alfred Wolfenstein (1888–1945) wrote expressionist prose, poetry and drama. He left Germany for Prague in 1933, moving to Paris in 1938. He was caught by the Nazis and spent three months in prison. He was released and spent the rest of the war on the run in Southern France and finally Paris, where he took his own life.

Marx and the Problem of Ideological Decay

1 Niels Lyhne was the main character of a novel by Jens Peter Jacobsen (see note 3, p. 240 above).

2 Gustav Freytag (1816–1895) was the author of *Soll und Haben* ('Debit and Credit'), an immensely popular work which showed the burgher as the kernel of the healthy German state.

A Correspondence with Anna Seghers

1 Anna Seghers (b. 1900) joined the German Communist Party in 1929; her books were banned and she emigrated to France in 1933 and was based there until 1940. She was active on the Republican side in the Spanish Civil War, spent the war years in Mexico, and returned to East Germany. She is known mainly for her novels, especially the best-selling *The Seventh Cross* (1942), which are written in a realist vein.

2 Seghers refers here to Lukács's essay 'Realism in the Balance' in which he attempted to deflect the debate on the political credentials of expressionism into a discussion on realism. It is available in English in Ernst Bloch et al., *Aesthetics and Politics*, London, 1977.

3 Alfred Durus (1895–1949) began his career as a contributor to the expressionist journal *Der Sturm*. In the twenties he was the editor of the *Rote Fahne* and a member of the League of Proletarian Revolutionary Writers. After 1933 he emigrated to the Soviet Union.

4 Ernst Gläser (1902–1962) was a journalist who wrote a well-known novel, *Jahrgang 1902*, describing the effects of the First World War on an adolescent. Having emigrated in 1933 he returned to Germany in 1939 and edited a soldiers' paper throughout the Second World War. Hans Marchwitza (1890–1965) was a Ruhr miner and a member of the German Communist Party; he wrote novels based on his experiences as a miner. Bernhard Brentano (1901–1964), a member of the literary family of that ilk, was a socialist who wrote political novels, essays and biographical works. Alfred Döblin (1878–1957) was the author of *Berlin Alexanderplatz* (1929) which used Joycean techniques whereas Vicki Baum (1888–1960) was a writer of popular fiction.

5 Lukács is referring to his essay 'Marx and the Problem of Ideological Decay' (see pp. 114–66 above).

6 Available in English in Georg Lukács, *Writer and Critic*, London, 1970.

Tribune or Bureaucrat?

1 Ivan Kaliayev was executed in 1905 for his part in the assassination of the Grand Duke Sergius; Theodor Leipart (1867–1947) was a trade-union leader up to 1933 when he was dismissed by the Nazis.

2 The story of the Brideau brothers is told in Balzac's *La Rabouilleuse* (translated into English as *The Black Sheep*, Harmondsworth, 1970); that of Rabourdin in *Les Employés*.

3 Lukács is referring to Ibsen's *When We Dead Awaken*.

Name Index

References to the Introduction are in italics

Adler, Friedrich, 85
Adler, Max, 85, 94, 97–8
Adorno, Theodor W., *2*
Aeschylus, 161
Arndt, Ernst Moritz, 34
Auerbach, Erich, *12*
Avenarius, Richard, 124
Averbach, Leopold, 29, 239n

Balzac, Honoré de, *10–11*, 40, 53, 66, 70, 121, 137–8, 143, 151, 210, 218, 224, 242n
Barbusse, Henri, 138, 186, 193
Barlach, Ernst, 111
Bassermann, Ernst, 80, 243n
Bastiat, Frédéric, 119
Baudelaire, Charles, 221, 223
Bauer, Bruno, 118
Baum, Vicki, 174, 245n
Bebel, August, 80
Becher, Johannes R., *13–14, 19*, 77, 242n
Bentham, Jeremy, 123
Bergson, Henri, 80, 83, 124
Berkeley, George (Bishop), 80
Bernstein, Eduard, 85, 199, 201
Blass, Ernst, 88, 243n
Bloch, Ernst, *9*, 176
Blüher, Hanns, 86, 243n
Boileau, Nicolas, 142
Bourget, Paul, 47, 70, 145
Brecht, Bertolt, *2–3, 9, 15–17, 20*, 66, 70–1, 239n, 240n, 241n

Bredel, Willi, *2, 13–16*, 23–32, 239n
Brentano, Bernhard, 174, 245n
Büchner, Georg, *2*
Bukharin, Nikolai, *1*
Bülow, Bernhard (Count) von, 80, 243n
Bürger, Gottfried August, 168
Byron, George Gordon (Lord), 181

Carlyle, Thomas, 121–2, 134, 181
Cervantes, Miguel, 158, 161, 175
Cohen, Hermann, 124
Copernicus, Nikolaus, 136
Corneille, Pierre, 184
Cromwell, Oliver, 67, 116
Cunow, Heinrich, 94

D'Annunzio, Gabriele, 187, 196
Danton, Georges-Jacques, 203
Darwin, Charles, 136
Defoe, Daniel, 147
Deutscher, Isaac, *19*
Dickens, Charles, 212
Diderot, Denis, 29, 70, 146, 214, 222, 237
Dimitrov, Georgi, *3*
Döblin, Alfred, 174, 245n
Dos Passos, John, 153, 174–6
Dostoyevsky, Fyodor, *5, 11*, 47–8, 240n
Dreyfus, Alfred (Captain), 213
Durus, Alfred, 173, 254n

Ebbinghaus, J., 80
Ehrenburg, Ilya, 45, 55, 74
Ehrenstein, Alfred, 103–4, 244n
Eisler, Hanns, 185
El Greco, 172
Eliot, George, *12*
Engels, Frederick, 34, 39–40, 42,
    49–50, 52–4, 56, 64–9, 116, 125,
    205–6, 210–11, 213, 230, 235,
    240n

Feher, Ferenc, *3, 10*
Fichte, Johann Gottlieb, *8, 20*
Fielding, Henry, 242n
Flake, Otto, 109, 244n
Flaubert, Gustave, *11*, 47, 70, 151,
    221, 223
Fontane, Theodor, *2*
Fourier, Charles, 121
France, Anatole, 47, 138, 149, 220–1
Francis of Assisi, 99
Freiligrath, Ferdinand, 34, 41, 239n
Freud, Sigmund, *20*, 137
Freytag, Gustav, 150, 245n

Galileo Galilei, 136
Ganghofer, Ludwig, 84, 243n
George, Stefan, *4–5, 7*, 84, 111
Gide, André, 226
Gläser, Ernst, 174, 245n
Goebbels, Joseph, 111
Goering, Hermann, 132
Goethe, August, 168
Goethe, Johann Wolfgang von, *8*, 80,
    114, 137, 140, 167–9, 172, 180–1,
    189, 194–5, 198, 212, 214, 218,
    221–4, 226, 237, 240n, 242n
Goncourt, Edmond and Jules, 70
Gorky, Maxim, *9, 11, 17*, 31, 74,
    141–3, 168, 179, 186, 192–3, 235,
    237, 240n, 242n
Gotsche, Otto, *14*, 28–32
Grillparzer, Franz, 157
Grünewald, Matthias, 111

Guizot, François, 115–17
Günderode, Karoline von, 168

Hamsun, Knut, 47
Harkness, Margaret, 40, 42
Hasenclever, Walter, 101, 106, 164,
    244n
Hauptmann, Gerhart, 106, 134
Haym, Rudolf, 80
Hebbel, Christian Friedrich, 157,
    240n
Hegel, Georg Wilhelm Friedrich, *8*,
    38, 40, 55, 59, 67–8, 72, 74, 78,
    114, 118, 136, 181, 219, 222
Heidegger, Martin, 124
Heine, Heinrich, *2, 9*, 29, 34, 123,
    181
Helvétius, Claude-Adrien, 122–3
Heraclitus, *20*
Herwegh, Georg, 34, 42, 239n
Herzog, Wilhelm, 88
Hess, Moses, *8*
Hettner, Hermann, 80, 146, 190
Hilferding, Rudolf, 94
Hiller, Kurt, 84, 88, 90–2, 100–1,
    243n
Hirschfeld, Georg, 106
Hobbes, Thomas, 122–3
Hoddis, Jakob van, 88, 243n
Hofmannsthal, Hugo von, *20*, 225–6
Holbach, Paul-Henri (Baron),
    122
Hölderlin, Friedrich, *8*, 168
Homer, 65, 175
Honigsheim, Paul, *4*
Hugo, Victor, 181
Husserl, Edmund, 80–1, 83, 124
Huysmans, Joris-Karl, 47, 70

Ibsen, Henrik, 138, 159–63, 221,
    223, 242n
Ivanov, Vsevolod, 141

Jacobsen, Jens Peter, 47, 240n

Johst, Hanns, 87, 243n
Jordan, Wilhelm, 156–7
Joyce, James, 145, 176

Kafka, Franz, *3, 20*
Kaganovitch, L. M., 228–9
Kaiser, Georg, 103, 164, 244n
Kaliayev, Ivan, 208, 245n
Kant, Immanuel, 37–8, 80, 85, 209
Kautsky, Karl, 94–5, 97, 99, 201
Keller, Gottfried, *2, 12,* 146–7, 190
Keyserling, Eduard (Count), 126
Kierkegaard, Søren, *5*
Kipling, Rudyard, 46
Kisch, Egon Erwin, *15*
Kleist, Heinrich von, 38, 168–70,
    181, 188
Knickerbocker, H. R., 53, 241n
Korsch, Karl, *9*

La Rochefoucauld, François (Duc
    de), 114
Lauff, Joseph von, 84, 243n
Leipart, Theodor, 207, 245n
Lenin, Vladimir Ilych, *10,* 31, 42–3,
    53, 64–7, 69, 72–4, 76, 84, 94, 99,
    107, 124, 136, 141, 143, 149, 155,
    198–237 *passim*
Lenz, Jakob, 168
Leonardo da Vinci, 213, 219, 237
Leonhard, Rudolph, 86, 243n
Lessing, Gotthold Ephraim, 29, 184,
    187–8, 195, 214, 217
Lichtenstein, Alfred, 88, 243n
Linguet, Simon-Nicolas-Henri, 121
Lipps, Theodor, 89
Locke, John, 122
Louis Bonaparte, 115
Löwy, Michael, *4, 10*
Lucian, 161
Ludwig, Emil, 25, 239n

Mach, Ernst, 63–4, 85, 108, 124, 153
Maeterlinck, Maurice, 152, 155

Malthus, Thomas, 121–2
Mann, Heinrich, 87, 138
Mann, Thomas, *3–4, 11, 19,* 138,
    149, 175, 179, 224–5
Manzoni, Alessandro, 181
Marat, Jean-Paul, 203
Marc, Franz, 173
Marchwitza, Hans, 174, 245n
Marinetti, Filippo, 187, 196
Marx, Karl, *5–6, 10,* 32, 37–9, 42,
    54, 64–9, 73, 114–25, 129–30,
    133, 143–4, 150, 154–7, 161, 205,
    211, 230, 235–6
Maupassant, Guy de, 70
Mehring, Franz, 35–40, 42, 239n
Mérimée, Prosper, 181
Michelangelo, 213, 237
Michels, Robert, 86
Mill, James, 117–19
Millerand, Alexandre, 199
Mirabeau, Honoré (Count), 203
Müller, Adam, 154

Napoleon Bonaparte, 67, 181
Neumann, Heinz, 25, 239n
Nicholas of Cusa, 136
Nietzsche, Friedrich, 80, 88, 92, 108,
    124, 137, 153, 156
Nolde, Emil, 111

Orwell, George, *16*
Otten, Karl, 98
Ottwalt, Ernst, *2, 15–17,* 45–75,
    240n, 241–2n

Panferov, Fyodor, 74, 242n
Pareto, Vilfredo, 92
Pfempfert, Franz, 108, 244n
Phidias, 182
Picard, Max, 96–7, 102, 107, 243n
Pinthus, Kurt, 88–90, 96–8, 102–3
Piscator, Erwin, *13, 15*
Plekhanov, Georgi, 207
Popper, Leo, *19*

Racine, Jean, 184
Radbruch, Gustav, 88
Ranke, Leopold von, 79
Raphael, 221
Rathenau, Walther, 82, 86
Rembrandt, 173, 182
Riazanov, David, *1*
Ricardo, David, 117–20
Rickert, Heinrich, 80–1
Riegl, Alois, 70
Riehl, Aloys, 124
Rilke, Rainer Maria, *20*, 131–3
Robespierre, Maximilien, 203
Rolland, Romain, 138, 175, 186,
    193, 224
Roscher, Wilhelm, G. F., 119
Rosenberg, Alfred, 108, 112
Rousseau, Jean-Jacques, 195, 214
Rubiner, Ludwig, 77, 88, 98, 242n
Ruge, Arnold, 156–7

Saltykov-Shchedrin, M. Y., 219
Sand, George, 45
Say, Jean-Baptiste, 119
Scheler, Max, 81
Schickele, René, 98
Schiller, Friedrich von, 36–7, 168,
    195
Schmidt, Conrad, 85
Schnitzler, Arthur, 215–16, 225
Scott, Walter, *11*, 181, 218
Seghers, Anna, *12*, 167–97 *passim*,
    245n
Seidler, Irma, *19*
Shakespeare, William, 143, 158, 175,
    217
Shaw, George Bernard, 138
Shelley, Percy Bysshe, 217
Simmel, Georg, *4*, 80, 82–3, 86
Sinclair, Upton, 45–6, 55, 61–2, 67
Sismondi, Jean-Charles, 83, 118–22
Slutsky, A. I., 32, 239n
Somlo, F., 88
Sorel, Georges, 85–6, 92

Spann, Othmar, 108
Spengler, Oswald, 108, 126, 137
Stalin, Josef, *9, 11*, 27, 32, 227–8,
    230–1, 235
Staudinger, Hermann, 85
Sterne, Laurence, 158
Stendhal (Henri Beyle), 29, 181
Sternheim, Carl, 103, 244n
Stirner, Max, 155
Storm, Theodor, *5*
Strasser, Otto, 112
Strindberg, August, 163–4
Südekum, A. O. W., 94
Sue, Eugène, 45, 138, 146
Swift, Jonathan, 147–8, 214, 219

Taine, Hippolyte, 151
Thälmann, Ernst, *14*, 25, 239n
Titian, 173, 221
Toller, Ernst, *4, 7–8*, 101, 244n
Tolstoy, Leo, *5, 10–12*, 40, 53,
    57–60, 72–3, 99, 137–8, 143, 152,
    169–70, 206, 209, 215, 218, 220,
    234
Tönnies, Ferdinand, *4*
Treitschke, Heinrich von, 79
Tretyakov, Sergei, *15*, 45, 61, 72,
    241n
Trotsky, Lev Davidovitch, 39, 43, 69

Vaihinger, Hans, 80
Van Gogh, Vincent, 226
Vauvenargues, Luc de Clapiers,
    142–3
Vergniaud, Pierre-Victurnien, 203
Verlaine, Paul, 186
Villon, François, 186
Vischer, F. T., 157
Vogelweide, Walther von der, 111
Voltaire (François-Marie Arouet),
    214

Walden, Herwarth, 108, 244n
Wassermann, Jacob, 72, 226, 242n

Weber, Max, *4*, 99, 126–9, 153, 208, 216

Wedekind, Frank, 164

Werfel, Franz, 86, 99–101, 243n

Werner, Zacharias, 168

Wilde, Oscar, 206, 222

Williams, Raymond, 7

Winckelmann, Johann, 172

Windelband, Wilhelm, 80

Wittfogel, Karl, *14*

Wolfenstein, Alfred, 110, 244n

Worringer, Wilhelm, 70, 76–7, 89–90, 102, 107

Zetkin, Clara, 65

Zhdanov, Andrey, *10, 17*

Ziegler, Leopold, 126

Zinoviev, Grigori, *1*

Zola, Emile, *11*, 45, 69–70, 138, 151, 214, 242n